MANAGING YOUR DIABETES

The Only Complete Guide to
Type 2 Diabetes for Canadians

M. SARA ROSENTHAL

Foreword by
Dr. James McSherry, MD, ChB, FCFP, FRCGP, FAAFP, FABMP,
Professor of Family Medicine, University of Western Ontario,
Chief of Family Medicine, London Health Sciences Centre

Macmillan Canada
Toronto

Canadian Cataloguing in Publication Data

Rosenthal, M. Sara
    Managing your diabetes : the only complete guide to type 2 diabetes
for Canadians

Includes index.
ISBN 0-7715-7560-2

1. Non-insulin-dependent diabetes – Popular works. I. Title.

RC660.4 R67 1998   616.4'62   C97–932194–4

Macmillan Canada wishes to thank the Canada Council, the Ontario Ministry of Culture and Communications and the Ontario Arts Council for supporting its publishing program.

This book is available at special discounts for bulk purchases by your group or organization for sales promotions, premiums, fundraising and seminars. For details, contact: Macmillan Canada, Special Sales Department, 29 Birch Avenue, Toronto, ON M4V 1E2. Tel: 416-963-8830.

Cover and inside design: David Vereschagin for CounterPunch
Composition: IBEX Graphic Communications Inc.
Author photograph: David Leyes

Macmillan Canada
A Division of Canada Publishing Corporation
Toronto, Ontario, Canada

1 2 3 4 5 TRI 02 01 00 99 98

Printed in Canada

Other books by M. Sara Rosenthal

The Thyroid Sourcebook (2nd edition, 1996)
The Gyneocological Sourcebook (2nd edition, 1997)
The Pregnancy Sourcebook (2nd edition, 1997)
The Fertility Sourcebook (2nd edition, 1998)
The Breastfeeding Sourcebook (1995)
The Breast Sourcebook (1996; 1997)
The Gastrointestinal Sourcebook (1997)

EDITORIAL BOARD:
(in alphabetical order)

Important Notice

The purpose of this book is to educate. It is sold with the understanding that the author and Macmillan Canada shall have neither liability nor responsibility for any injury caused or alleged to be caused directly or indirectly by the information contained in this book. While every effort has been made to ensure its accuracy, the book's contents should not be construed as medical advice. Each person's health needs are unique. To obtain recommendations appropriate to your particular situation, please consult a qualified health care provider.

ACKNOWLEDGEMENTS

If it weren't for the commitment, hard work and guidance of the following people, this book would never have been written.

Anne Kenshole, MB, BS, FRCPC, FACP, Medical Director of TRIDEC, Professor of Medicine, University of Toronto, bravely reviewed several portions of this work. Dr. Kenshole pointed out countless crucial aspects of Type 2 diabetes management that have been missing in other consumer health books.

Robert Panchyson, BScN, RN, Nurse Clinician, Diabetes Educator, Hamilton Civic Hospitals, Hamilton General Division, was my knight in shining armour, who went miles out of his way to make sure I understood this disease from both the "politically correct" and politically *incorrect* perspective. His years of experience in the trenches come through loud and clear in this book.

James McSherry, MD, ChB, FCFP, FRCGP, FAAFP, FABMP, Medical Director, Victoria Family Medical Centre, Chief of Family Medicine, The London Health Sciences Centre, brings the sensitivity and caring of truly *patient*-centred family medicine to this work.

Robert Silver, MD, FRCPC, Endocrinologist, Division of Endocrinology and Metabolism, The Toronto Hospital, was a pleasure to deal with and tackled one of the most difficult chapters in this book.

Stuart Harris, MD, MPH, CCFP, ABPM, Assistant Professor, Departments of Family Medicine and Epidemiology and Biostastics, University of Western Ontario, and former Medical Director, University of Toronto Sioux Lookout Program, made it possible for me to address diabetes in Aboriginal Canada, and I cherish his expertise and commitment. Irwin Antoine, MD, CCFP, Assistant Professor, Department of Family Medicine, University of Western Ontario, took the time to give me a "nod," an "okay" and encouraged a chapter about diabetes in Aboriginal Canada.

Anne Levin, BScPT, MCPA, Physiotherapist and Certified Hydrotherapist, Baycrest Centre for Geriatric Care, Coordinator, Arthritis Education and Exercise Program, and Lecturer, Physical Therapy, Faculty of Medicine, University of Toronto, is 100% gold and I was lucky to have her!

Barbara Mcintosh, RN, BScN, CDE, Nurse Coordinator, Adult Diabetes Education Program, Grand River Hospital, Kitchener, Ontario, helped me sleep at night by making my life ... less complicated, while Diana Phayre, Clinical Nurse Specialist, Diabetes Education Centre, The Doctor's Hospital, helped with more "ups and downs."

And, now, the "food editors": Brenda Cook, RD, University of Alberta Hospitals, offered several fat-cutting tips to make the book a little leaner and meatier. Tasha Hamilton, BaSc, RD, Diabetes Educator-Dietitian, Tri-Hospital Diabetes Education Centre, left no stone unturned when it came to meal planning; thorough and impeccable best describes her work. Barbara Theedom, RD, CDE, a tough cookie with a big heart and eyes like a hawk, offered many important suggestions, and Karen Faye, LPN, AFFA (U.S.), Fitness Practitioner, who herself has maintained an 80-pound weight loss for 15 years, provided much of the groundwork for food and fitness.

I'd also like to thank my editorial assistant, Larissa Kostoff; my very patient editor, Nicole de Montbrun, and my copy editor Liba Berry.

Special thanks to Gary May, MD, FRCP, Clinical Assistant Professor of Medicine, Department of Medicine, Division of Gastroenterology, University of Calgary, who provided some of the ground-work for this text through his role as Medical Advisor on a past work. Gillian Arsenault, MD, CCFP, IBCLC, FRCP, Simon Fraser Health Unit, served as a past advisor on two works and has never stopped advising and sending me valuable information. Irving Rootman, PhD, Director, Centre for Health Promotion, University of Toronto, put me in touch with several experts and always encourages my interest in primary prevention and health promotion issues.

To all the people interviewed for this book: your stories, struggles, and important suggestions were very much appreciated.

In the moral support department—my husband, Gary S. Karp, and all the relatives and friends who cheered me on.

FOREWORD

Diabetes and the Family Doctor

Managing Your Diabetes is a timely book indeed. Demographic trends tell us that the number of Canadians with Type 2 diabetes is going to increase dramatically over the next decade as the baby boomers move into middle age and beyond. Fortunately, there have been important developments in the management of Type 2 over the past several years and it is now clear that the serious complications of diabetes are potentially avoidable or at least treatable in a way that was impossible only a short time ago.

The gradual reductions in government funding for medical education that have occurred in the past decade have important implications for the way in which medical care is going to be provided in the future—there will be fewer medical specialists and their role will change from care provider to consultant.

Surveys tell us that 95 percent of Canadians consult their family physicians as their preferred point of entry into the health care system. Additionally, about 20 percent of Canadians with Type 1 diabetes and 80 percent with Type 2 receive their medical care from their family physicians at present; those figures are likely to increase as the scope of specialist practice changes. Family physicians, working as important members of a diabetes care team that includes nurses, diabetes educators, pharmacists, chiropodists and other health professionals, have already begun to prepare themselves for greater responsibilities in the care of patients with diabetes and other diseases.

With scientific advances, and likely changes in how medical care is going to be organized, has come the realization that diabetic care begins with the diabetic patient. The well-informed person with diabetes is his or her own biggest asset in dealing with a disease that has potentially serious consequences. It is surely no secret that doctors can't look after patients who don't—or won't—look after themselves.

The next biggest asset is a well-informed and interested family physician who is not only knowledgeable about diabetes but who is proactive in organizing medical care by scheduling routine examinations, performing screening procedures for complications, and notifying diabetic patients when annual influenza immunizations are due.

Sara Rosenthal is to be commended for writing this book. I sincerely hope that it will help Canadians with diabetes increase their knowledge, become interested in developing new skills, and come to a fresh awareness of what they can do to help themselves. I also hope that new knowledge and attitudes will stimulate development of an effective partnership between persons with diabetes and their family physicians. The effective patient–doctor relationship, founded on mutual respect and trust, requires patients to assume responsibility for all of the things they can and should do for themselves, and it requires doctors to be interested, well-informed, skilled clinicians—and good communicators. Are we all ready for that? I believe we are.

Dr. James McSherry, MD, ChB, FCFP, FRCGP, FAAFP, FABMP, Professor of Family Medicine, University of Western Ontario, Chief of Family London Health Sciences Centre

CONTENTS

INTRODUCTION

What is Type 2 Diabetes?

You've just come home from your doctor's office. You can't remember anything he or she said other than those three horrible words: "You have diabetes." What does this mean? How will your life change? You've never been any good at diets, meal plans or exercising. And since you can't stand the sight of blood, how can you be expected to prick your finger every day to monitor your blood sugar? (The frequency of testing depends.)

By 2004, one in four Canadians over the age of 45 will be diagnosed with Type 2 diabetes. Currently, 1.5 million Canadians have been diagnosed with Type 2 diabetes; an additional 750,000 Canadians have the disease but don't know it. Whether you've just been diagnosed, or have been living with it for years, this is a difficult disease to understand. In fact, it is the most complicated condition

I've ever written about, and I've tackled some tough health topics, including AIDS and cancer.

Why is Type 2 diabetes so difficult to understand? Part of the problem is that there are so many names for this one disease, and so many *other* types of diabetes, which also have more than one name, it's easy to lose track of what kind of diabetes you have. So I'm going to begin this book by clearing up all points of confusion regarding names, labels and definitions. Clearing up this confusion is the first step in managing Type 2 diabetes. When Canada's Dr. Frederick G. Banting first got the idea to develop a therapy for diabetes in 1921, diabetes, like the world war, wasn't yet numbered. It was long known, however, that there was a "milder" diabetes, and a more severe form. But diabetes wasn't officially labelled *Type 1* and *Type 2* until 1979.

Type 2 diabetes means that your pancreas is functioning. You are making plenty of insulin. In fact, you are probably making too much insulin, a condition called *hyperinsulinemia* ("too much insulin"). Insulin is a hormone made by your *beta cells*, the insulin-producing cells within the *islets of Langerhans*—small islands of cells afloat in your pancreas. The *pancreas* is a bird beak–shaped gland situated behind the stomach.

Insulin is a major player in our bodies. One of its most important functions is to regulate the blood sugar levels. It does this by acting as a sort of courier, "knocking" on your cells' door, and announcing: "Sugar's here; come and get it!" Your cells then open the door to let sugar in from your bloodstream. That sugar is absolutely vital to your health, and provides you with the energy you need to function.

But what happens if the cells don't answer the door? Two things. First, the sugar in your bloodstream will accumulate, having nowhere to go. It's the kind of situation that develops when your newspapers pile up outside your door when you're away. Second, your pancreas will keep sending out more couriers to try to get your cells to open that door and take in the "newspapers." The result of the cell's not complying is a pile of newspapers *and* a line-up of unsuccessful couriers by your door. When the cell doesn't answer the door, this is called *insulin resistance*; the cell is resisting insulin. Why this is happening is discussed in Chapter 2. The end result, however, is *diabetes*, which means "high blood sugar." A synonym for diabetes is *hyperglycemia*, which also means "high blood sugar." If insulin resistance goes on for too long, the pancreas can become overworked and eventually may not make enough, or any, insulin. In effect, it's like a courier strike. And finally, the liver, being the good neighbour that it is, will lend a bowl or two of sugar to the sugar-deprived cell. (See Chapter 2.) But this can exacerbate existing high blood sugar.

Type 2 diabetes, a genetic disease, is a completely different disease than Type 1 diabetes, an autoimmune disease. In Type 1, the immune system attacks the beta cells in the pancreas, causing them to be impaired or defective. The result is that no insulin is produced by the pancreas at all. That means no couriers are sent to knock at the cell's door. In this case, the result is a pile of newspapers without the line-up of couriers.

Type 1 diabetes is usually diagnosed before age 30, often in childhood. For this reason, Type 1 diabetes was once known as *juvenile diabetes*, or *juvenile-onset diabetes*. Because people with Type 1 diabetes depend on insulin injections to live, it was also called *insulin-dependent diabetes mellitus* (IDDM). The word *mellitis* comes from the Greek meaning "sweet," a leftover term from the days when diabetes was diagnosed by "urine tasters"; the urine becomes sweet when blood sugar is dangerously high, something that doesn't usually occur in Type 2. Only 10 percent of all people with diabetes have Type 1 diabetes.

Type 2 diabetes, on the other hand, accounts for 90 percent of all people with diabetes. Since Type 2 diabetes doesn't usually develop until after age 45, it was once known as *mature-onset diabetes* or *adult-onset diabetes*. In rare cases when Type 2 develops before age 30, it is called *mature-onset diabetes in the young* (MODY). Since Type 2 diabetes is a disease of insulin resistance, rather than no insulin, it often can be managed through diet and exercise, without insulin injections. For this reason, Type 2 diabetes was also known as *non-insulin-dependent diabetes mellitis* (NIDDM).

Here's where it gets really confusing! When you are told that you have non-insulin dependent diabetes, it's logical to conclude that you will never need to have an insulin injection. But this just isn't so. In fact, about one-third of all people with Type 2 diabetes will eventually need to begin insulin therapy, for reasons I explain in Chapter 2. Does this mean you now have insulin-dependent diabetes, or Type 1? After all, if you need insulin, aren't you now insulin-dependent, which, by definition, means Type 1? This is a logical conclusion, *but it's wrong.* As stated above, Type 2 diabetes is a genetic disease; Type 1 diabetes is an autoimmune disease. Type 2 diabetes cannot "turn into" Type 1 diabetes any more than an apple can turn into a banana. So what do you call it when someone with Type 2 diabetes requires insulin? Try *insulin-requiring Type 2 diabetes.*

Something else you need to understand about Type 2 diabetes is that the high blood sugar that results from insulin resistance can lead to a number of other diseases, including cardiovascular disease (heart disease and stroke) and peripheral vascular disease (PVD), which means that the blood doesn't flow properly to other parts of your body. This can create a number of problems, discussed in Chapter 7. Many people who suffer a heart attack or stroke have Type 2 diabetes.

Screening studies show that Type 2 diabetes is prevalent all over the world, particularly in countries that are becoming westernized. What's so disturbing is that Type 2 diabetes is increasing in the developed world at an annual rate of about 6 percent, while the number of people with Type 2 diabetes doubles every 15 years. Roughly 6 percent of all Caucasian adults have Type 2 diabetes, but the disease affects African–North Americans at a rate of 12 to 15 percent, Hispanics at a rate of 20 percent, and aboriginal North Americans at a rate exceeding 30 percent. In some aboriginal communities, up to 70 percent of adults have Type 2 diabetes. This is why I've devoted an entire chapter to this population.

It's taken months of research, from hundreds of sources, for me to understand Type 2 diabetes. If you feel confused and overwhelmed by the topic, this book will help change that. My goal is to make the information you must have to manage Type 2 diabetes accessible to all Canadians.

Unless you live in a large Canadian city, you may not have immediate (or any!) access to the right health care professionals. With further cuts in our health care system, diabetes education centres, in many hospitals, may be shut down, while many people are on a waiting list to see a diabetes educator. Take heart—there are other ways to get the information you need to manage your disease. Every manufacturer of a diabetes product, be it a glucose meter, insulin pen or diabetes medication, has a 1-800 customer care line. These are excellent sources of information. As well, the Canadian Diabetes Association (CDA) is one of the rare non-profit organizations that is truly there for the patient. Make this the first call once you're diagnosed. CDA divisions and branches are listed in the resource section at the back of the book. You can also get a lot of information through the Internet; useful websites are listed in the resource section as well.

As I'll stress again and again in the book, Type 2 diabetes is a genetic disease; but by modifying your lifestyle and diet, you may be able to delay or even prevent the onset of the disease.

Chapter 1

WHY YOU SHOULD BE WORRIED ABOUT TYPE 2 DIABETES

I liken Type 2 diabetes in some ways to AIDS; many people with Type 2 diabetes won't find out they have it until they have "full-blown Type 2," meaning that the disease has progressed to the point where they are experiencing complications, or what I refer to as "Type 2–defining illnesses." Indeed, many HIV-positive persons don't know they've been exposed to the virus until they develop an AIDS-defining illness, such as pneumocystis carini pneumonia (PCP). Similarly, you should be worried about Type 2 diabetes because of what the disease most often leads to: cardiovascular disease and peripheral vascular disease. People with Type 2 diabetes are four times more likely to develop heart disease and five times more likely to suffer a stroke than people without Type 2 diabetes.

If you consume a diet higher in fat than carbohydrates, and low in fibre, you increase your risk for Type 2 diabetes if you are genetically predisposed to the disease. If you weigh at least 20 percent more than you should for your height and age (the definition of "obese"), are sedentary and over the age of 45, you are considered at high risk for Type 2 diabetes. Your risk further increases if you are:

- of aboriginal descent (this is true for aboriginal peoples all over the world, from Australia to North America; in Canada, First Nations people are at highest risk; in the United States, the Pima Indians are at highest risk);
- of African or Hispanic descent;
- have a family history of Type 2 diabetes;
- are obese and female (73 percent of all women with diabetes are obese);
- are pregnant (one in twenty women will develop gestational diabetes by their third trimester; this number increases with age, while gestational diabetes can predispose you to Type 2 diabetes later in life).

There are several co-factors that contribute to your risk profile, which can change your risk from higher to lower. The purpose of this chapter is to give you a clear idea of where you fit into this risk puzzle. That way, you'll be more aware of early warning signs of the disease, which will make it easier for you to get an accurate diagnosis. If you've already been diagnosed with Type 2 diabetes, this chapter will help you understand why you developed the disease, and what you can do today to eliminate some of the factors that may be aggravating your condition. But to really understand why diet and lifestyle have so much do to with your risk of contracting the disease, you need a bit of background. After all, you didn't create the modern diet; you were born into it. In fact, the root word of diet comes from the Greek "diatta," meaning "way of life."

The Good Times Disease

Type 2 diabetes is referred to as the Good Times Disease partly because of the work of Dr. Bouchardat, a French physician in the 1870s, who noticed that his diabetic patients seemed to do rather well in war. When their food was rationed, the sugar in Dr. Bouchardat's diabetic patients' urine disappeared. It was at this point that a connection between food *quantity* and diabetes was made. This observation paved the way for special low-carbohydrate diets as a treatment for diabetes, but it seemed to be effective only in eliminating sugar from the urine in "milder" diabetes, which was what Type 2 diabetes was called before the disease was better understood.

Economies and Scales

Bouchardat's observations were observed throughout Europe a few decades later. Many European countries experienced a significant drop, not just in "mild" diabetes, but in a number of obesity-related diseases during the First and Second World Wars, when meat, dairy food and eggs became scarce in large populations. Wartime rations forced people to survive on brown bread, oats and barley meal and home-grown produce.

Had it not been for the Depression, we may indeed have seen an increase in Type 2 diabetes much earlier than we did in North America. The seeds of sedentary life were already planted in the 1920s, as consumer comforts, mainly the automobile and radio, led to more driving, less walking and more sedentary recreation. The Depression interrupted what was supposed to be prosperous times for everyone. It also intercepted obesity and all diseases related to obesity, as most industrialized nations barely ate enough to survive.

The Depression years, which ended in Canada when Britain declared war on Germany in 1939, combined with six long years of war, led to an unprecedented yearning for consumer goods such as cars, refrigerators, stoves, radios and washing machines. As the boys marched home, they were welcomed with open arms into civilian bliss. By 1948, university enrolment had doubled in a decade, leading to an explosion in desk jobs and the commuter economy that exists today. The return of the veterans led to an unprecedented baby boom, driving the candy, sweets and junk-food markets for decades to come. Moreover, a sudden influx of money from Victory Bond investments and veteran's re-establishment grants coincided with the first payments of government pensions and family allowances. Never before had North Americans had so much money.

Manufacturers and packaged-goods companies were looking for better ways to compete and sell their products. The answer to their prayers arrived in the late 1940s with the cathode ray tube: television. In the end, television would become the appliance most responsible for dietary decline and sedentary lifestyle as it turned into a babysitter that could mesmerize the baby boom generation for hours.

The Diet of Leisure

Naturally, after the war, people wanted to celebrate. They gave parties, they drank wine. They smoked. They went to restaurants. More than ever before, our diets began to include more high-fat items, refined carbohydrates, sugar, alcohol and chemical additives. And as women began to manage large families, easy-fix meals in boxes and cans were being manufactured in abundance and sold on television to millions.

The demand for the diet of leisure radically changed agriculture, too. Today, 80 percent of our grain harvest goes to feed livestock. The rest of our arable land is used for other cash crops such as tomatoes, sugar, coffee and bananas. Ultimately, cash crops have helped to create the modern Western diet: an obscene amount of meat, eggs, dairy products, sugar and refined flour.

Since 1940, chemical additives and preservatives in food have risen by 995 percent. In 1959, the Flavour and Extract Manufacturers Association of the United States (FEMA) established a panel of experts to determine the safety status of food flavourings to deal with the overwhelming number of chemicals that companies wanted to add to our foods.

One of the most popular food additives is monosodium glutamate (MSG), the sodium salt of glutamic acid, an amino acid that occurs naturally in protein-containing foods such as meat, fish, milk and many vegetables. MSG is a flavour enhancer that researchers believe contributes a "fifth taste" to savoury foods such as meats, stews, tomatoes and cheese. It was originally extracted from seaweed and other plant sources to function in foods the same way as other spices or extracts. Today, MSG is made from starch, corn sugar or molasses from sugar cane or sugar beets. MSG is produced by a fermentation process similar to that used for making products such as beer, vinegar and yogurt. While MSG is labelled Generally Recommended As Safe (GRAS) by the United States Food and Drug Administration (FDA), questions about the safety of ingesting MSG have been raised because food sensitivities to the substance have been reported. This fact notwithstanding, the main problem with MSG is that it arouses our appetites *even more*. Widespread in our food supply, MSG makes food taste better. And the better food tastes, the *more we eat*.

Hydrolyzed proteins are also used as flavour enhancers. These are made by using enzymes to chemically digest proteins from soy meal, wheat gluten, corn gluten, edible strains of yeast or other food sources. This process, known as *hydrolysis*, breaks down proteins into their component amino acids. Today, there are several hundred additive substances like these used in our food, including sugar, baking soda and vitamins (see Chapters 5 and 9).

Of course, one of the key functions of food additives is to preserve foods for transport. The problem is, once we begin to eat foods that are not indigenous to our country, the food loses many of its nutrient properties. Refrigerators make it possible for us to eat tropical foods in Canada and Texas-raised beef in Japan. As a result, few industrialized countries eat "indigenously" anymore.

Minimum wage, maximum fat

The legacy of the Western diet of leisure is that it has become cheaper to eat out of a box or can than off the land. In the developed Western world, where there's minimum wage, there is also maximum fat. At one time, fat was a sign of prosperity and wealth. Today, wealth is defined by thinness and fitness. Ironically, low-fat foods, diet programs and fitness clubs attract the segment of our population least affected by obesity. In fact, eating disorders tend to plague women who live in higher income brackets.

In 1997, the Coalition for Excess Weight Risk Education, a Washington-based organization comprising the American Diabetes Association, the American Association of Diabetes Educators, the American Society for Clinical Nutrition, the North American Association for the Study of Obesity and four pharmaceutical manufacturers issued statistics on obesity in the United States. The data can be used to interpret obesity patterns throughout the Western world. Based on a 33-city survey, the National Weight Report found that cities with high unemployment rates and low per capita income tended to have higher rates of obesity. Areas with high annual precipitation rates and a high number of food stores also contributed to obesity. (More rainy or snowy days leads to more snacking in front of the television set!) The study also revealed:

- Restaurant-rich New Orleans had the United States' highest obesity rate, where 37.5 percent of its adult residents were obese, while Denver, known for its outdoor living had the lowest rate of obesity, where only 22.1 percent of its residents were obese.
- Eating meals away from home and equating high-fat, fried food to a sense of "family" was most commonly reported among obese adults. (This suggests that our commuter society increases fast-food eating, while stress and a lack of emotional support leads people to eat for comfort rather than hunger.)
- Ethnic food (despite the fact that much of it can be lower in fat) tempted Cleveland, Ohio, residents (31.5 percent of Cleveland's adults are obese), while many people blamed their obesity on the cold climate, which made them crave meat, biscuits and french fries to help them fuel up.

■ People in hot climates, such as Phoenix, Arizona, where 24.3 percent of its adult population is obese, reported that they gained weight when the weather got too hot for outdoor exercise. (This is a case for eating *seasonably*. Heavy foods in hot climates are unnecessary. This "eating on location" concept is discussed in detail in Chapter 9.)

Other statistics reveal that 35 percent of North American men and 27 percent of North American women are obese. Unfortunately, obesity, physical inactivity and dietary-fat intake are factors we have to look at when trying to understand why 6 percent of Canadian adults (the number is much higher in aboriginal populations) between ages 18 and 74 currently have diabetes, and why 12 percent of Canadian adults suffer from *impaired glucose tolerance*, discussed later in the chapter.

Risk Factors You Can Change

Type 2 diabetes more than meets the requirements of an epidemic. In 1985, the World Health Organization (WHO) estimated that roughly 30 million people globally had Type 2 diabetes. By 1993, that number jumped to 98.9 million people, and it's estimated that 250 million people worldwide will have Type 2 diabetes by 2020.

As mentioned earlier, one in four Canadians over the age of 45 will be diagnosed with diabetes by 2004. And, unless more people modify their risk factors, that number is likely to increase by 2020.

Thirty-two percent of people with diabetes have at least three of the risk factors that can *double* their risk of developing Type 2 diabetes, while 89 percent of people with the disease have at least one *modifiable* risk factor. That means you can lower your risk of developing diabetes by changing your lifestyle or diet.

Calculating your risk of getting a particular disease is very tricky business. To simplify matters, I've divided this chapter into two sections: modifiable risk factors—risk factors you can change; and risk markers—risk factors you cannot change, such as your age or genes. It's also crucial to understand that risk estimates are only guesses that are not based on you personally, but on people *like* you, who share your physical characteristics or lifestyle patterns. It's like betting on a horse. You look at the age of the horse, its vigour and shape, its breeding, its training and where the race is being run. Then you come up with odds. If you own the horse, you can't change your horse's colour or breeding, but you can change its training, its diet, its jockey and, ultimately, where it's being raced, when and how often. Chance, of course, plays a role in horse racing. You can't control acts of God. But you can decide whether you're going to tempt fate by racing your horse during a thunderstorm.

Chronic Dieting

The road to obesity is paved with chronic dieting. It is estimated that at least 50 percent of all North American women are dieting at any given time, while one-third of North American dieters initiate a diet at least once a month. The very act of dieting in your teens and twenties can predispose you to obesity in your thirties, forties, and beyond. This occurs because most people "crash and burn" instead of eating sensibly. In other words, they're chronic dieters.

The crash-and-burn approach to diet is what we do when we want to lose a specific number of pounds for a particular occasion or outfit. The pattern is to starve for a few days and then eat what we normally do. Or, we eat only certain foods (like celery and grapefruit) for a number of days and then eat normally after we've lost the weight. Most of these diets do not incorporate exercise, which means that we burn up some of our muscle as well as fat. Then, when we eat normally, we gain only fat. And over the years, that fat simply grows fatter. The bottom line is that when there is more fat on your body than muscle, you cannot burn calories as efficiently. It is the muscle that makes it possible to burn calories. Diet it away, and you diet away your ability to burn fat.

If starvation is involved in our trying to lose weight, our bodies become more efficient at getting fat. Starvation triggers an intelligence in the metabolism; our body suddenly thinks we're living in a war zone and goes into "super-efficient nomadic mode," not realizing that we're living in North America. So, when we return to our normal caloric intake, or even a *lower*-than-normal caloric intake after we've starved ourselves, *we gain more weight*. Our bodies say: "Oh look—food! Better store that as fat for the next famine." Some researchers believe that starvation diets slow down our metabolic rates far below normal so that weight gain becomes more rapid after each starvation episode.

This cycle of crash or starvation dieting is known as the yo-yo diet syndrome, the subject of thousands of articles in women's magazines throughout the last 20 years. Breaking the pattern sounds easy: Combine exercise with a sensible diet. But it's not that easy if you've led a sedentary life most of your adult years. Ninety-five percent of the people who go on a diet gain back the weight they lost, as well as extra weight, within two years. As discussed in Chapter 9, the failure often lies in psychological and behavioural factors. We have to understand why we need to eat before we can eat less. The best way to break the yo-yo diet pattern is to educate your children early about food habits and appropriate body weight. Experts say that unless you are significantly overweight to begin with or have a medical condition, *don't diet*. Just eat well. (Technically, "obese" means you weigh 20 percent more than your ideal body weight for your height and age.)

But if you're gonna diet

A recent study suggests that prepackaged balanced meals can help you stick to a meal plan more easily if you do indeed need to lose weight. Therefore, plan your meals in advance with a nutritionist and try to prefreeze or refrigerate them. This will help curb impulse eating. If you're contemplating a diet, you should also consider the following:

- What is a reasonable weight for you, given your genetic makeup, family history, age and culture? A smaller weight loss in some people can produce dramatic effects.
- Aim to lose weight at a slower rate. Too much too fast will probably lead to gaining it all back.
- Incorporate exercise into your routine, particularly activities that build muscle mass.
- Eat your vitamins. Make sure you're meeting the Canadian Recommended Nutrient Intakes (RNIs). Many of the popular North American diets of the 1980s, for example, were nutritionally inadequate (the Beverly Hills Diet contained zero percent of the U.S. recommendation for vitamin B_{12}).

Eating Disorders

Imagine three steps. Chronic dieting is the bottom step; eating disorders are the middle step; obesity is the top step. Many women become obese after dieting on and off for several years. Many other women develop eating disorders after chronic dieting, and then go on to become obese later in life.

For 2 percent of the female population in North America, starving and purging are considered a normal way to control weight. Only a small portion of women are obese because of truly hereditary factors. Most women who think they are overweight are, in fact, at an *ideal* weight for their height and body size. In Western society, the fear of obesity is so crippling that 60 percent of young girls develop distorted body images between grades one and six, believing that they are "fat"; 70 percent of all women begin dieting between the ages of 14 and 21. A U.S. study of high-school girls found that 53 percent were unhappy with their bodies by age 13; and by age 18, 78 percent were dissatisfied. The most disturbing fact, revealed in the 1991 critically acclaimed Canadian documentary *The Famine Within*, is that when given a choice, most women *would rather be dead than fat!* Eating disorders are so widespread that abnormal patterns of eating are increasingly accepted in the general population. There are parents who are actually *starving* their young daughters in an effort to keep them thin.

The two most common eating disorders involve starvation. They are *anorexia nervosa* ("loss of appetite due to mental disorder"), and bingeing followed by purging, known as *bulimia nervosa* ("hunger like an ox due to mental disorder"). Women will purge after a bingeing episode by inducing vomiting, abusing laxatives, diuretics and thyroid hormone. The most horrifying examples occur in women with Type 1 diabetes who sometimes deliberately withhold their insulin to control their weight.

Perhaps the most accepted weight-control behaviour is *over-exercising*. Today, rigorous, strenuous exercise is used as a method of "purging," and has become one of the tenets of socially accepted feminine behaviour in the 1990s. A skeleton with biceps is the current ideal.

Why are we doing this?

Eating disorders are diseases of control that primarily affect women, although more men are becoming vulnerable in recent years. Bulimics and anorexics are usually overachievers in other aspects of their lives, and view excess weight as an announcement to the world that they are "out of control." This view becomes more distorted as time goes on, until the act of eating food in public (in bulimia) or at all (in anorexia) is equivalent to a loss of control.

In anorexia, the person's emotional and sensual desires are perceived through food. These unmet desires are so great that the anorexic fears that once she eats she'll never stop since her appetite will know no natural boundaries; the fear of food drives the disease.

Most of us find it easier to relate to the bulimic than the anorexic; bulimics express their loss of control through bingeing in the same way that someone else may yell at his or her children. Bulimics then purge to regain their control. There is a feeling of comfort for bulimics in both the binge and the purge. Bulimics are sometimes referred to as "failed anorexics" because they'd starve if they could. Anorexics, however, are masters of control. They never break. I once asked a recovering anorexic the dumb question, "But didn't you get *hungry*?" Her response was that the hunger pangs made her feel powerful. The more intense the hunger, the more powerful she felt; the power actually gave her a "high."

The role of runways

Most women have a desired weight goal set at roughly ten pounds *under* their ideal weight; many women who think they are overweight are either at an ideal weight or ten pounds underweight. Supermodels like Kate Moss, who are seriously underweight, don't help much. The epidemic of eating disorders is fuelled by the fashion industry, which imposes impossible standards of beauty on the average woman. Normal body fat for a healthy woman is 22 to 25 percent; most models and actresses have roughly 10 percent body fat. In order to achieve model-thinness, women will resort to the unhealthy habits discussed above.

To help establish what is a reasonable weight for *you*, experts suggest you ask yourself four questions:

1. What is the lowest weight you have maintained as an adult for at least one year?
2. What is the largest size of clothing you feel you can "look good" in and how much do you need to weigh to wear that size?
3. Think of someone your age and height whom you know (versus a model or actress) who appears to be a "normal" weight. What does that person *actually* weigh?
4. What weight can you live with?

The message is this: accepting a normal body weight in your twenties and thirties can prevent obesity in your forties and fifties.

Binge Eating Disorder (BED)

When we hear "eating disorder," we usually think about anorexia or bulimia. There are many people, however, who binge without purging. This is also known as binge eating disorder (a.k.a. compulsive overeating). In this case, the bingeing is still an announcement to the world that "I'm out of control." Someone who purges is hiding his or her lack of control. Someone who binges and never purges is *advertising* his or her lack of control. The purger is passively asking for help; the binger who doesn't purge is aggressively asking for help. It's the same disease with a different result. (For further discussion, see Chapter 9.)

Obesity

Many obese people say that they've "dieted themselves up" to their present weight. Obesity is the strongest risk factor for developing Type 2 diabetes. Basically, the longer you've been obese, the more you are at risk. I am not referring to people who need to lose a few pounds for cosmetic reasons; I'm referring to people who weigh at least 20 percent more than their ideal weight for their age and height. If this describes you, don't panic. No one is asking you to lose *all* your weight, or any weight at once. As discussed above, start low and go slow. Instead of aiming to lose ten pounds, just aim for five. Even five pounds will allow your body to use insulin more effectively.

Why we like our fat

Fat tastes good. Fat also *feels* good in our mouths. Foods that have the particular texture and taste of fat are more acceptable than foods that don't. This is why packaged-good manufacturers describe their products as "smooth, creamy, moist, tender and rich." All the foods that boast these qualities, from ice cream or chocolate, to cheese, give us that unique feeling of satiety and satisfaction that makes us feel good.

Eating is a sensual experience. When we enjoy our food, our brains produce endorphins, "feel good" hormones that are, ironically, also produced when we exercise. Eating fat is analogous to having a "mouth orgasm." To many of us, without the taste and texture of fat, eating is an empty experience. And when we're in emotional pain or need, the texture and taste of fat become even more important, as I discuss in Chapter 9. Bingeing or falling off the diet wagon is not due to "losing control" but to regaining lost "good feelings." Food, as millions of overeaters will tell you, is our friend. It's always there; it never lets us down. (For dozens of fat-cutting tips, see Chapter 9.)

The impact of "low-fat" products

Since the late 1970s, North Americans have been deluged with low-fat products. In 1990, the United States government launched Healthy People 2000, a campaign to urge manufacturers to double their output of low-fat products by the year 2000. Since 1990, more than a thousand new fat-free or low-fat products have been introduced into North American supermarkets annually.

Current guidelines tell us that we should consume less than 30 percent of calories from fat, while no more than one-third of fat calories should come from saturated fat (see Chapter 9). According to U.S. estimates, the average person gets between 34 to 37 percent of calories from fat and roughly 12 percent of all calories from saturated fat. Data shows that in terms of "absolute fat," the intake has increased from 81 g per day in 1980 to 83 g per day in the 1990s. Total calorie intake has also increased from 1,989 per day in 1980 to 2,153 calories per day. In fact, the only reason that data shows a drop in the percentage of calories from fat is because of the huge increase in calories per day. The result is that we weigh more today than in 1980, despite the fact that roughly 10,000 more low-fat foods are available to us now than in 1980.

Most of these low-fat products, however, actually encourage us to eat more. For example, if a bag of regular chips has 9 g of fat per serving (1 serving usually equals about 5 chips or one handful), you will more likely stick to that one handful. However, if you find a low-fat brand of chips that boasts "50 percent less fat" per serving, you're more likely to eat the whole bag (feeling good about eating "low-fat" chips), which can easily triple your fat intake.

Low-fat or fat-free foods trick our bodies with ingredients that mimic the functions of fat in foods. This is often achieved by using modified fats that are only partially metabolized, if at all. While some foods reduce the fat by removing the fat (skim milk, lean cuts of meat), most low fat-foods require a variety of "fat copycats" to preserve the taste and texture of the food. Water, for example, is often combined with carbohydrates and protein to mimic a particular texture or taste, as is the case with a variety of baked goods or cake mixes. In general, though, the low-fat "copycats" are either carbohydrate-based, protein-based or fat-based.

Carbohydrate-based ingredients are starches and gums that are often used as thickening agents to create the texture of fat. You'll find these in abundance in low-fat salad dressings, sauces, gravies, frozen desserts and baked goods. Compared to natural fats, which are at about 9 calories per gram, carbohydrate-based ingredients run anywhere from zero to 4 calories per gram.

Protein-based low-fat ingredients are created by "doing things" to the proteins that make them behave differently. For example, by taking proteins such as whey or egg white, and heating or blending them at high speeds, you can create the look and feel of "creamy." Soy and corn proteins are often used in these cases. You'll find these ingredients in low-fat cheese, butter, mayonnaise, salad dressings, frozen dairy desserts, sour cream and baked goods. They run between 1 to 4 calories per gram.

Low-fat foods that use fat-based ingredients tailor the fat in some way so that we do not absorb or metabolize it fully. These ingredients are found in chocolate, chocolate coatings, margarine, spreads, sour cream and cheese. You can also use these ingredients as low-fat substitutes for frying foods (you do this when you fry eggs in margarine, for example). Olestra, the new fat substitute currently being test-marketed in the United States, is an example of a fat substitute that is not absorbed by our bodies, providing no calories (see Chapter 9).

Caprenin and salatrim are examples of partially absorbed fats (they contain more long-chain fatty acids; see glossary), and are the more traditional fat-based low-fat ingredients. These are roughly 5 calories per gram.

There's no question that low-fat foods are designed to give you more freedom of choice with your diet, supposedly allowing you to cut your fat without compromising your taste buds. Studies show that taste outperforms "nutrition" in your brain. Yet, many experts believe that low-fat products create more of a barrier to weight loss in the long term.

Researchers at the University of Toronto suggest that these products essentially allow us to increase our calories even though we are reducing our overall fat intake. For example, in one study, women who consumed a low-fat breakfast food ate more during the day than women who consumed a higher-fat food at breakfast.

The good news about low-fat or fat-free products is that they are, in fact, *lower in fat*, and are created to substitute for the "bad foods" you know you shouldn't have but cannot live without. The boring phrase "everything in moderation" applies to low-fat products, too. Balancing these products with "good stuff" is the key. A low-fat treat should still be treated like its high-fat original. In other words, don't have double the amount because it's low-fat. Instead, have the same amount as you would of the original.

What about the fat hormone?

A study reported in a 1997 issue of *Nature Medicine*, showed that people with low levels of the hormone leptin may be prone to weight gain. In this study, people who gained an average of 50 pounds over three years started out with lower leptin levels than people who maintained their weight over the same period. Therefore, this study may form the basis for treating obesity with leptin. Experts speculate that 10 percent of all obesity may be due to a leptin resistance. Leptin is made by fat cells and apparently sends messages to the brain about how much fat our bodies are carrying. Like other hormones, it's thought that leptin has a stimulating action that acts as a thermostat of sorts. In mice, adequate amounts of leptin somehow signalled the mouse to become more active and eat less, while too little leptin signalled the mouse to eat more while becoming less active.

Interestingly, Pima Indians who are prone to obesity and also at highest risk for Type 2 diabetes in the United States, were shown to have roughly one-third less leptin in blood analyses. Human studies of injecting leptin to treat obesity are in the works right now, but to date have not been shown to be effective.

Right now, researchers are working on using leptin as a prevention drug for Type 2 diabetes. Not only does leptin block the formation of fat in body tissues, but it apparently lowers blood sugar levels, too. It's believed that leptin somehow improves the function of insulin-producing cells in the pancreas, which helps the body to use insulin more effectively. Since you won't find leptin on your drugstore shelves just yet, you're going to have to be your own fat hormone and do the difficult work of losing some weight.

Anti-obesity pills

The U.S. government recently approved an anti-obesity pill that blocks the absorption of almost one-third of the fat people eat. One of the side effects of this new prescription drug, called orlistat (Xenical), causes rather embarrassing diarrhea each time you eat fatty foods. To avoid the drug's side effects, simply avoid fat! The pill can also decrease absorption of vitamin D and other important nutrients, however.

Not yet available in Canada, orlistat is the first drug to fight obesity through the intestine instead of the brain. Taken with each meal, it binds to certain pancreatic enzymes to block the digestion of 30 percent of the fat you ingest. How it affects the pancreas in the long term is not known. Combined with a sensible diet, people on orlistat lost more weight than those not on orlistat. This drug is not intended for people who need to lose a few pounds; it is designed for medically obese people (see page 14). (Orlistat was also found to lower cholesterol, blood pressure and blood sugar levels.)

Another obesity pill, called Redux, alters brain chemicals to trick the body into feeling full. A similar competitor, sibutramine, is expected to be approved by the end of 1998.

One of the most controversial anti-obesity therapies was the use of fenfluramine and phentermine (Fen/Phen). Both drugs were approved for use individually more than 20 years ago, but since 1992, doctors have tended to prescribe them together for long-term management of obesity. In 1996, U.S. doctors wrote a total of 18 million monthly prescriptions for Fen/Phen. And many of the prescriptions were issued to people who were not obese. This is known as "off-label" prescribing. In July 1997, the United States Food and Drug Administration, researchers at the Mayo Clinic and the Mayo Foundation made a joint announcement warning doctors that Fen/Phen can cause heart disease. On September 15, "Fen" was taken off the market. The Fen/Phen lesson: diet and lifestyle modification are still the best pathways to wellness.

In light of the safety concerns regarding current anti-obesity drugs, diet and lifestyle modification are still considered the best pathways to wellness.

High Cholesterol

Cholesterol is a whitish, waxy fat made in vast quantities by the liver. That's why liver or other organ meats are high in cholesterol! Cholesterol is needed to make hormones as well as cell membranes. If you have high cholesterol, the excess cholesterol in your blood can lead to narrowed arteries, which can lead to a heart attack. Saturated fat, discussed in detail in Chapter 9, is often a culprit when it comes to high cholesterol. But the highest levels of cholesterol are due to a genetic defect in the liver. Since people with diabetes are four times more likely to develop heart disease and five times more likely to suffer a stroke, lowering your cholesterol, especially if you're already at risk for Type 2 diabetes, is a good idea.

Insulin's role in "fat control"

Insulin not only keeps blood sugar in check, it also keeps the levels of "good" cholesterol (HDL—high-density lipoproteins), "bad" cholesterol (LDL—low-density lipoproteins) and triglycerides in check. When you're not making enough insulin or your body isn't using insulin efficiently, your LDL levels and your triglycerides rise, but more important, *your HDL levels fall*, which can lead to heart disease. When diabetes is in control, cholesterol levels will return to normal, which will cut your risk of heart disease, and stroke, as well.

Checking your cholesterol

Cholesterol levels are checked through a simple blood test. Soon, home cholesterol tests may be available in Canada. The magic number is 200 milligrams per decilitre (200 mg/dl) or lower. At this level, you can have your cholesterol levels checked every five years.

If your blood cholesterol is between 200 and 239 mg/dl, so long as you don't smoke, are not obese, have normal blood pressure, are a premenopausal female and do not have a family history of heart disease—you're fine! But chances are, you do not meet all these criteria. In this case, discuss with your doctor how often you need to have your cholesterol levels checked.

A high cholesterol reading should always be followed up with an HDL-LDL analysis. If your LDL number is below 130 mg/dl, you're fine, but if LDL levels are between 130 and 160 mg/dl, you are considered a "borderline" case of high cholesterol. Once your LDL levels reach 160, you should definitely be on a treatment plan to lower your cholesterol.

Hypertension (a.k.a. High Blood Pressure)

About 12 percent of Canadian adults suffer from hypertension, or high blood pressure. What is blood pressure? The blood flows from the heart into the arteries (blood vessels), pressing against the artery walls. The simplest way to explain this is to think about a liquid-soap dispenser. When you want soap, you need to pump it out by pressing down on the little dispenser pump, the "heart" of the dispenser. The liquid soap is the "blood" and the little tube, through which the soap flows, is the "artery." The pressure that's exerted on the wall of the tube is therefore the "blood pressure."

When the tube is hollow and clean, you needn't pump very hard to get the soap; it comes out easily. But when the tubing in your dispenser gets narrower as a result of old, hardened, gunky liquid soap blocking the tube, you have to pump down much harder to get any soap, while the force the soap exerts against the tube is increased. Obviously, this is a simplistic explanation of a very complex problem, but essentially, the narrowing of the arteries, created by higher blood pressure, forces your heart to work harder to pump the blood. If this goes on too long, your heart muscle enlarges and becomes weaker, which can lead to a heart attack. Higher pressure can also weaken the walls of your blood vessels, which can cause a stroke.

The term hyper*tension* refers to the tension or force exerted on your artery walls. (Hyper means "too much," as in "too much tension.") Blood pressure is measured in two readings: X over Y. The X is the systolic pressure, which is the pressure that occurs during the heart's contraction. The Y is the diastolic pressure, which is the pressure that occurs when the heart rests between contractions. In "liquid soap" terms, the systolic pressure occurs when you press the pump down; the diastolic pressure occurs when you release your hand from the pump and allow it to rise back to its "resting" position.

Normal blood pressure readings are 120 over 80 (120/80). Readings of 140/90 or higher are generally considered borderline, although for some people this is still considered a normal reading. For the general population, 140/90 is "lecture time," when your doctor will begin to counsel you about dietary and lifestyle habits. By 160/100, many people are prescribed a hypertensive drug, which is designed to lower blood pressure.

Let's examine some of the causes of hypertension. The same factors that put you at risk for Type 2 diabetes, such as obesity, can also put you at risk for hypertension. Hypertension is also exacerbated by tobacco and alcohol consumption, too much sodium or salt in the diet. (People of African descent tend to be more salt-sensitive.)

If high blood pressure runs in the family, you're considered at greater risk of developing hypertension. High blood pressure can also be caused by kidney disorders (which may be initially caused by diabetes) or pregnancy (known as pregnancy-induced hypertension). Medications are also common culprits. Estrogen-containing medications (such as oral contraceptives), non-steroidal anti-inflammatory drugs (NSAIDs), such as ibuprofen, nasal decongestants, cold remedies, appetite suppressants, certain antidepressants and other drugs can all increase blood pressure. Be sure to check with your pharmacist.

How to lower your blood pressure without drugs

- Change your diet and begin exercising (see discussion of obesity, above).
- Limit alcohol consumption to no more than 2 oz of liquor or 8 oz of wine or 24 oz of beer per day, and lower still, for "liver health."
- Limit your salt intake to about $1\frac{1}{2}$ teaspoons per day. Cut out all foods high in sodium, such as canned soups, pickles, soy sauce and so on. Some canned soups contain 1,000 mg of sodium, for example. That's a lot!
- Increase your intake of calcium or dairy products and potassium (i.e., bananas). Some still-unproven studies suggest that people with hypertension are calcium- and potassium-deficient.
- Lower your stress levels. Studies show that by lowering your stress, your blood pressure decreases.

Sedentary Lifestyle

What's the definition of sedentary? *Not moving!* If you have a desk job or spend most of your time at a computer, in your car or watching television (even if it is PBS or CNN), you are a sedentary person. If you do roughly 20 minutes of exercise less than once a week, you're relatively sedentary. You need to incorporate some sort of movement into your daily schedule in order to be considered active. That movement can be anything: aerobic exercise, brisk walks around the block or walking your dog. If you lead a sedentary lifestyle, and are obese, you are at significant risk of developing Type 2 diabetes in your forties, if you are genetically predisposed. If you are not obese, your risk is certainly lowered, but you are then predisposed to a number of other problems, particularly if you're female. Chapter 6 discusses exercise and Type 2 diabetes in detail.

Smoking

Smoking and diabetes is a toxic combination. You already know that smoking leads to heart attacks. But what you might not know is that if you have Type 2 diabetes, and do not smoke, you are *already* four times more likely to have a heart attack than a person without diabetes. If you smoke, *and* have Type 2 diabetes, you have an even greater risk of having a heart attack than nonsmokers without diabetes.

Smoking and obesity

Smoking and obesity often coexist. Women, in particular, begin to smoke in their teens as a way to lose weight. A 1997 study done by the Department of Psychology and Preventive Medicine at the University of Memphis in Tennessee shows that this approach doesn't work. Smoking teens are just as likely to become obese over time as non-smokers. Ironically, it was found that the more a person weighed, the more cigarettes he or she smoked. In fact, the heavier the person, the more cigarettes he or she smoked. In the long run, smokers often wound up weighing more than non-smokers because they substituted food for nicotine when they quit or attempted to quit.

Sleep Deprivation or Sleep Disorders

There are studies linking obesity and, hence, Type 2 diabetes, to lack of sleep, snoring, loss of REM sleep and a range of other sleep disorders. When you don't sleep well or get enough sleep—particularly REM sleep (rapid eye movement, which occurs in deep sleep)—you will be irritable and drowsy during the day. That means you'll eat more and will likely crave fast-energy foods high in sugar or starch. By visiting a sleep disorder clinic or, in some cases, by going to a time management seminar, you should be able to get your sleep.

Vitamin Deficiency

Blood samples from people with diabetes show a tendency toward "oxidative stress," meaning that people with diabetes tend to be antioxidant-deficient. Antioxidants are vitamins found in coloured (i.e., non-green) fruits and vegetables, discussed in more detail in Chapter 5.

Many people make the mistake of cutting out nutrients along with the fat in their diets. Experts recommend that to meet all vitamin needs through food alone, you need 1,200 calories per day if you're female and 1,500 calories per day if you're male. (Unless you need more or less vitamins due to a medical condition). Studies reveal that when diets fall to 1,000 calories, these vitamins dropped to approximately 60 percent of their recommended levels. This is where vitamin supplements, meal replacement drinks or health bars come in. They're designed to give you your daily requirement of vitamins and minerals. If you're on a low-fat diet, make sure that you're not cutting out all protein, calcium or carbohydrates. You do need some of these! (See Chapter 9.)

Studies also show that approximately 25 percent of North Americans skip breakfast, while an additional 38 percent skip lunch. Eating breakfast will help you to lower your fat intake because this reduces that impulsive snacking in the late afternoon and actually improves your nutrient absorption.

Age can also interfere with vitamin intake. Research shows that seniors (over 65) tend to be deficient in vitamins A, C, D, protein and calcium. Yet these nutrients can boost the immune system, and improve bone density, cardiovascular health and a thousand other things.

Risk Factors You Can't Change

By *modifying* any of the modifiable risk factors above, you can help to offset your risk of developing Type 2 diabetes if you have any of the following risk markers. While you can't change your genetic makeup, medical history or age, you can significantly reduce the odds of these factors predisposing you to Type 2 diabetes.

Age

The risk of developing Type 2 diabetes increases with age. Perhaps at no other time in history have we seen so many people over age 45—the so-called baby boom generation. This may, in part, account for the increase we're seeing in Type 2 diabetes, as well as other age-related diseases. However, the lifestyle and dietary habits you practise before age 45 count—either against you or for you. So, by changing your diet and becoming more active before age 45, you may not necessarily be able to prevent your genetic fate, but you may certainly be able to delay it. And in the event that you develop Type 2 diabetes, a healthy diet and active lifestyle will go a long way in controlling the disease.

It's crucial to keep in mind that studies regarding diet, lifestyle and Type 2 diabetes are still unclear, although experts certainly agree that there is a strong relationship between genetic markers for diabetes and environmental factors, such as activity levels, weight and diet.

Menopause

When women reach menopause, estrogen loss can lead to some well-documented problems, such as osteoporosis (estrogen helps to maintain calcium levels) and heart disease (estrogen raises HDL levels, or "good" cholesterol, which protects premenopausal women from heart disease). Estrogen also helps to protect against insulin resistance. Even if you decide against hormone replacement therapy, diet and lifestyle changes can lower your risks of heart disease, osteoporosis and Type 2 diabetes substantially. (See Chapter 9 for more details on dietary fat and healthful eating.)

Genes

Type 2 diabetes is a genetic disease, which means you have the "wiring" installed for Type 2 diabetes at birth. Fortunately, we do understand some of the outside factors that can trip the Type 2 switch. Body shapes, diet and activity levels are strong switch-trippers. On the other hand, if you don't have any Type 2 diabetes genes (in other words, you're not "wired" for this disease), these outside factors cannot, by themselves, cause you to develop Type 2 diabetes. For instance, there are plenty of obese and sedentary people walking around who do not have Type 2 diabetes, nor will they develop the disease in the future.

When underdeveloped populations become urbanized and adopt a Western lifestyle, there is an explosion in Type 2 diabetes. But the genes must be present in order to "allow" for the disease in the first place. This is more proof that there is a genetic-environmental combo platter at work when it comes to this disease. The question is, what aspect of westernization triggers Type 2 diabetes in these regions? "Western" means many things, including a higher-fat diet, less physical activity, as well as access to medical care, which means populations are living longer.

And what role does earlier screening and better detection of Type 2 diabetes play in the global increase of the disease? As one doctor put it, "When you don't look for it, you don't find it." More and more evidence points to the fact that Type 2 diabetes has been around for a long time.

What are the odds?

Type 2 diabetes is caused by multiple factors. The odds of developing it have to do with some genes interacting with some environmental factors. Obesity, excess calories, deficient calorie expenditure and aging can all lead to a resistance to insulin. If you remove the environmental risks, however, you can probably modify the risk of Type 2 diabetes.

Who are you?

As discussed earlier, aboriginal cultures develop Type 2 diabetes at far higher rates than other Canadians. On some reserves, Type 2 diabetes is present in 70 percent of the adult population. Approximately 15 percent of African–North American adults have Type 2 diabetes, while about 20 percent of all North American Hispanics have Type 2 diabetes.

The "thrifty gene" is thought to be responsible for the higher rates of Type 2 diabetes in the aboriginal and African–North American populations. This means that the more recently your culture has lived indigenously or nomadically (that is, living off the land you came from and eating seasonally), the more efficient your metabolism is. Unfortunately, it is also more sensitive to nutrient excess. If you're an aboriginal North American, only about 100 years have passed since your ancestors lived indigenously. This is an exceedingly short amount of time to ask thousands of years of hunter-gatherer genes to adjust to a Western diet. If you're African–North American, your ancestors haven't lived here any longer than about 400 years; prior to that, they were living a tribal, nomadic lifestyle. Again, 400 years is *not* a long time.

As for Hispanic populations or other immigrant populations, many come from families who have spent generations in poverty.

Their metabolisms adjusted to long periods of famine, and are often overloaded by Western foods. The other problem is poverty in North America. Aboriginal, African and Hispanic populations tend to have much lower incomes, and are therefore eating lower-quality food, which, when introduced to the "thrifty gene," can trigger Type 2 diabetes.

What about Easterners?

Type 2 diabetes seems to occur in South-East Asian populations at Western rates even when the diet is Eastern. East Indians, in particular, have very high rates of heart disease. In fact, India has the largest Type 2 population in the world. Urbanization is cited as a major factor.

Multiracial North Americans

Your risk of developing Type 2 diabetes depends on your mix of genes and your current and past lifestyle and diet. If you are part aboriginal and part European, for example, you will probably need to be more conscientious about your diet than if you were part Asian and part European. Studying your family tree and family history of Type 2 diabetes is the best way to assess the "damage" and make the necessary changes in your own diet and lifestyle to repair it.

Other medical conditions

There are certain diseases such as Prader-Willi, Down's syndrome, Turner's syndrome, Cushing's disease or acromegaly (large face, long arms and hands) that can lead to diabetes in the long term. In this case, diabetes is a presenting feature of the disorder. Many diseases run together and this is another example of that.

Gestational Diabetes

Many women may be worried that a history of gestational diabetes means they will eventually develop Type 2 diabetes.

If you developed (or will develop) gestational diabetes during pregnancy, consider yourself put on alert. Approximately 20 percent of all women with gestational diabetes develop Type 2, presuming no other risk factors. If you are genetically predisposed to Type 2 diabetes, then a history of gestational diabetes can raise your risk of eventually developing the disease. Gestational diabetes develops more often in women who were overweight prior to pregnancy, and women who are over 35; gestational diabetes increases with maternal age. If your mother had gestational diabetes, you are more likely to develop it. For a more detailed discussion, see Chapter 2.

Impaired Glucose Tolerance (IGT)

One in three people with impaired glucose tolerance (IGT) will develop Type 2 diabetes. A diagnosis of IGT is sometimes mistakenly called "borderline diabetes." For the record, there is no such thing as borderline diabetes. You either have diabetes or you don't. IGT is what many doctors refer to as the "gray zone" between normal blood sugar levels and "full-blown diabetes." And there are even two different subtypes of IGT that have been identified. IGT is to Type 2 diabetes what HIV is to AIDS. IGT means that you could progress to Type 2 diabetes, but no one knows when that day will come. Therefore, starting prophylactic therapy is your best defence; this means having a frank discussion with your doctor about your risk of developing Type 2 diabetes, as well as which lifestyle modifications or early therapies are available for optimum health.

Diagnosing IGT

In the past, oral glucose tolerance tests were used to diagnose IGT. But today, a fasting blood glucose test, which is a simple blood test, is all that's necessary. The only time oral glucose tolerance tests are used anymore is to screen pregnant women for IGT or gestational diabetes. An oral glucose tolerance test involves taking a sugary drink, and having the blood sugar tested at regular intervals over the next two hours. In the United States, jelly beans are sometimes used instead of the drink, but this is not yet approved by the American or Canadian Diabetes Association.

Normal fasting blood glucose readings (what your levels are before you've eaten) are between 3 to 5 millimoles (mmol), a unit of measurement that counts molecular volume per litre. Three fasting blood glucose levels between 5 and 7.8 mmol means that you have IGT. A fasting blood glucose level over 7.8 mmol or a random (any time of day) blood glucose level greater than 11.1 mmol mean that you have diabetes.

It's also possible to have abnormally low blood glucose levels, which is called *hypoglycemia* (discussed in detail in Chapter 4).

Pancreatitis

Diabetes can be caused by a condition known as pancreatitis, which means inflammation of the pancreas. This occurs when the pancreas's digestive enzymes turn on you and attack your own pancreas. This can cause the gland to bleed, as well as serious tissue damage, infection and cysts. (Other organs, such as your heart, lungs and kidneys could be affected in severe cases.) Pancreatitis is most often chronic, as opposed to acute (sudden), caused by years of alcohol abuse. In fact, 90 percent of all chronic pancreatitis affects men between 30 and 40 years of age. In rare cases, chronic pancreatitis is inherited, but experts are not sure why this is. People with chronic pancreatitis tend to have three main symptoms: pain, weight loss (due to poor food absorption and digestion), as well as diabetes (the type depends on how much damage was done to your islet or insulin-producing cells).

The treatment is to first stop drinking. Then you will need to be managed like any other diabetes patient: blood glucose monitoring, meal planning and, possibly, insulin injections.

"Side-Effect Diabetes"

This is a term I've coined to describe what's known as "secondary diabetes." This occurs when your diabetes is a *side effect* of a particular drug or surgical procedure.

A number of prescription medications, including steroids or Dilantin, can raise your blood sugar levels, which would affect the outcome of a blood sugar test, for example. Make sure you tell your doctor about all medications you're on prior to having your blood sugar checked.

If you've had your pancreas removed (a pancreatectomy), diabetes will definitely develop. It may also develop if you've experienced the following:

- severe injury to your pancreas;
- severe pancreatitis (see above);
- liver disease;
- iron overload;
- brain damage.

Signs and Symptoms

By now you should have a pretty good idea of your risk profile for Type 2 diabetes. But knowing the signs of Type 2 diabetes is crucial. If you have any of the symptoms listed below, request to be screened for Type 2 diabetes.

- Weight gain. When you're not using your insulin properly, you may suffer from excess insulin, which can increase your appetite. This is a classic Type 2 symptom.
- Blurred vision or any change in sight.
- Drowsiness or *extreme* fatigue at times when you shouldn't be drowsy or tired.

- Frequent infections that are slow to heal. (Women should be on alert for recurring vaginal yeast infections.)
- Tingling or numbness in the hands and feet.
- Gum disease. High blood sugar affects the blood vessels in your mouth, causing inflamed gums; the sugar content can get into your saliva, causing cavities in your teeth.

Your Child's Risk of Type 2

As discussed earlier, Type 2 diabetes is certainly a genetic disease. But, as mentioned, there are many outside factors that can "trip" the switch. The most influencial factors are eating habits and lack of physical activity, which, thankfully, can be modified.

There is also a rare kind of Type 2 diabetes known as mature-onset diabetes of the young (MODY). This means that a person under age 30 develops non-insulin-dependent diabetes. If one parent has MODY, your child has a 50 percent chance of developing it, too.

Teach Your Children Well

You can't change your child's genes, but you can help to offset the genetic tendency towards Type 2 diabetes by teaching your child good habits early. Since you control much of your child's diet and environment, you can make sure that you lower these odds.

For example, in young children, try to limit what I call the Sugar Shows—television programming for children that is basically a vehicle to sell sugar cereals and junk food. Some foods aimed at children contain as much as 22 g of fat and 1,500 mg of sodium. And selling pies and cakes as "breakfast foods" to children raises some ethical questions as well.

Instead, play that Disney video another time or limit programs to "safe channels" (with that V-chip being marketed). Some of the worst damage is done during network Saturday-morning cartoons. You can also practise Fast-Food Control by ordering some of the healthier foods for your kids when they're begging for it. For instance, pizza, tacos or falafel are healthier choices than greasy hamburgers, fried chicken or fries. Try to resist fat-in-a-box meals that boast enough grease to kill your whole family, *plus* a free chocolate layer cake when you buy two!

Everything your child eats today counts in adulthood. Research shows that even infant eating patterns can lead to obesity years later. One famous baboon study found that baboons overfed early in life became obese later on. This didn't happen with baboons who were fed a normal diet in infancy.

Stop Parenting With Food

Many bad habits begin with parents forcing children to finish food when they say they're full. We all start with biological mechanisms that tell us when we're hungry or full. But if we hear things like "Clean your plate" when we say, "But I'm full, Mom," and worse, "Good girl/boy" when we do cram that last bit of food in to "please," we *wreck* those biological signals designed to stop us from becoming obese. In essence, you're teaching your child not to follow natural instincts about food and eating. When your child is hungry, he or she will eat. If a food isn't palatable, unless your child is living in war or famine, don't force the food on your child. And, *never* punish a child by withholding food or, worse, *rewarding* a child with dessert. By saying, "No chocolate until you finish your carrots" you're programming your child to feel *emotional* rewards when he or she eats that chocolate. In other words, both these terrible parenting methods (which we learned from our parents) are recipes for eating disorders, chronic dieting or obesity down the road.

A word about "schedules"

There are parents out there who set feeding schedules for their children. In one case, a grandmother was forbidden by the mother to feed a healthy snack to a three-year-old who was crying and begging for food out of sheer hunger (in an affluent North American suburb, I might add!). The mother apparently only allowed the child to eat at certain times. This is a recipe for disaster in later life. *Don't do this!*

Feed your children well

Why is your toddler eating toys, mud and crayons? Because that toddler is communicating that, as a human being, he or she needs a *variety* of foods in his or her diet. And, fortunately, because we're not living in war or famine, we can give this to our children. Introduce a wide variety of "normal" foods (all colours of vegetables and fruits; whole grains, pastas and so on). Without a varied diet, a child will not consume the vitamins and minerals he or she needs. The lack of a varied diet could also lead to obesity in childhood, as the child loads up on carbohydrates, fat and junk foods.

Babes in arms

Breastfeed your baby. And do so for as long as possible. Lots and lots of studies say breastfed children are healthier and have fewer diseases (including obesity-related diseases) than formula-fed babies. Breast milk is perfectly balanced to satiate your baby; the "foremilk" is more watery, while the "hindmilk" is creamier and fattier—the perfect meal for someone with no teeth. (And, breast milk is more watery in hot climates for hydration, and creamier in cold climates for calories!)

A recent study concludes that nutrition is most important in infancy and adolescence. For example, the amount of salt in a newborn's diet could affect blood pressure later in life. The formula Similac contains 27 mg of sodium per 5-oz serving, too high for a baby!

Chapter 2

WHAT'S MY TYPE?

If you have been diagnosed with diabetes, the good news is that you are living at a time when self-managing your diabetes has never been easier. There are not only brand-new treatment options available, but dozens of upgraded products to make your diabetes a lot easier to monitor. The bad news is that only *you* can manage your diabetes. This is one of those diseases that can't be managed by only your doctor. You have to take charge, while your doctor supervises from afar. For this reason, being diagnosed with diabetes may feel like being pushed out of an airplane without a parachute. Think of this chapter as basic training. It will tell you what you need to know in order to plan for a safe landing. It will also serve as a user's guide to your diabetes equipment: glucose monitors (optional), pills and, in some cases, insulin and all of its gear.

Type Casting

As discussed in the Introduction, there are several labels for Type 2 diabetes. The most common is non-insulin dependent diabetes mellitus (NIDDM), a genetic disease that is completely different from Type 1 diabetes, insulin-dependent diabetes mellitus (IDDM), which is an autoimmune disease. That means that unlike Type 2, environmental factors, such as a sedentary lifestyle or obesity, do not influence the onset of Type 1 diabetes.

Type 2 diabetes is a genetic disease that *is* triggered by environmental factors, such as obesity or a sedentary lifestyle. Lean, fit, healthy people who are genetically predisposed to Type 2 diabetes can still develop it, but they may also prevent the disease by modifying one or more environmental factors, discussed in Chapter 1. Type 2 diabetes is also a disease of insulin resistance, discussed below.

There are two other kinds of diabetes. Diabetes can be a side effect of something else, such as pancreatic surgery (see page 34). Diabetes can also develop during pregnancy, known as *gestational diabetes mellitis* (GDM), which occurs between the 24th and 28th week of pregnancy.

Insulin Resistance Versus No Insulin

It wasn't until the 1960s when researchers discovered that most people with Type 2 diabetes suffered from a *resistance* to insulin, not necessarily a lack of insulin. In fact, Type 2 diabetes is usually a disease of insulin resistance rather than "no insulin." The disease causes your body to overproduce insulin. Too much insulin has led to a decrease in insulin-receptor sites, small "keyholes" on the surface of your insulin-producing cells, into which insulin (the "key") fits. Sometimes there are simply not enough receptor sites; other times, something is wrong with the connection or link between the key and keyhole.

In the Introduction, I explain the relationship between insulin and glucose, comparing insulin to a courier knocking on the cell's door with a message to "let sugar in." Again, insulin resistance occurs when there is no answer at the door. The insulin is there; the cell isn't responding to it. The result is diabetes—too much sugar in the blood. This causes all the classic symptoms of diabetes (see Chapter 1), which may have led your doctor to diagnose diabetes or screen you for the disease.

Some experts believe that insulin resistance actually causes obesity, which is why obesity is such a risk factor. When the body uses insulin properly, it not only lowers blood sugar but assists in the distribution of fat and protein. Therefore, when your body doesn't use insulin properly, obesity can be the by-product.

By the time you're diagnosed with Type 2 diabetes, it may be that you have inadequate or unreliable insulin secretion from your pancreatic beta cells.

Although Type 2 diabetes is usually a disease of insulin resistance, it is sometimes caused by a liver gone awry, a scenario in which the liver actually takes it upon itself to make glucose, increasing your levels of blood sugar. This is often the case in alcoholics.

Having Type 2 diabetes doesn't mean that you have only high blood sugar. This condition can cause other problems such as hypertension (high blood pressure), high cholesterol and insulin resistance in your muscles and liver. So even if you manage to get your blood sugar levels under control, you still may need to be treated for these other conditions, which can be greatly alleviated through diet and exercise. However, you don't have to have any symptoms to be diagnosed with Type 2 diabetes.

When you have Type 2, but require insulin

Insulin resistance, characterized by the body's inability to use insulin, sometimes leads to a condition in which the pancreas stops making insulin altogether. The cells' resistance to insulin causes the pancreas to work harder, causing too much insulin in the system (a.k.a. hyperinsulinemia) until it's just plumb tuckered out, as the saying goes. Your pancreas is making the insulin and knocking on the door, but the cells aren't answering. Your pancreas will eventually say, "Okay, fine! I'll shut down production since you obviously aren't using what I'm making."

But this isn't always the reason you need insulin. Often the problem is that your body becomes increasingly more resistant to the insulin your pancreas is producing. This is sometimes exacerbated by medications or the disease over time. Controlling your blood sugar becomes harder and harder until, ultimately, you need to inject insulin.

Type 2 can also become an insulin-requiring disease if you go for long periods with high blood sugar levels. In this case sugar toxicity occurs—or, in other words, the sugar poisons the cells of the body, including the insulin-producing cells in the pancreas, destroying them forever. The result is no insulin and hence, insulin-requiring Type 2 diabetes. This is not the same thing as insulin-dependent diabetes, or Type 1 diabetes, which is a completely different, autoimmune disease.

If you have been told that you need insulin, and you are over age 45, or you were told you had impaired glucose tolerance and now need insulin, this is what probably happened to you.

Almost Diabetes?

As discussed in the last chapter, there is no such thing as "borderline diabetes" or a "touch of diabetes." You either have diabetes or you don't. Many people have what's clinically known as impaired glucose tolerance (IGT), a condition in which blood sugar levels are higher than normal, but are still not high enough to be classified as diabetes (see Chapter 1).

Gestational Diabetes Mellitus (GDM)

Gestational diabetes refers to diabetes that is first diagnosed during the 24th to 28th week of pregnancy. If you had diabetes prior to your pregnancy (Type 1 or Type 2), it is known as *pre-gestational diabetes*, which is a completely different story in that the risks to the fetus exist throughout pregnancy. In this case, you'll need to have excellent control of your blood sugar before you get pregnant, and will need to discuss the risks of pregnancy with your diabetes managment team (Chapter 3) prior to conception.

What is GDM?

Gestational diabetes is "high blood sugar (hyperglycemia) first recognized during pregnancy." Three to 12 percent of all pregnant women will develop gestational diabetes. During pregnancy, hormones made by the placenta can block the insulin the pancreas normally makes. This forces the pancreas to work harder and manufacture three times as much insulin as usual. In many cases, the pancreas isn't able to keep up and blood sugar levels rise. Gestational diabetes is therefore a common pregnancy-related health problem, and is in the same league as other pregnancy-related conditions that develop during the second or third trimesters, such as high blood pressure.

GDM usually takes the form of Type 2 diabetes in that it can be managed through diet and blood sugar monitoring. However, recent research on California women with gestational diabetes shows that only one-third were able control their condition through diet and blood glucose monitoring. Therefore, insulin may be necessary if your GDM cannot be controlled. GDM will usually disappear once you deliver, but it recurs in future pregnancies two out of three times. In some cases, GDM is really the unveiling of Type 2 or even Type 1 diabetes *during* pregnancy.

If you are genetically predisposed to Type 2 diabetes, you are more likely to develop Type 2 in the future after a bout of gestational diabetes.

Moreover, if you have GDM, you're more at risk for other pregnancy-related conditions such as hypertension (high blood pressure), pre-eclampsia and polyhydramnios (too much amniotic fluid). And if you're carrying more than one fetus, your pregnancy is even more at risk. It's wise to seek out an obstetrician if you have GDM. In very high-risk situations, a perinatologist (an obstetrician who specializes in high-risk pregnancies) may have to be consulted.

Diagnosing GDM

The symptoms of gestational diabetes are extreme thirst, hunger or fatigue, all of which can be masked by the normal discomforts of pregnancy. Therefore, all women should be screened for GDM during weeks 24 to 28 of their pregnancy, via a urine test or oral glucose tolerance test, discussed in the previous chapter. This is particularly crucial if:

- you are of aboriginal, African or Hispanic descent;
- your mother had GDM;
- you previously gave birth to a baby with a birth weight of more than 9 pounds;
- you've miscarried or had a still birth;
- you're over 25 years of age;
- you're overweight or obese (20 percent above your ideal weight);
- you have high blood pressure.

Since blood sugar levels rise steadily throughout pregnancy, it's entirely possible to have normal levels at week 24 and high levels at week 28. Some doctors believe it isn't necessary to screen a woman for GDM if she has no symptoms or any of the risk factors above; the attitude is that universal screening can create unnecessary anxiety. However, U.S. studies show that by screening only women with risk factors, almost half of all gestational diabetes is missed.

Risks to the fetus

Fortunately, because gestational diabetes occurs well after the baby's body has been formed, birth defects are not a risk with GDM (although they are with pre-gestational diabetes). Gestational diabetes is only linked to heart defects when the condition is severe enough to necessitate insulin treatment in the last trimester.

The main risk to the fetus with GDM is that the high blood sugar levels cross the placenta and feed the fetus too much glucose, causing it to grow too fat and large for its gestational age. This condition is called *macrosomia*, which is technically defined by a birth weight greater than 4,000 g.

Babies with macrosomia are usually not able to fit through the birth canal because their shoulders get stuck (known as *shoulder dystocia*). As a result, most women with macrosomic babies will need to deliver by Cesarean section.

The extra glucose that gets into the baby can also cause its pancreas to work harder, which can cause hypoglycemia after birth.

Treating GDM

The treatment for GDM is controlling blood sugar levels through diet, exercise, insulin (if necessary) and blood sugar monitoring. To do this, you must be under the care of a pregnancy practitioner (obstetrician, midwife, etc.), a diabetes specialist and a dietitian. Guidelines for nutrition and weight gain during a diabetic pregnancy depend on your current health, the fetal size and *your* weight.

Managing Type 2 Diabetes

Your goal in managing Type 2 diabetes is to control your blood sugar levels and weight through diet and exercise, and to prevent long-term complications of your disease. One of the most important Type 1 diabetes research projects ever undertaken is the Diabetes Control and Complications Trial (DCCT). This trial proved beyond a doubt that when people with Type 1 diabetes kept their blood sugar levels as normal as possible, as often as possible, they could dramatically reduce the odds of developing small blood-vessel diseases related to diabetes such as kidney disease, eye problems and nerve disease, all discussed in Chapter 7. Many experts believe that frequent self-testing of blood sugar may one day prevent the large blood-vessel diseases, such as cardiovascular disease, that plague people with Type 2. At this time, however, there is simply no data to support this theory.

Two management philosophies have emerged regarding frequent self-testing of blood sugar and Type 2 diabetes. Many physicians feel that until there's a good case to be made for it, frequent self-testing of blood sugar in Type 2 diabetes only complicates Type 2 diabetes management. In other words, it interferes with more crucial goals, such as getting your diet under control and incorporating exercise into your routine. Other physicians feel that the more involved you become in managing your blood sugar, the better off you'll be in the long run and, therefore, they support frequent self-testing of blood sugar in their Type 2 patients. The Canadian Diabetes Association also recommends that people with Type 2 diabetes self-test their blood sugar. In fact, in a newly diagnosed person with Type 2 diabetes frequent daily testing will show *individual patterns* of glucose rises and dips. This information may help your health care team tailor your meal plans, exercise routines and medication regimens. And if you do have to take insulin in the future, you will need to get into the habit of testing your own blood sugar anyway. (Of course, by getting your diet under control, you can avoid requiring insulin.)

Regardless of your doctor's approach to self-testing blood sugar, the DCCT has caused an explosion in easy-to-use home blood sugar monitors, which could potentially eliminate that weekly trip to the doctor. Many people with Type 2 diabetes who would go to the doctor's for a blood sugar test once a week, or sometimes once a month, can now check their own blood sugar at home. And there's certainly no harm in testing your sugar frequently if you want to.

What About My Weight?

Statistics suggest that about 80 percent of people with Type 2 diabetes weigh 20 percent more than their ideal weight, the technical definition of "obese." If you begin a meal-planning program—which means eating the right combination and amount of food—with a diabetes educator and dietitian, as well as incorporate exercise into your routine, you'll lose weight. Weight loss can greatly improve your body's ability to use insulin. However, there is no need to start a crash diet or panic about your weight. Meal planning is managing your diabetes; weight loss will become a fringe benefit. As you lose weight, your blood sugar levels will drop, which may affect any diabetes medication you're on. For example, if you're taking pills that stimulate your body to make insulin, weight loss without adjusting your dosage may result in hypoglycemia (low blood sugar) discussed in Chapter 4. Weight loss will also decrease the odds of developing complications from diabetes, such as heart disease.

Staying symptom-free

The first step to managing your diabetes is to eliminate your diabetes symptoms and to remain as symptom-free as possible. Meal planning (Chapter 5) combined with exercise (Chapter 6) is the best way to remain symptom-free. This will help you lose weight if you need to, as well as distribute an even amount of calories to your body throughout the day. By not putting any unusual strain on your body's metabolism, you will likely *not* experience any surprises when it comes to your blood sugar levels. Exercise makes insulin much more available to your cells, while your muscles use sugar as fuel.

If you can't seem to keep your blood sugar levels below 8 mmol/l, you are probably a candidate for an anti-diabetic pill or an oral hypoglycemic pill (discussed below, as well as in Chapter 4).

Highs and Lows

Once you begin meal planning and exercising, your body is going to be operating more efficiently, which could mean that your blood sugar levels go too low, especially if you're taking an oral hypoglycemic agent. A blood sugar level less than 4 mmol/l is too low. Immediately ingesting sugar in the form of juice, candy or a sweet soft drink will raise your sugar to normal levels again. In addition, if you're taking insulin, it will be some time before you get "good" at it, and you may also suffer from a "low." For this reason, I devote all of Chapter 4 to hypoglycemia, which will explain what happens during a low, what to do when it occurs and how to avoid it in the future.

Management errors can cause high blood sugar (hyperglycemia), as well, which will cause all the classic diabetes symptoms discussed in Chapter 1. Early signs of high blood sugar are extreme thirst, dry and flushed skin, mood swings or unusual fatigue. But many people notice no symptoms at all.

Common reasons for a change in blood sugar levels revolve around the following:

- overeating or eating more than usual;
- a change in exercise routine;
- missing a medication dose or an insulin shot (if you're taking insulin);
- an out-of-the-ordinary event (illness, stress, upset, excitement);
- a sudden mood change (extreme fright, anger or sadness);
- pregnancy.

In response to unusual strains or stress, your body taps into its stored glucose supplies for extra energy. This will raise your blood sugar level as more glucose than usual is released into your system. Whether you're fighting off a flu or fighting with your mother, digesting all that food you ate at that all-you-can-eat buffet or running away from a black bear, your body will try to give you the extra boost of energy you need to get through your immediate stress.

Don't worry about ketones

When blood sugar levels are very high in people with Type 1 diabetes, they form ketones (a.k.a. ketone bodies), poisonous chemicals the body manufactures in desperation, as a source of energy when no glucose is available for energy. Ketones are the by-product when the body breaks down fat. The body tries to get rid of them through the kidneys by flushing them into the urine. High ketones along with high blood glucose cause *diabetic ketoacidosis* (DKA), which is an emergency situation. Signs of DKA include frequent urination (polyuria), excessive thirst (polydipsia), excessive hunger (polyphagia) and a fruity smell to the breath.

But people with Type 2 diabetes do *not* form ketones. That's because the cells never think they are "starving" since insulin still comes to knock at the door, and the liver continues to make glucose.

Sick Days

Blood sugar levels naturally rise when you're ill. In the event of a cold, fever, flu or injury, you'll need to adjust your routine to accommodate high blood sugar levels, especially if vomiting or diarrhea is occurring. In some cases, you may need to go on insulin temporarily. When you're ill and you have Type 2 diabetes, it's crucial to see your doctor.

Monitoring Your Performance

If you want to test your own blood sugar, discuss with your health care practitioner how frequently to test yourself. Use Table 2.1 as a general outline for testing times.

TABLE 2.1
What constitutes diabetes, impaired glucose tolerance (IGT) or normal blood sugar? Have a look:

	DIABETES	IGT	NORMAL
Fasting	<7.8	<7.8	>7.8
2 hours after meals	<7.8	7.8–<11.1	≥11.1

When to Test Your Blood Sugar

In the days when diabetes patients went to their doctors' offices for blood sugar testing, they were usually tested first thing in the

morning before eating (called a fasting blood sugar level) or immediately after eating (known as a postprandial or postmeal blood
sugar level). It was believed that if either the fasting or postprandial levels were normal, the patient was stable. This is now known
to be completely false. In fact, your blood sugar levels can bounce
around all day long. Because your blood sugar is constantly changing, a blood sugar test in a doctor's office is pretty useless because
it measures what your blood sugar is only for that nanosecond. In
other words, what your blood sugar is at 2:15 p.m. is not what it
might be at 3:05 p.m.

It makes the most sense to test yourself before each meal, so you
know what your levels are before you eat anything, as well as about
two hours after meals. Immediately after eating, everybody's blood
sugar is high, so this is not the ideal time to test anybody. In a person
without diabetes, blood sugar levels will drop about two hours after
eating, in response to the natural insulin the body makes. Similarly,
test yourself two hours after eating to make sure that you are able to
"mimic" a normal blood sugar pattern, too. Ideally, this translates into
at least four blood tests daily:

When you wake up
After breakfast/before lunch (i.e., two hours after breakfast)
After lunch/before dinner (i.e., two hours after lunch)
After dinner/or at bedtime (i.e., two hours after dinner)

*The most revealing information about your blood sugar control is in the
answers to the following questions:*
1. What is your blood sugar level as soon as you wake up? (It should
    be at its lowest point.)
2. What is your blood sugar level two hours *after* a meal? (It should
    be much lower two hours after eating than one hour after
    eating.)
3. What is your blood sugar level when you feel ill? (You need to
    avoid dipping too low or high since your routine is changing.)

Variations on the theme

- Test yourself 4 times a day (times indicated above) 2 to 3 times a week, and then test yourself 2 times a day (before breakfast and before bedtime) for the remainder of the week.
- Test yourself twice a day 3 to 4 days a week in a rotating pattern (before breakfast and dinner one day; before lunch and bedtime the next).
- Test yourself once a day every day, but rotate your pattern (day 1 before breakfast; day 2 after dinner; day 3 before bedtime, and so on).
- Test yourself 4 times a day (times indicated above) 2 days a month.

While there is still no conclusive proof that frequent blood sugar testing is helpful for people with Type 2 diabetes, testing at home will certainly eliminate some of your trips to the doctor or lab. And that's less stress for you. The equipment you need for self-testing blood sugar is a good glucose monitor. There are several on the market; your doctor, pharmacist or diabetes educator can recommend the right brand for you. When you get your glucose monitor, experts suggest you compare your results to one regular laboratory test, to make sure you've purchased a reliable and accurate machine.

A Brief History of Blood Sugar Testing

Twenty years ago, the only way you could test your blood sugar level yourself was by testing your urine for sugar, which meant that you had reached your renal threshold (kidney limit), where sugar spilled into your urine. The limitations of urine testing are that one can only test for *really* high blood sugar levels, over 11 mmol/l. Urine testing is also useless for checking low blood sugar. Far more accurate home blood sugar testing became available with the development of glucose meters in 1982.

The first models measured glucose levels in whole blood, while laboratories were still measuring glucose levels in blood plasma. The difference is technical and not important to you personally. What you need to know, however, is that the readings vary. This meant that doctors needed to add about 12 percent to the glucose meter's recordings in order to get an accurate picture. This is changing. Today, most glucose meters measure glucose levels in plasma. What this means for you, personally, is that if you're a self-testing veteran, your next glucose meter may suddenly be giving you readings that are 12 percent higher than your last meter. This doesn't mean that you are losing control of your disease; rather, that your meter is measuring glucose levels in your plasma instead of whole blood. As a rule, before you purchase a new glucose meter, make sure you ask the pharmacist: "Is this a whole blood test or a plasma test?"

Choosing and Using Your Glucose Meter

As in the computer industry, glucose meter manufacturers tend to come out with technological upgrades every year. In fact, you can now purchase systems that download the time, date and blood sugar values for the last 125 glucose tests right onto your personal computer. This information can help you gauge whether your diet and exercise routine is working, or whether you need to adjust your medications or insulin. Of course, new upgrades cost money, but if you can't afford the "Pentium," a reliable "386" is fine. *All* glucose monitors will provide the following:

- a battery-powered, pocket-sized device;
- an LED screen (that is, a calculator-like screen);
- accurate results in 30 to 60 seconds;
- the date and time of your test result;
- a recall memory of at least your last 10 readings;
- at least a one-year warranty;
- the opportunity to upgrade;
- a 1-800 customer service hotline;

- mailings and giveaways every so often; and
- a few free lancets ("finger-pricker thingies") with your purchase; you may have to separately purchase what's known as a lancing device, a sort of Pez dispenser for your lancets. (Eventually, you'll run out of lancets and have to buy those, too.)

No matter which glucose meter you choose, these instructions can serve as a general guideline:

- Wash your hands with an antibacterial soap.
- Pierce your finger on the side rather than top, and obtain a "hanging" drop of blood (some newer devices "suck out" your blood for you).
- Smear or blot your drop of blood onto a plastic strip that looks like a strip of tape without the sticky side. (Whether you smear or wipe depends on your glucose meter.)
- Turn on your glucose meter and place the strip into the machine.
- The results will show up on the calculator-like screen.
- Record these results in a logbook.

Hint: A good result before meals ranges from 4 to 7 mmol/l; a good result after meals ranges from 5 to 10 mmol/l.

Factors That Can Taint Your Results

Most people are not testing their blood sugar under squeaky-clean laboratory conditions. The following outside factors may interfere with your meter's performance.

Other medications you're taking

Studies show that some meters can be inaccurate if you're taking acetaminophen, salicylate, ascorbic acid, dopamine or levodopa. As a rule, if you're taking any medications, check with your doctor, pharmacist and glucose meter manufacturer (call their 1-800 number) about whether your medications can affect the meter's accuracy.

Humidity

The worst place to keep your meter and strips is in the bathroom where humidity can ruin your strips, unless they're individually wrapped in foil. Keep your strips in a sealed container away from extreme temperatures. Use your "video" rules; don't store your meter and strips, for example, in a hot glove compartment. Don't keep them in the freezer, either.

Bright light

Ever tried to use a calculator or portable computer in bright sunlight? It's not possible because the light interferes with the screen. Some meters are photometric, which means they are affected by bright light. If you plan to test in sunlight, get a biosenser meter that is unaffected by bright light (there are several).

Touching the test strip

Many glucose meters come with test strips that cannot be touched with your fingers or a second drop of blood. If you're all thumbs, purchase a meter that is unaffected by touch and/or allows a second drop of blood.

Wet hands

Before you test, thoroughly dry your hands. Water can dilute your blood sample.

Motion

It's always best to test yourself when you're standing still. Testing on planes, trains, automobiles, buses and subways may affect your results, depending on the brand of glucose meter.

Dirt, lint and blood

Particles of dirt, lint and old blood can sometimes affect the accuracy of a meter, depending on the brand. Make sure you clean the meter regularly (follow the manufacturer's cleaning directions) to remove build-up. Make sure you change your batteries, too! There are meters on the market that do not require cleaning and are unaffected by dirt, but they may cost a little more.

Glycosylated Hemoglobin

The most detailed blood sugar test cannot be done at home yet. This is a blood test that checks for glycosylated hemoglobin (glucose attached to the protein in your red blood cells), known as *glyco-hemoglobin* or HbA_{1c} levels. This test can tell you how well your blood sugar has been controlled over a period of 2 to 3 months by showing what percentage of it is too high. I compare this test to cars with special gas-tank meters that can tell you what percentage of your last quarter tank is left before you need to refuel. That information is far more telling than just "F," "$\frac{1}{2}$," "$\frac{1}{4}$" and "E." It's recommended that you get an HbA_{1c} test every 3 months. This test is discussed in more detail in Chapter 3.

When You're Not Managing Very Well

When you're diagnosed with Type 2 diabetes, changing your lifestyle is the optimum therapy. That means meal planning and exercising. If you can do that, you probably won't need any medication, and your body may begin to use its own insulin efficiently again. But less than 10 percent of people with Type 2 diabetes are prepared to make the necessary lifestyle changes to keep their diabetes under control. First, the older people get, the harder it is for them to change their eating habits. Second, many people may not be able to incorporate exercise or physical activity into their routine.

Today there are pills to help you manage your diabetes, if the lifestyle changes you've made aren't doing the trick. Going on diabetes medication is in no way a cure-all; taking a pill will help you stay as healthy as possible in the event that you cannot or will not make the necessary lifestyle changes.

Diabetes Medications

There are four kinds of medications that may be prescribed to you. (The next chapter discusses dosages, side effects, ideal and inappropriate candidates for these medications in more detail.) It's crucial to note, however, that these medications can only be prescribed to people who still produce insulin. They have no effect on people with Type 1 diabetes, or insulin-dependent diabetes.

Sulphonylureas (e.g., chlorpropamide and glibenclamide):

Pills that help your pancreas release more insulin. These pills are known as oral hypoglycemic agents (OHAs) and account for about 75 percent of all prescriptions for people with Type 2 diabetes. This medication can make your insulin-producing cells more sensitive to glucose, and stimulate them to secrete more insulin, which will lower your blood sugar. If your average blood-glucose levels are greater than 8 mmol/l, you will likely be prescribed an OHA. About 15 percent of people on OHAs will not respond to them, while an additional 3 to 5 percent of people on OHAs will stop responding to them. The major risk with OHAs is hypoglycemia, discussed in greater detail in Chapter 4.

Biguanides (Metformin):

Pills that help your insulin work better. These pills primarily stop your liver from producing glucose, which will help to lower your blood sugar levels and increase glucose uptake by your muscle tissue. These pills also help your tissues respond better to your insulin. Ultimately, biguanides can lower premeal and postmeal blood sugar levels in about 75 to 80 percent of people with Type 2 diabetes. This medication also seems to lower the "bad" cholesterol levels. These pills do not increase insulin levels and will not directly cause low blood sugar.

Alpha-glucosidase inhibitors (a.k.a. acarbose or Prandase):

Pills that delay the breakdown of sugar in your meal. Introduced in 1996, acarbose is the first anti-diabetic medication to come along since the mid-1950s, when sulphonylureas and biguanides were developed. Acarbose is very similar in structure to the sugars found in foods. The main sugar in blood, glucose, is a *simple sugar* that is made from starch and sucrose (table sugar). Starch and sucrose are turned into glucose by enzymes in the lining of the small intestine called alphaglucosidases. What acarbose does is stall this process by forcing the starch and sugar you eat to "take a number" before they're converted into glucose. Why do this? Well, this will slow down the absorption of glucose into the cells, preventing a rise in blood glucose after a meal. But in order to work, acarbose must be taken with the first bite of each main meal. You'll also need to test your blood sugar two hours after eating to see how well you're responding to the medication. Research is under way to determine if acarbose can be used worldwide as a preventive for people with impaired glucose tolerance (IGT).

Thiazoladinediones (troglitazone or Rezulin):

Pills that make your cells more sensitive to insulin. These pills make your cells more sensitive to insulin, thereby improving insulin resistance. And when this happens, more glucose gets into your tissues, and less glucose hangs around in your blood. The result is that you'll have lower fasting blood glucose levels, without the need to increase insulin levels. Troglitazone works by stimulating muscle tissue to "drink in" glucose. It also decreases glucose production from the liver, and makes fat tissue more receptive to glucose. This drug is reserved for people with Type 2 diabetes who must take insulin to reduce their blood sugar levels. (See page 58.) Troglitazone is being touted as a new wonder drug because you only need one tablet a day for the pill to work its wonders! In fact, researchers are currently investigating troglitazone as a drug that can delay or prevent the onset of Type 2 diabetes altogether.

Natural alternatives

If you don't like the idea of taking pills to control your diabetes, you can try to incorporate more natural methods to see if you can prevent taking medication. You'll have to discuss this approach with your doctor, of course, but here are some options:

- *Guar gum.* This is a high source of fibre (see Glossary), made from the seeds of the Indian cluster bean. When you mix guar with water, it turns into a gummy gel, which slows down your digestive system, similar in effect to acarbose (see above). Guar has often been used as a natural substance to treat high blood sugar as well as high cholesterol. Guar can cause gas, some stomachache, nausea and diarrhea. (These are also side effects of acarbose, discussed in Chapter 3.) The problem with guar is that there are no scientific studies, to date, concluding that it improves blood sugar control. Nevertheless, most experts agree that it can certainly provide some marginal benefits.

- Delay glucose absorption by eating more fibre, avoiding table sugar (sucrose) and eating smaller meals more often to space out your calories. Meal planning is discussed in detail in Chapter 5.

When You Need to Take Insulin

Right now, 40 to 50 percent of all people with Type 2 diabetes require insulin injections to manage their condition. Until troglitazone is more widely prescribed and in use, this is the reality. As discussed earlier, insulin resistance eventually may lead to requiring insulin from an outside source. You'll need to discuss the various insulins available with your doctor, as well as be trained in giving yourself insulin injections.

The newest insulin is known as insulin lispro, an insulin analogue ("copycat"). This is a synthetic insulin that does not have an animal or human source. It's made by reversing the order of two amino acids (LYS and PRO) in the human insulin molecule.

With traditional human insulins (animal insulin is not readily available, and is discussed in the next chapter), you need to be extremely good at calculating when you're going to eat, how much you're going to eat and how much insulin to inject. Basically, you need to be in excellent control of your diabetes. The problem with traditional, longer-acting insulin is that you can wind up with too much of it your system, which can cause insulin shock, or hypoglycemia (low blood sugar). (See Chapters 4 and 5.) Insulin lispro is a very short-acting insulin, which means that you inject it about 15 minutes before you eat (while you're cooking dinner or when ordering food in a restaurant). Therefore some experts consider it an easier insulin to work with.

That said, insulin is highly individualized. It's simply not possible for me to tell you which insulin you need to be on any more than I can tell you what, exactly, you need to eat each day. This is why a diabetes health care team, discussed in the next chapter, is so crucial. Your meal plans, medications and insulin (when needed) is tailored to suit *you*. And that has everything to do with who you are, not which brand of insulin is popular.

Your insulin gear

If you've graduated to insulin therapy, here's what you'll need to buy:

- really good glucose monitor that is made for people who test frequently;
- lancets and a lancing device for testing your blood sugar;
- insulin pens and cartridges (this is far easier) or traditional needles and syringes (a diabetes educator will need to walk you through the types of products available);
- the right insulin brand for you (see Chapter 3 for more details).

You'll also need to be trained in injecting insulin and in rotating your injection sites. *Do not attempt insulin injections without a training session with your doctor or diabetes educator!*

Travelling with insulin
When travelling, you'll need to make sure you pack enough insulin for your trip, as well as identification (a doctor's note) that clearly states you have diabetes, so you don't get harassed over carrying needles, syringes and vials. In fact, many experts suggest that for a trip, you switch to an insulin pen, which is far easier to carry and less obvious. In some cases, even lancets and a glucose meter may be suspect without identification. Experts recommend the following supplies for travel:

- a back-up supply of insulin *on you*, as well as extra cartridges, needles, syringes and testing supplies; vials break, baggage gets lost, and planes, trains or buses get delayed;
- a doctor's written prescription for your insulin and a doctor's note explaining why you're carrying your equipment;
- a Medic Alert tag or card stating that you have diabetes;
- a day's supply of food (especially if you're flying);
- an extra sugar source, such as dextrose tablets;
- a list of hospitals in your travel–destination areas.

It's also important never to part with your insulin; always carry it with you in carry-on baggage. Dividing your supplies between two bags is best in case vials break. If you're flying, drink lots of liquids prior to boarding, as well as one glass of non-alcoholic liquid for every hour of flight. And don't order a special meal; these have a nasty habit of never making it to your plane. Bring food with you and pick at the plane food you're served. You should also stroll up and down the cabin as much as possible to avoid high blood sugar. (This bit of exercise will use up some sugar.) If you're travelling to a different time zone, consult your doctor or diabetes educator about adjusting insulin injections to the new time zone.

Breaking News in Diabetes

Diabetes treatment and prevention is rapidly changing. By the year 2000, today's research may dramatically affect future treatment. For example, non-invasive blood glucose monitoring may soon be available at your local pharmacy. In this case, a glucose monitor would pass a beam of light into your body, which could then detect your glucose levels. This technology was developed for the food industry to determine the sugar content of potatoes or orchard fruit prior to picking.

In other exciting news, Canadian researchers have not only uncovered the diabetes genes, which could play a role in preventing the disease, but an Alberta research team is experimenting with islet cell transplantation, which could free all people needing insulin from requiring insulin injections. One Montreal research team has even identified the gene responsible for regenerating insulin-producing islet cells in the pancreas. This gene, named INGAP, for Islets NeoGenesis-Associated Protein, could lead to a definitive cure for diabetes. And in the United States, small, pale, pink ceramic beads that encase a collection of insulin-producing cells are being studied as implant material.

Finding Diabetes Earlier

Perhaps the most important change in the future of diabetes is revising the Clinical Practice Guidelines for Diabetes. This means that doctors will need to change the way they manage and treat diabetes. For example, the new guidelines may require that all health care providers:

- Routinely screen for Type 2 diabetes in high-risk individuals (See Chapter 1). This means screening based on risk factors instead of symptoms.
- Provide prevention education to anyone at high risk for Type 2 diabetes. This means you'll be sent on a diabetes education course, even if you don't have the disease.

- Encourage people with Type 2 diabetes to self-monitor their blood sugar levels, if data proves this is useful.
- Not prescribe medication to people with Type 2 diabetes unless meal planning and lifestyle modification have been tried first, and have not worked.
- Revisit who should use insulin and who can avoid it, and not prescribing insulin with pills.
- Prevent, at all costs, complications by making sure that Type 2 diabetes patients understand how to change their diet and lifestyle.
- Lobby to make more diabetes educators and special care centres available across Canada.

Having Type 2 diabetes is a 24-hour, 7-day-a-week job. Despite this, 70 percent of people with Type 2 diabetes never receive any diabetes education whatsoever. Clearly, diabetes is taking its toll on our health care system. Experts predict that as more people age and are diagnosed with Type 2 diabetes, less education will be available as doctors and diabetes educators become overburdened with patients.

The next chapter focuses on how to maximize your relationships with all your health care providers. Developing a good relationship with your doctor means *helping your doctor help you!* Actively managing your diabetes involves keeping health logs, choosing the right doctor to begin with, knowing the right questions to ask your doctors, educators and pharmacists and avoiding duplication of efforts.

Chapter 3

WHO IS A

DIABETES DOCTOR?

There is really no such thing as one "diabetes doctor" who manages the disease completely. Your primary care physician often acts as overall supervisor of your condition, but, ideally, this doctor should be working with a team of health care professionals, which includes:

- *A Certified Diabetes Educator* (CDE): CDEs come from a variety of backgrounds. They can be dietitians, nurses, pharmacists, social workers or any other professional in the health care system who has an interest in diabetes education. CDEs are absolutely vital to managing diabetes. They will help you gain control of your disease by teaching you how to adjust your diet, incorporate physical activity into your routine, test your blood and record the results, as well as manage any medication or insulin that's been prescribed. CDEs can be found through the Canadian Diabetes Association, or you can be referred through your primary care doctor or endocrinologist.

- *A **dietitian**:* In addition to a CDE, you should see a dietitian regularly during your first year with diabetes. If you learn to meal-plan accordingly, you may be able to control your diabetes without taking any medications.
- *An **exercise/fitness instructor**:* This is any professional who can tailor a fitness program that suits your lifestyle and level of ability. Check with your CDE, the Canadian Diabetes Association, the YMCA/HA or your local community centre for lists of fitness instructors. You do not need a referral to one; you can simply make an appointment independent of your doctor.
- ***Community Health Representative*** *(CHR):* This is someone from your community who works with you and your family, as well as with other health care professionals, to educate you about diabetes. CHRs are usually found in rural areas where access to doctors is poor. CHRs attend a four-day training session and complete a skills test. The are required to review and update their skills annually. CHRs are common in aboriginal Canadian communities.
- *An **endocrinologist and other specialists**:* This is discussed further on page 70.
- ***Pharmacist**:* Since you may be expected to do home glucose tests, your pharmacist will recommend the right glucose meter for you, and will become a valuable source of information on drug interactions and their effects on your blood sugar. Finding a diabetes care centre in your neighborhood is an ideal place to purchase your diabetes products and consult with a pharmacist.

While clearly there is treatment for Type 2 diabetes, it is a complex disease that can only be managed through a multi-layered approach. The goal of treatment is not just to relieve symptoms, but to prevent a range of other diseases down the road. Self-managing your disease while maintaining your quality of life can only happen if you're willing to learn and to change. That means asking questions and participating in your treatment.

There are various stops along this treatment highway. How many times you stop depends on how well you can control your blood sugar. Some of you may be able to control diabetes solely through diet and exercise (Chapters 5 and 6). Some of you may need to combine diet and lifestyle modification with diabetes pills, while some of you may need to use insulin to control your disease.

This chapter will guide you through the maze of treatments and health care professionals you'll encounter. It will also feed you the right questions so you can get the right answers. Only then can you be expected to participate more fully in decisions that affect your diabetes and the rest of your life.

The Right Primary Care Doctor

A primary care doctor is the doctor you see all the time. For example, you would see this doctor for a cold, flu or an annual physical; this is the doctor who refers you to specialists.

In Canada, primary care doctors today are *general practitioners* (4 years of medical school and one year of internship), *family practitioners* (4 years of medical school, and a two-year residency in family medicine) or *internists* (4 years of medical school, and a four-year residency in internal medicine). During medical training, rotations are done in a variety of specialities, such as psychiatry, endocrinology, obstetrics and gynecology, emergency medicine, and so on. During a residency, the years are spent in a teaching hospital, under the supervision of teaching faculty (assistant, associate or full professors of medicine) who teach one specialty. The number of years spent in a residency program after 4 years of medical school varies on the university and specialty. To qualify as a specialist, such as an endocrinologist, a doctor must do a residency in endocrinology. After, a fellowship year is required, and that doctor must be eligible to write exams for Fellowship of the Royal College of Physicians of Canada. The letters "F.R.C.P." stand for Fellow of the Royal College of Physicians. ("F.R.C.S." stands for Fellow of the Royal College of Surgeons). In the United States, the "R" is replaced with "A" for American (College of Physicians/Surgeons).

Eighty percent of all people with Type 2 diabetes are cared for by their primary care doctors, but the quality of care may vary. What you'll find today is that most primary care doctors in Canada become very good at treating a few conditions. Some see a lot of patients with diabetes; others see more pregnant women; still others see more elderly patients requiring palliative care. It all depends on the magic phrase "patient population." *Where* is the doctor's practice located? *Who* are the people in that neighbourhood?

Therefore, a primary care physician may not be the best doctor to manage your diabetes, if that doctor doesn't see many diabetes patients. Some doctors are also behind the times when it comes to diabetes, and do not immediately recognize early warning signs or high-risk groups. Nor do all primary care doctors counsel their patients about newer approaches to therapy, namely, self-monitoring of blood glucose levels, which though optional in Type 2 diabetes, may not be discussed as an option. (See Chapter 2.)

When you're diagnosed with diabetes, ask your doctor the following questions. It will help determine whether you should stay with your doctor or look for another one:

1. ***What is your philosophy about blood sugar monitoring?*** Any doctor who does not discuss the option of your purchasing a glucose meter and self-monitoring your blood sugar levels may not be up-to-date. As discussed in the last chapter, the Canadian Diabetes Association recommends that people with Type 2 diabetes get into the habit of self-testing their blood sugar. A discussion about it with your doctor is warranted, even though self-testing remains optional pending more convincing data. A good family doctor should present the facts to date: "Here's what some people think; here's what I think; here are my recommendations." (Ultimately, the decision is yours.)

2. *How often will you be checking my glycosylated hemoglobin or glycohemoglobin levels?* If your doctor says "Huh?" get out of there and find another doctor! This is a blood test (HbA_{1c}) that should be done every 3 to 6 months. (Note: in Quebec, family doctors report that this test is not uniformly available.)

3. *Will you be referring me to a specialist?* The answer should be "Yes!" If you've been diagnosed with diabetes, you need to see other health care professionals as soon as possible: Freqently, an endocrinologist who specializes in diabetes, a certified diabetes educator and a dietitian, and an opthalmologist (or optometrist if the former isn't available). If your doctor says, "I can manage your condition without referring you elsewhere," get out of that office and go elsewhere.

4. *Where can I go for more information?* Any doctor who does not tell you to call the Canadian Diabetes Association as soon as you're diagnosed with diabetes is not worth seeing.

The alarm bells

If you hear the following words come out of your doctor's mouth, go elsewhere:

- You have borderline diabetes or "just a touch of sugar." (There's no such thing. There *is* such a thing as impaired glucose tolerance, discussed in chapters 1 and 2.)
- You don't need to change your diet; I'll just give you a pill. (In general, no medication should be prescribed until you've been sent to a dietitian, who will work with you to modify your diet and lifestyle. In cases where medication is warranted immediately, you must still see a dietitian.)
- You don't need to see a specialist. (You *do* need to see a specialist.)
- You have a recurrent yeast infection. This is perfectly normal. (Chronic vaginal yeast infections are a classic sign of diabetes in postmenopausal women.)

Your Rights

When it comes to your diabetes care, you have rights. Make sure whoever is on your diabetes health care team knows that you're entitled to:

As much information about your diabetes as you want. Any doctor who is reluctant to give you literature, videos and a referral to a diabetes educator and dietitian is not giving you proper care.

Answers to your questions about diabetes. If there isn't time during an exam or check-up, make another appointment that serves as a question and answer period.

Regular assessments. When you have diabetes, you should be seen at least every three months for a check-up or at regular intervals. It's important to ask how much advance booking time you need to get an appointment.

Participate in treatment plans. You'll need to educate yourself about your diabetes before you can participate, but you have many options in treatment.

Decent emergency care and a meeting with your doctor's substitute. Who looks after you when your doctor is on holidays or sick?

Privacy and confidentiality. Diabetes often taints relationships with employers, co-workers and insurance companies. Find out what your doctor's legal obligations are with respect to health records—and what are *yours*?

Know about fees and costs. What is covered by the province and what is not? How much of your medication and equipment are covered by your drug plan? Your doctor should be able to give you an estimate for your diabetes care products in case you are not covered. He or she should also be able to give you cheaper products if you cannot afford what is being prescribed. Pharmacists and the Canadian Diabetes Association are also helpful.

Be seen on time. If you're on time for an appointment, your doctor should be as well. Do you generally have to wait more than 30 minutes in the reception area before your doctor will see you?

Although this sometimes can't be helped, the doctor should be aware that waiting creates anxiety. Especially if appointments are timed close to meals, and you are taking insulin.

To switch doctors. If you're unhappy with your current doctor, or simply need a change, you have every right to switch. Make sure you arrange for your records to be transferred. Some costs may be involved, however.

A second opinion, or a consultation with a specialist. No family doctor should deny you a referral to a specialist.

Your Doctor's Rights

Your doctor has the right to expect the following from you:

Honesty. If you're not being truthful about how often you're checking your blood sugar levels, what you're eating or you are "cooking" your log to avoid a lecture, your doctor can't be blamed if your health deteriorates.

Courtesy and respect. Treat your doctor like a business associate. If you make an appointment, show up; if you need to cancel, give 24 hours' notice. If you have a problem, go through reasonable channels; dial the after-hours emergency number the doctor leaves with the answering service, or call your doctor's office during business hours.

Good reporting. Don't tell you're doctor "you're not feeling well" and expect a diagnosis. Tell your doctor what your *specific symptoms* are. Better yet, write them down before you visit your doctor.

Questions. If you don't ask a particular question, you can't blame your doctor for not answering it.

Follow-through. If you don't follow your doctor's advice, you can't blame the doctor if you experience side effects to medications, or worsening symptoms. If you don't think your doctor's advice is reasonable, say so and discuss it. Maybe your doctor doesn't have a full understanding of your condition; maybe you don't have a full understanding of your doctor's suggestions.

Self-Management. Don't call your doctor ten times a day with every little change in your blood sugar levels. You should be able to monitor your blood sugar levels and adjust your diet and medication regimen accordingly. Emergencies or illness are different situations, however, and your doctor should be notified since even a common virus will elevate your blood sugar level.

Your Diabetes Specialist

A diabetes specialist is an endocrinologist who subspecializes in diabetes. Endocrinologists are hormone specialists. Some see more thyroid patients than diabetes patients. Some specialize in reproductive endocrinology (male and female hormones). Therefore, it's important that you wind up with someone who almost exclusively manages diabetes patients. The shortest route to a diabetes specialist is to ask your primary care doctor for a referral. If your primary care doctor refuses to refer you (this, by the way, is not unusual), call the Canadian Diabetes Association and ask them for a list of endocrinologists in your area.

If you live in an underserviced area (there are several of these in Canada!), ask people you know if they know someone with diabetes. And then, call them! Who are *they* seeing? You may need to go outside your area to a larger city. But it's worth the trip to avoid being mismanaged.

Your primary care doctor can continue to manage the rest of your referrals to ophthalmologists (for diabetes eye disease), podiatrists for footcare, and so on. (See Chapter 7 for more details.)

Getting Along with Your Specialist

You may find your endocrinologist a little intimidating because he or she is more academic; he or she may use more technical terms to explain your disease and treatment. Endocrinologists often teach or run residency programs, are active in research, frequently lecture and regularly publish articles and books in their field. These doctors are usually harder to get in touch with; they're usually booked months in advance. That's why it's crucial to maximize the time you *do* have. The best way to do this is to tape-record your appointment. That way, you can replay the information in the comfort of your own home. It's also important to take a list of questions with you. If there isn't time for all your questions to be answered, schedule a separate Q&A session. Finally, ask your specialist to draw you a picture of your condition. Visualizing your disease, and seeing how various medications may interact in your body, will help you understand what's going on, and what's being recommended.

A *dozen good questions to ask*
Of course, it's difficult to prepare questions in advance when you don't know what to ask. So here are few good questions to get you started:

1. *How severe is my diabetes?* (In other words, if you are experiencing other health problems as a result of your diabetes, the disease is likely more advanced.)
2. *Does my hospital or treatment centre have a multidisciplinary diabetes education care team?* (This means that a number of health care professionals—Certified Diabetes Educators, Clinical Nurse Specialists, dietitians, endocrinologists and other relevant specialists discuss your case together and recommend treatment options.)
3. *What treatment do you recommend, and why?* (For example, if insulin therapy is being recommended over oral hypoglycemic agents, find out why. And find out how this particular treatment will reduce the odds of complications.)
4. *How will my treatment help the risks/side effects associated with diabetes and who will help me adjust my medications or insulin?*
5. *How long do you recommend this particular treatment? (Lifelong? On a wait-and-see basis?)*

6. *What if I forget to take a pill or insulin shot? What are the consequences?*
7. *What other health problems should I look out for?* (You'll want to watch for symptoms of high or low blood sugar, as well as symptoms of long-term complications, such as eye problems or numbness in your feet.)
8. *How can I contact you between visits?*
9. *Can I take other medications? Or, how will my pills or insulin affect other medications I'm taking?*
10. *What about alcohol? How will alcohol consumption affect any pills or insulin I'm on? How do I compensate for it?*
11. *Will I be able to participate in new studies or clinical trials using new drugs or therapies?*
12. *Are there any holistic approaches I can turn to as a complement to diabetes pills or insulin therapy?*

Other Specialists

Since diabetes can involve a variety of complications down the road, you may need to consult some or all of the following specialists:

Internist: This is a doctor who specializes in non-surgical treatment of a variety of medical problems, including diabetes.

Ophthalmologist: This is an eye specialist, someone who will be able to monitor your eyes and make sure that you're showing no symptoms of diabetes eye disease (see Chapter 7). If you are, this is the specialist who will treat your condition.

Cardiologist: This is a heart specialist. People with Type 2 diabetes are four times more likely to suffer from heart attacks. You may be sent here if you are experiencing symptoms of heart disease or angina.

Nephrologist: This is a kidney specialist. Since kidney disease is a common complication of diabetes, you may be sent here if you're showing symptoms of kidney disease (protein in your urine).

Gastroenterologist: This is a G.I. (gastrointestinal) specialist. Diabetes often results in a number of chronic gastrointestinal ailments. You may be sent here if you have symptoms of chronic heartburn, reflux, and other gastric aches and pains.

Neurologist: This is a nerve specialist whom will see you if you're experiencing nerve damage as a result of your diabetes.

Gerontologist: This is a doctor who specializes in diseases of the elderly. If you are over 65 and have a number of other health problems, this doctor will help you balance your various medications and conditions, in conjunction with your diabetes.

Obstetrician/Gynecologist: If you develop diabetes during pregnancy, you'll need to be under the care of an obstetrician for the remainder of your pregnancy. All women should see a gynecologist regularly for Pap smears, breast health and consultation regarding sexual health, contraception and hormone replacement therapy after menopause.

Urologist: This is a doctor who specializes in, among other things, male reproduction problems. Impotence is often a complication with diabetes, and this is the doctor who will be able to determine the cause of your impotence.

Orthopedist: This is a foot doctor who can help you monitor "foot health." If you're experiencing severe problems with your feet (see Chapter 7), your podiatrist may likely send you here.

When You Want a Second Opinion

Getting a second opinion means that you see two separate doctors about the same set of symptoms. If you answer yes to one of the questions below, you're probably justified in seeking a second opinion.

1. *Is the diagnosis uncertain?* If your doctor can't give you a straight answer about what's going on, you're justified in seeing someone else.
2. *Is the diagnosis life-threatening?* In this case, hearing the same news from someone else may help you cope better with your illness, or come to terms with the diagnosis.

3. *Is the treatment controversial, experimental or risky?* You might not question the diagnosis, but have problems with the recommended treatment. For example, if you're not comfortable with treatment approach A, perhaps another doctor can recommend treatment approach B.

4. *Is the treatment not working?* If your oral hypoglycemic agents can't seem to control your blood sugar levels, maybe it's time for insulin. In this case, getting a second opinion may help to clear up the problem.

5. *Are risky tests or procedures being recommended?* If you find a particular test or procedure frightening, a second opinion will either help confirm your suspicions, or confirm your original doctor's recommendations.

6. *Do you want another approach?* If you have poor control over your diabetes, your doctor may want you to begin taking insulin, while another doctor may prescribe dietary changes along with anti-diabetic medication.

7. *Is the doctor's competence in question?* If you suspect that your doctor doesn't know what he or she's doing, go somewhere else to either reaffirm your faith in your doctor, or confirm your original suspicions.

Self-Service

Doctors cannot manage your diabetes; you have to do this yourself. That means you need to adjust your diet and lifestyle habits, quit smoking, and so on. You should also begin a health diary, in which you record any unusual symptoms, and the times and dates those symptoms occur. Without your diary or health record, your doctors could be working in the dark and may not be able to design the right therapy program for you.

Control Yourself

You should start with tight control over your blood sugar levels. A healthy pancreas measures its owner's blood sugar levels once a second or 3,600 times an hour. It then produces exactly the right amount of insulin for that second. In light of this, testing your blood sugar (see Chapter 2 for details on blood sugar testing) may prove useful, and for now is an option that the Canadian Diabetes Association thinks is worth considering for people with Type 2 diabetes.

What Your Health Diary Should Reveal

The most important information your health diary will contain is the pattern of your blood sugar's peaks and valleys. Dates and times of these peaks and valleys may be important clues to establish the pattern. Your meal plan, exercise routine and medication regimen should be tailored to anticipate these peaks and valleys. You may need to incorporate a snack to prevent a low, or go for a 20-minute walk after dinner to prevent a high. Since there are a variety of factors that can affect your blood sugar levels, your diary should also record:

- any medication you're taking;
- unusually high or low readings that fall outside your pattern;
- stressful life events or situations;
- illness;
- out-of-the-ordinary happenings (no matter how insignificant);
- changes in your health insurance or status;
- severe insulin reactions (if you're taking insulin);
- general medical history (surgeries, tests you've had done, allergies, past drug reactions).

When to Call Your Doctor

As discussed in Chapter 2, if you have Type 2 diabetes, it's important to call your doctor whenever you're sick with even just a cold or flu. Fighting off the commonest viruses will elevate your blood sugar levels and will require some juggling of your regular routine.

Until you can get in to see your doctor, stay on your meal plan. If that's not possible, drink about a half a cup of calorie-free broth, or diet or regular soda every hour you are awake. Over-the-counter medications may alter your blood sugar levels unless they are sugar-free. You should also test your blood sugar every four hours when you're ill to accommodate higher blood sugar levels. If you're taking any medication, stick to your usual plan and take it as prescribed at the usual times. You may need to go on insulin temporarily if your blood sugar levels remain high. This would not be the case with a cold, but may be necessary if you're laid up with a flu.

When you're not ill, but you have an unusually high blood sugar reading (over 11 mmol/l), it's time to see your doctor, too.

What the Doctor Orders

Throughout the year, your managing doctor (primary care physician or endocrinologist) should be ordering a variety of blood tests to make sure that your blood sugar levels are as controlled as they can be, and that no complications from diabetes are setting in.

The Hemoglobin A_{1c} (HbA$_{1c}$) test

The most important test is one that checks your glycolsylated hemoglobin levels, known as the hemoglobin A_{1c} test or the HbA$_{1c}$ test. Hemoglobin is a large molecule that carries oxygen to your bloodstream. When the glucose in your blood comes in contact with the hemoglobin molecule, it conveniently sticks to it. The more glucose stuck to your hemoglobin, the higher your blood sugar is. The HbA$_{1c}$ test actually measures the amount of glucose stuck to hemoglobin. And since each hemoglobin molecule stays in your blood about 3 to 4 months before it is replaced, this test can show you the average blood sugar level over the last 3 to 4 months. Therefore this test is recommended at least every 6 months. If you have cardiovascular problems, you will need to have the HbA$_{1c}$ test more often.

A similar test, known as a fructosamine test, can show the amount of glucose stuck to a molecule in your blood known as albumin. Albumin gets replaced every 4 to 6 weeks, however, so this test can therefore give you an average of blood sugar levels only over the last 4 to 6 weeks.

What's a good HbA$_{1c}$ result?

Just like your glucose monitor at home, the goal of the HbA$_{1c}$ test is to make sure that your blood sugar "average" is as close to normal as possible. Again, the closer to normal it is, the less likely you are to experience long-term diabetes complications.

This test result is slightly different than your glucose meter result. For example, an HbA$_{1c}$ level of 7.0 percent is equal to 8 mmol/l on your blood glucose meter. A result of 9.5 percent is equivalent to 13 mmol/l on your blood glucose meter. In a person without diabetes, an HbA$_{1c}$ ranges from 4.3 percent to 6.1 percent. The results are often expressed as percentages of "normal" such as <110 percent, 111–140 percent or >140 percent.

TABLE 3.1
What's a Good Glycosylated Hemoglobin Test (HbA$_{1c}$) result?

NON-DIABETIC RANGE	GREAT CONTROL	OKAY CONTROL	POOR CONTROL
4.3%–6./1%	6.0–7.5%	7.5–9.0%	>9.1%
≤100%	<110%	111–140%	>140%

Source: Adapted from *Clinical Practice Guidelines*, 1992.

The Canadian Diabetes Advisory Board recommends that values of 7.8 percent or less are good results and mean that your blood sugar is perfectly under control. Meanwhile, anything higher than 9.0 percent is alarming; this would be a poor result and means that your diabetes is not under control. Studies show that when your HbA$_{1c}$ result is 9.0 percent or higher, you have a greater than 75 percent chance of developing long-term complications. In fact, for every 10 percent drop in your HbA$_{1c}$ average (that is, 8.1 percent down from 9.1 percent), the risk of long-term complications falls by about 40 percent.

Problems with the HbA$_{1c}$ test

If your child came home with a report card showing a B average, it doesn't mean your child is getting a B in every course; it means that he or she could have received a D in one course and an A+ in another. Similarly, the HbA$_{1c}$ test is just an "average mark." You could have a decent result, even though your blood sugar levels may be dangerously low one day and dangerously high the next.

If you suffer from sickle-cell disease or other blood disorders, the HbA$_{1c}$ results will not be accurate, either. In this case, you may wind up with either false high or low readings.

And at any time, if your home blood sugar tests (if you've opted for self-testing) over the past two or three months do not seem to match the results of the HbA$_{1c}$ test, be sure to check the accuracy of your meter, and perhaps show your doctor or Certified Diabetes Educator how you are using the meter in case your technique needs some refining.

Other Important Tests

It's important to have the following routine tests done at least once a year, and more often if you are at high risk for complications.

Glucose meter checkup

If you've opted to test your own blood sugar, it's important to compare your home glucose meter's test results to a laboratory blood glucose test. In fact, it's a good idea to do this every 6 months. All you do is bring your meter to the lab when you're having a blood glucose test done. After the lab technician takes your blood, do your own test within about 5 minutes and record the result. Your meter is working perfectly so long as your result is within 15 percent of the lab test (if your meter is testing whole blood, as opposed to plasma).

Blood pressure

As discussed in Chapter 1, high blood pressure can put you at greater risk for cardiovascular problems. Diabetes can also cause high blood pressure. That's why it's important to have your blood pressure checked every 4 to 6 months.

Kidney tests

One of the most common complications of diabetes is kidney disease, known in this case as *diabetic nephropathy* (diabetic kidney disease). This condition develops slowly over the course of many years, but there are usually few symptoms or warning signs. To make sure no damage to the kidneys has occurred, it's important to have your urine tested regularly to check the health of your kidneys.

Cholesterol

As discussed in Chapter 1, high cholesterol is a problem for people with diabetes, while diabetes can also trigger high cholesterol. Your cholesterol is checked through a simple blood test that should be done once upon diagnosis, and once a year thereafter. See Chapter 1 and Table 3.2 for more details.

TABLE 3.2
Checking Your Cholesterol

	GOOD	POOR
Total Cholesterol	below 5.2	above 6.2
LDL Cholesterol	below 3.4	above 4.1
HDL Cholesterol	above 1.1	below 1.0
Triglycerides	below 2.0	above 2.6

Foot exam

When you have diabetes, nerve damage and poor circulation can wreak havoc on your feet. Be sure to have a thorough foot exam each year to check for reduced sensation or feeling, circulation, evidence of calluses or sores. See Chapter 7 for more details.

Eye exam

Since diabetes can cause what's known as diabetes eye disease or diabetic retinopathy (damage to the back of your eye), annual eye exams are crucial. Your eye exam should also rule out cataracts and glaucoma.

When caught early, laser treatment can be used to treat diabetic eye disease, and prevent blindness. If your exam uses the term *absent* on your chart, it means your retina is just fine. If you see the word *background*, it means that mild changes have occurred to your eye(s) and that you need more regular monitoring. If the terms *pre-proliferative* or *proliferative* are used, it means that there is some damage to one or both eyes and you will require treatment and regular exams. See Chapter 7 for more details.

When Your Doctor Tells You to Take a Pill

When diet and lifestyle changes make no impact on your your blood sugar levels, you may be prescribed pills. While Chapter 2 provides you with an overview of the kinds of pills prescribed for Type 2 diabetes, this section covers who should take these pills, appropriate dosages, side effects and questions to ask your doctor and/or pharmacist.

Before you fill your prescription for anti-diabetic pills, you should know that between 40 to 50 percent of all people with Type 2 diabetes require insulin therapy after ten years. Continuing insulin resistance may cause you to stop responding to oral medications. Furthermore, these pills are meant to complement your meal plan, exercise routine and glucose monitoring; they are not a substitute.

Bear in mind, too, that physicians who prescribe the medications discussed in this section, without also working with you to modify your diet and lifestyle, are not managing your diabetes properly. These medications should be prescribed only after you've been unsuccessful in managing your Type 2 diabetes through lifestyle modification and frequent blood sugar testing.

If you cannot get down to a healthy body weight, you are probably a good candidate for anti-diabetic medication. And anyone with Type 2 diabetes who cannot control his or her blood sugar levels *despite* lifestyle changes is also a good candidate.

Oral Hypoglycemic Agents (OHAs)

As discussed in Chapter 2, sulphonylureas and biguanides are common oral hypoglycemic agents (OHAs). Sulphonylureas are pills that help your pancreas release more insulin; biguanides help your insulin work better. Initially, 75 percent of people with Type 2 diabetes will respond well to sulphonylureas, while biguanides will lower blood sugar in 80 percent of people with Type 2 diabetes. But about 15 percent of all people treated with OHAs fail to respond to them at all, while 3 to 5 percent of all people on OHAs will stop responding to them each year. So don't get too comfortable on these pills.

Sulphonylureas would generally be the initial oral agent of choice in people who are not obese and/or have high blood sugar levels (or suffer from symptoms of high blood sugar). A biguanide is appropriate in people who *are* obese and have milder levels of high blood sugar. That's because biguanides do not not result in the weight gain, which is typically associated with sulphonylurea and insulin therapy.

Dosages for sulphonylureas

There is no fixed dosage for sulphonylureas. It all depends on your brand. For example, it's perfectly common to take anything from 80 to 320 mg a day. If you are taking a dosage higher than the recommended initial dose, indicated in Table 3.3, you should divide your dose into two equal parts. Your pills should be taken before or with meals, and your doctor should start you on the lowest effective dose. If your blood sugar levels are high when you start your pills, it's a good idea to have a short trial period of about 6 to 8 weeks to make sure your drug is working.

TABLE 3.3
Sulphonylureas, a common class of oral hypoglycemic agent

	DAILY/MG	INITIAL	PER DAY
Acetohexamide*	250–1,500	250	1–2
Chlorpropamide*	100–500	250	1
Gliclazide**	40–320	160	1–2
Glyburide**	2.5–20	5	1–2
Tolbutamide*	500–3,000	1,000	1–3

First generation-not prescribed very much*
Second generation-more commonly prescribed**

Source: *Compendium of Pharmaceuticals and Specialities*, 1996.

Dosages for biguanides (Metformin)

There is only one biguanide available in Canada, which goes by the trade name Metformin. In this case, the usual dose is 500 mg 3 or 4 times a day or 850 mg 2 or 3 times a day. Your dose is not to exceed 2.5 g a day. If you're elderly, a lower dose will probably be prescribed.

When OHAs should not be used

If you've had Type 2 diabetes longer than ten years, this is not the time to start OHAs. And, of course, nobody with Type 1 or insulin-dependent diabetes (IDDM) should ever take OHAs; they will not work. OHAs should never be taken under the following conditions, either:

- alcoholism;
- pregnancy;
- kidney or liver failure (Metformin only).

Side effects

Sixty percent of people taking OHAs continue to have high blood sugar levels 2 hours after meals. These pills can also cause increased appetite and weight gain. However, the main side effect with first generation OHAS is hypoglycemia (low blood sugar), which occurs in one in five people treated with OHAS. If you're over age 60, hypoglycemia may occur more often, which is why it's dangerous for anyone over age 70 to take certain OHAS.

About one-third of all people taking OHAS will experience gastrointestinal side effects (no appetite, nausea, abdominal discomfort and, with Metformin, diarrhea). Adjusting dosages and taking your pills with your meals, or afterward, often clears up these symptoms.

Acarbose (a.k.a. Alpha-Glucosidase Inhibitors)

As discussed in Chapter 2, these are pills that delay the breakdown of sugar in your meal by delaying the conversion of starch and sucrose into glucose. This reduces high blood sugar levels after you eat. Acarbose is prescribed to people who cannot seem to get their after-meal (that is, postmeal or postprandial) blood sugar levels down to acceptable levels. A major benefit of acarbose is that it may reduce the risk of hypoglycemic episodes during the night, particularly in insulin users. Investigators are studying whether acarbose may be used one day as a substitute for that "morning insulin." The usual rules apply here: acarbose should complement your meal plan and exercise routine; it is not a substitute or way out, and does not, by itself, cause hypoglycemia.

Who should take acarbose?
- anyone who cannot control his or her blood sugar through diet and lifestyle modification alone;
- anyone who is on OHAS but is still experiencing high blood sugar levels after meals;
- anyone who cannot take OHAS and in whom diet/lifestyle modification has failed;
- anyone not doing well on an OHA, who wants to prevent the advent of starting insulin treatment.

Who should not take acarbose?

Anyone with the following conditions should not be taking this drug:

- inflammation or ulceration of the bowel (that is, inflammatory bowel disease, ulcerative colitis or Crohn's disease);
- any kind of bowel obstruction;
- any gastrointestinal disease;
- kidney or liver disorders;
- hernias;
- pregnancy or lactation;
- Type 1 diabetes.

Dosage

The usual starting dosage for acarbose is 25 mg (half of a 50 mg tablet), with the first bite of each main meal. After 4 to 8 weeks, your dosage may be increased to 50 mg, three times a day. Or you may start by taking one 50-mg tablet once daily with supper. If that's not working, you'll move up to two 50-mg tablets twice daily with your main meals or three 50-mg three times daily with main meals. The maximum dosage of acarbose shouldn't go beyond 100 mg three times a day.

For best results, it's crucial that you take acarbose with *the first bite* of each main meal. In fact, if you swallow your pill even 5 to 10 minutes before a meal, acarbose will pass through your digestive system and have no effect. It's also important that you take acarbose with a carbohydrate; the medication doesn't work if there are no carbohydrates in your meal. You shouldn't take acarbose between meals, either; it won't work. Nor should acarbose be used as a weight-loss drug.

Side effects

The good news is that acarbose doesn't cause hypoglycemia. However, since you may be taking this drug along with an OHA, you may still experience hypoglycemia, as acarbose doesn't prevent it, either. (See Chapter 4 for warning signs and treatment for hypoglycemia.)

The only side effects acarbose, by itself, causes are gastrointestinal: gas, abdominal cramps, softer stools or diarrhea. But acarobose combined with Metformin can produce unacceptable gastrointestinal symptoms. You'll notice these side effects after you've consumed foods that contain lots of sugar. Avoid taking antacids; they won't be effective in this case. Adjusting the dosage and making sure you're taking acarbose correctly will usually take care of the side effects.

Thiazoladinediones (Troglitazone or Rezulin)

This is a brand-new drug for Type 2 diabetes that makes your cells more sensitive to insulin. It is also being studied as a drug to use in people with impaired glucose tolerance (IGT), so that Type 2 diabetes can be prevented.

Not yet widely used in Canada (it was approved here in 1997), clinical trials suggest that troglitazone is effective in just a single daily dose of 200-, 400-, 600- or 800-mg tablets. You can also split a dosage into two, such as 200 or 400 mg twice daily.

Studies show that the drug is effective with people who have IGT. One study showed that one 400-mg tablet every morning for a six-week period improved blood sugar to normal readings in 75 percent of study participants. After 12 weeks of treatment, 80 percent of study participants with IGT showed normal glucose levels.

Side effects

Studies show that when taken at doses of 600 and 800 mg a day, troglitazone can raise LDL ("bad") cholesterol. Anyone with cardiovascular problems should not be on this drug, nor should anyone with liver disease take it. White blood cell counts also went down in people taking the highest dosage of 800 mg daily. Therefore, high doses of this drug are not recommended for people who are immune-suppressed for any reason, and the drug may also trigger an infection in healthy people as a result. Headaches were also reported in users, but for the most part, troglitazone is a well-tolerated drug with a low incidence of adverse side effects.

Questions to Ask About Diabetes Drugs

Before you fill your prescription, it's important to ask your doctor or pharmacist the following:

1. *What does this drug contain?* If you are allergic to particular ingredients, such as dyes, it's important to find out the drug's ingredients before you take it.

2. *Are there any medications I shouldn't combine with this drug?* Be sure to ask about interactions with cholesterol or hypertension medications, as well as any antidepressants or antipsychotics.

3. *If this drug doesn't work well, am I a candidate for combination therapy?* This means that your drug could be combined with another drug. Common combo-platters include: a sulphonylurea and biguanide; acarbose and an OHA. Either the first drug you started is raised to its maximum dosage, before the second drug is started at its lowest dosage, or both drugs are started at their lowest dosages and then raised gradually.

4. *If this drug doesn't work well, would insulin ever be prescribed along with this pill?* It remains controversial whether combining insulin with a pill has any benefits. Nevertheless, some studies have shown that there is some benefit.

5. *How will you measure the effectiveness of my drug?* You should be testing your blood sugar with a glucose monitor, particularly two hours after eating, to make sure that the lowest effective dose can be prescribed. Your doctor should also be doing a glycosylated hemoglobin or HbA_{1c} test 2–3 times per year (see above).

6. *How should I store my drugs?* All pills should be kept in a dry place at a temperature between 15°C and 25°C. Keep these drugs away from children, don't give them out as "samples" to your friends and don't use tablets beyond their expiry date.

7. *What symptoms should I watch out for while on these drugs?* You'll definitely want to watch for signs of high or low blood sugar.

When Your Doctor Prescribes Insulin

Let me dispel a common fear about insulin: Since insulin is not a blood product, you don't have to worry about being infected with a blood-borne virus such as HIV *or hepatitis.*

Many doctors often delay insulin therapy for as long as possible by giving you maximum doses of the pills discussed above. This isn't considered good diabetes management. If you need insulin, you should take insulin. The goal is to get your disease under control. Therefore, anyone with the following conditions is a candidate for insulin:

- high blood sugar levels, despite maximum doses of oral hypoglycemic agents;
- fasting glucose levels consistently over 9 mmol/l;
- illness or stress (insulin may be needed until you recover);
- major surgery;
- complications of diabetes (see Chapter 7);
- pregnancy (insulin may be temporary).

If going on insulin will affect your job security, you should discuss this with your doctor so that appropriate notes or letters can be drafted to whom it may concern. You should also keep in mind that if insulin therapy does not bring your diabetes under control within 6 months of treatment, it may be necessary to return to your drug therapy, after all.

The Right Insulin

The goal of a good insulin program is to try to mimic what your pancreas would do if it were working properly. Blood sugar rises in a sort of "wave" pattern. The big waves come in after a big meal; the small waves come in after a small meal or snack. The insulin program needs to be matched to your own particular wave pattern. So what you eat— and when—has a lot to do with the right insulin program. Therefore, the right insulin for someone who eats three square meals a day may not be appropriate for someone who tends to "graze" all day. And the right insulin for an active 47-year-old man in a stressful job may not be the right insulin for a 67-year-old woman who does not work, and whose heart condition prevents her from exercising regularly.

You and your health care team will also need to decide how much control you need over your blood sugar. Insulin "recipes" depend on whether you need tight control (3 to 6 mmol), medium control (4 to 10 mmol) and even loose control (11 to 13 mmol). Loose control is certainly not encouraged, but on rare occasions, when a person is perhaps quite elderly and suffering from a number of other health problem, it is still "done." To determine the appropriate insulin recipe for you, your health care team should look at who you are as a person—what you eat, where you work (do you work shifts?), your willingness to change your eating habits and other lifestyle factors.

There are many kinds of insulins available. Every manufacturer has a different brand name of insulin and a separate letter code for the insulin action. To make things as easy to understand as possible, I've provided a table on page 94 with a translation of all these codes. Once you and your diabetes health care team choose the right insulin for you, you will need to have a minicourse on how to use and inject insulin. This is usually done by a Certified Diabetes Educator (CDE).

Human insulin

All human insulin is biosynthetic, which means that the biochemically created "product" normally made by the human pancreas has been re-created in a test tube through DNA technology.

Today, most manufacturers produce only these insulins which are considered the purest form of insulin available. Human insulins come in three different actions: short-acting (clear fluid), intermediate-acting (cloudy fluid) and long-acting (cloudy fluid). Short-acting means that it stays in your body for the shortest duration of time; long-acting means that it stays in your body for the longest duration of time. (See Table 3.5 for details.)

TABLE 3.4
Breaking the Codes

R: This stands for "regular" biosynthetic human insulin. Regular means that it is short-acting insulin.

"ge" Toronto: "ge" is the name Connaught-Novo gives to all of its biosynthetic insulin. It stands for "genetically engineered." Toronto is the brand name of this company's short-acting insulin, like "Kraft" or "President's Choice."

Insulin Lispro: This is a very new and "super short-acting" insulin under the brand name Humalog, which starts to work in 15–30 minutes. (See the previous chapter.) It is a biosynthetic insulin made from two amino acids, lys and pro. It's ideal for people with Type 1 diabetes.

N or nph: "nph" are simply the initials of the man who invented this type of insulin, which is an intermediate-acting insulin that is said to have an "abrupt" peak. ("ge-nph" stands for genetically engineered nph.)

L or Lente: This is also an intermediate-acting insulin that is very similar to nph except it has a more "lumbering" peak. ("ge-Lente" stands for genetically engineered Lente.)

Beef/pork: This is animal insulin made from cows or pigs. It's still available in Canada from Eli Lilly but isn't readily available at most pharmacies unless it's a special order.

Humulin 10/90: This is a premixed insulin, meaning that it is 10 percent regular and 90 percent nph. Also available in 20/80, 30/70, 40/60 and 50/50. (Note: Many people with Type 2 diabetes do well on 30/70.)

Novolin 10/90 "ge": Exactly the same as above, except "ge," which stands for genetically engineered, is the label Connaught-Novo gives to its biosynthetic insulin.

Novolin ultra "ge": Connaught-Novo's long-acting insulin, which starts acting in 4 hours, peaks within 8–24 hours and exits within 28 hours. Again, "ge" stands for genetically engineered.

Ultra Lente "ge": The same as above except it peaks in 10–30 hours and exits in 36 hours.

Semi Lente-nph: This is a very long-acting insulin that is rarely used. Most diabetes educators haven't seen someone on this stuff for years!

Beef/pork insulin

The only people who should be on animal insulin are people who began using it years ago. These are likely people with Type 1 diabetes who developed a rhythm with their animal insulin and are reluctant to switch to human insulin or an insulin analogue. If you're newly diagnosed with Type 2 diabetes, or you have just started to take insulin, this is not the right insulin for you. Animal insulin is less pure and has a higher incidence of hypoglycemia. If you're currently on animal insulin and would like to switch, you must discuss this with your managing physician first. On the flip side, you shouldn't feel pressured into switching insulins if you're happy on animal insulin.

Premixed insulin

Premixed insulin means that both the short-acting insulin and the intermediate-acting insulin are mixed together. These are extremely popular insulins for people with Type 2 diabetes for reasons explained in Table 3.5. These work well for people who have a very set routine and don't want to take more than one or two insulin injections daily.

Both human and animal insulin are available in premixed formats. They are labelled as 10/90 (10 percent short-acting; 90 percent intermediate-acting), 20/80, 30/70, 40/60 and 50/50. Premixed insulin is always cloudy. It's also possible to mix together short-acting with long-acting; or long-acting with intermediate-acting.

Learning to Use Insulin

Insulin must be injected. It cannot be taken orally because your own stomach acids digest the insulin before it has a chance to work. Your doctor, pharmacist, CDE or someone at a diabetes care centre will teach you how to inject yourself painlessly. Don't inject insulin by yourself without a training session. The most convenient way to use insulin is with an insulin pen. In this case, your insulin (if human or biosynthetic) will come in a cartridge. If you decide against a pen, your insulin will come in a bottle and you will need a needle and syringe. Always know the answers to these questions before you inject your insulin:

1. How long does it take before it starts to work? (Known as the *onset of action*.)
2. When is this insulin working the hardest? (Known as the *peak*.)
3. How long will my insulin continue to work? (Known as the *duration of action*.)

How many injections will I need?

This really depends on what kind of insulin you're taking and why you're taking it. A sample routine may be to take an injection in the morning, a second injection before supper and a third before bed. What you want to prevent is low blood sugar while you're sleeping. You may need to adjust your insulin if there is a change in your food or exercise routine (which could happen if you're sick). Your insulin schedule is usually carefully matched to your meal times and exercise periods.

Where to Inject It

The good news is that you do not have to inject insulin into a vein. As long as it makes it under your skin or in a muscle, you're fine. Thighs and tummies are popular injection sites. These are also large enough areas that you can vary your injection site. (You should space your injections about 2 to 3 cm apart.) Usually you establish a little rotating pattern. Other injection sites are the upper outer area of the arms, the upper outer surfaces of the buttocks and lower back areas. Insulin injected in the abdomen is absorbed more quickly than insulin injected in the thigh. In addition, strenuous exercise will speed up the rate of absorption of insulin if the insulin is injected into the limb you've just "worked out." Other factors that can affect insulin's action is the depth of injection, your dose, its temperature (insulin should be room temperature or body temperature) and what animal your insulin came from (human, cow or pig).

Experts also suggest you massage the injection site to increase the rate of insulin absorption. If you notice a hardening of skin due to overuse, this will affect the rate of absorption. Your doctor or CDE will show you how to actually inject your insulin (angles, pinching folds of skin, and so on). There are lots of tricks of the trade to optimize comfort. With the fine needle points available today, this doesn't have to be an uncomfortable ordeal.

Side Effects

The main side effect of insulin therapy is low blood sugar, which means that you must eat or drink glucose to combat symptoms. This side effect is also known as insulin shock. Low blood sugar or hypoglycemia is discussed in Chapter 4.

You may also notice something called *lipodystrophy* (a change in the fatty tissue under the skin) or *hypertrophy* (an enlarged area on your skin). Rotating your injection sites will prevent these problems. A sunken area on your skin surface may also occur, but is usually only present with animal insulin. Rashes can sometimes occur at injection sites, too. Less than 5 percent of all insulin users notice these problems.

Questions to Ask About Insulin

The answers to these questions will depend on your insulin brand. Pharmacists and doctors should know the answers to all these questions, but if they don't, I recommend calling the customer care 1-800 number provided by your insulin manufacturer.

- How do I store this insulin?
- What are the characteristics of this insulin (that is, onset of action, peak and duration of action)?

- When should I eat after injecting this insulin?
- When should I exercise after injecting this insulin?
- How long are opened insulin bottles/cartridges safe at room temperature?
- What about the effect of sunlight or extreme temperatures on this insulin?
- Should this insulin be shaken or rolled?
- What should I do if the insulin sticks to the inside of the vial/cartridge?
- Should this insulin be clear or cloudy? And what should I do if the appearance looks "off" or has changed?
- What happens if I accidentally inject out-of-date insulin?
- What other medications can interfere with this particular brand?
- Who should I see about switching insulin brands?
- If I've switched from animal to human insulin, what dose should I be on?

TABLE 3.5
Getting to Know Your Insulin

Short-acting insulin (This is the "hare." It gets there fast but tires easily.)
Starts working in: 30 minutes (insulin lispro: <15–30 minutes)
Peaks in: 2 to 4 hours. (insulin lispro: 30 minutes–2.5 hours)
Duration of action: 6 to 8 hours (insulin lispro: 3–4 hours)
When to eat: within 30 minutes of injecting
Peak effect (maximum action): 1½ to 5 hours
Exits body in: 8 hours
Appearance: Clear. Don't use if cloudy, slightly coloured or if solid chunks are visible.

Intermediate-acting insulin (This is the "tortoise." It gets there at a slower pace, but it lasts longer.)
Starts working in: 1 to 2 hours
Peaks in: 4 to 12 hours (usually around 8 or less)
Duration of action: 24 hours (or less)
When to eat: within 2 hours
Exits body in: 24 hours
Appearance: Cloudy. Do not use if the white material remains at the bottom of the bottle after mixing, leaving a clear liquid above; or if clumps are floating in the insulin after mixing or if it has a "frosted" appearance.

Long-acting insulin (This is the "two-legged turtle." It's *really* slow. And it hangs around for a long time.)
Starts working in: 8 hours
Peaks in: 18 hours
Duration of action: 36 hours
When to eat: within 8 hours
Exits body in: 36 hours or more
Appearance: Cloudy. Do not use if the white material remains at the bottom of the bottle after mixing, leaving a clear liquid above; or if clumps are floating in the insulin after mixing or if it has a "frosted" appearance.

For information about brand names, premixed insulins and specific products, consult your doctor, pharmacist, diabetes educator or insulin manufacturer.

Chapter 4

THE FLIP SIDE:

HYPOGLYCEMIA

When you're diagnosed with Type 2 diabetes, whether your treatment revolves around lifestyle modification, oral hypoglycemic or insulin therapy, you may experience an episode of low blood sugar. This is clinically known as *hypoglycemia*. Hypoglycemia can sometimes come on suddenly, particularly overnight. If left untreated, hypoglycemia can also result in coma, brain damage and death. Hypoglycemia is considered the official cause of death in about 5 percent of the Type 1 population. In the past, hypoglycemia was a more common problem among people with Type 1 diabetes. But since 40 to 50 percent of all people with Type 2 diabetes will eventually graduate to insulin therapy, the incidence of hypoglycemia has increased by 300 percent in this group. Moreover, hypoglycemia is a common side effect of oral hypoglycemic pills, the medication the majority of people with Type 2 take when they are first diagnosed.

This chapter will explain exactly what happens when you have low blood sugar, who's at risk, how to treat it and how to avoid it.

The Lowdown on Low Blood Sugar

Any blood sugar reading below 3.8 mmol/l is considered too low. A hypoglycemic episode is characterized by two stages: the warning stage and what I call the *actual* hypoglycemic episode. The warning stage occurs when your blood sugar levels begin to drop, and can occur as early as a blood sugar reading of 6 mmol/l, in people with typically higher than normal blood sugar levels. When your blood sugar drops to the actual 3 mmol/l range, you are *officially* hypoglycemic.

During the warning stage, your body responds by piping adrenaline into your bloodstream. This causes symptoms such as trembling, irritability, hunger and weakness, some of which mimic drunkenness. The irritability can simulate the rantings of someone who is drunk, while the weakness and shakiness can lead to the lack of coordination seen in someone who is drunk. For this reason, it's crucial that you carry a card or wear a bracelet that identifies that you have diabetes. (See pages 105 and 106.) Your liver will also release any glucose it has stored for you; but if it doesn't have enough glucose to get you back to normal, there won't be enough glucose for your brain to function normally and you will feel confused, irritable or aggressive.

Once your blood sugar is 3 mmol/l and falling, you'll notice a more rapid heartbeat, trembling and sweating. As the levels become lower, your pupils will begin to dilate, and you will begin to lose consciousness, and could perhaps experience a seizure. No one with diabetes is immune to hypoglycemia; it can occur in someone with long-standing diabetes just as much as in someone newly diagnosed. The important thing is to be alert to the warning signs, be prepared and try to avoid future episodes.

Who's at Risk?

Since hypoglycemia can be the result of too high an insulin dose, it is often called insulin shock (or insulin reaction). This is a misleading term, however, because it implies that only people who take insulin can become hypoglycemic. For the record, all people with Type 1 or Type 2 diabetes can become hypoglycemic. If you are taking more than one insulin injection a day, you are at greater risk of developing hypoglycemia. But hypoglycemia can be triggered just as easily by:

- delaying or missing a meal or snack (see Chapter 5);
- drinking alcohol (see Chapter 5);
- exercising too long (without compensating with extra food) (see Chapter 6);
- taking too high a dose of an oral hypoglycemic agent (this can happen if you lose weight but are not put on a lower dose of your pill).

If you're taking pills

About 15 percent to 30 percent of all people taking sulphonylureas (see Chapters 2 and 3), are vulnerable to hypoglycemia because this drug stimulates the pancreas to produce insulin. This is synonymous with taking an insulin injection. Furthermore, if you lose weight after you begin taking sulphonylureas, but don't lower your pill dosage, you could also experience hypoglycemic episodes. That's because losing weight will make your body more responsive to insulin.

Yet, biguainides (see Chapters 2 and 3) do not typically cause hypoglycemic episodes, since they work by preventing the liver from making glucose rather than stimulating anything to make insulin. Similarly, acarbose does not, by itself, cause hypoglycemia. It works by delaying the breakdown of starch and sucrose into glucose. That's not to say, however, that hypoglycemia can't happen to you if you're taking biguainides or acarbose; you can still develop it if you miss meals, snacks or overexercise without compensating for it, although this is rare.

As discussed in Chapter 3, your diabetes pills may also react with other medications. For example, some of the older oral hypoglycemic agents may work less or more effectively when combined with certain medications including: blood thinners (anticoagulants), oral contraceptives, diuretics, steroids, aspirin and various anticonvulsive or antihypertensive medications.

Another factor is the half-life of your oral medication. By knowing when the drug peaks in your body, you'll be able to prevent hypoglycemia from occurring. For example, tolbutamide is a short-acting oral hypoglycemic agent. It begins to work about an hour after you take it and lasts for about 12 hours, peaking between 5 to 6 hours after you ingest it.

Acetohexamide starts working about an hour after you take it, and stays in your body for about 14 hours and peaks at about 5 hours. Glyburide goes to work in about 1.5 hours, stays in your body for 24 hours and peaks at about 3 hours. Finally, chlorpropamide has the longest half-life. It starts to work an hour after you take it, stays in your body for 72 hours and peaks within 35 hours.

Combination therapy

Roughly 40 percent of all people taking a combination of oral hypoglycemic agents experience hypoglycemic episodes, while 33 to 47 percent of people who combine insulin with sulphonylureas experience hypoglycemic episodes. These are higher odds than if you were taking one oral hypoglycemic agent only.

Hypoglycemia without diabetes

Yes, people can have chronic hypoglycemia without having diabetes. This is a commonly diagnosed condition in the general, non-diabetic population. In this case, hypoglycemia is caused by overactive glucose absorption in the body. The symptoms of hypoglycemia, in this case, will be similar to the symptoms seen in people with diabetes, but not as dramatic. Non-diabetic people are not likely to become unconscious, for example, but they will definitely feel shaky and irritable if they don't eat. Non-diabetics affected by hypoglycemia will need to carry snack packs with them, as well, and space out their meals as judiciously as someone with diabetes, to prevent the onset of symptoms. People who do not have diabetes yet have hypoglycemia will also react more strongly to sugar in their diets; this will create a "high" and then a "crash." If you have hypoglycemia, a good diet, carefully planned out with a nutritionist, is your best treatment. Eating good stuff (fruits, vegetables, grains, etc.) in regularly spaced meals will keep your symptoms away.

Recognizing the Symptoms

If you can begin to recognize the warning signs of hypoglycemia, you may be able to stabilize your blood sugar before you lose consciousness. Watch out for the adrenaline symptoms: initially you will be hungry and headachy, then sweaty, nervous and dizzy. Those who live with or spend a lot of time with you should learn to notice sudden mood changes (usually extreme irritability, "drunklike aggression" and confusion) as a warning that you are "low."

One of the best examples of "hypoglycemia on film" is in the movie *Steel Magnolias*, in which Julia Roberts portrays a woman with Type 1 diabetes opposite Sally Fields, who plays her mother. At the local beauty parlour, amidst happy chatter over Roberts's upcoming wedding, her character suddenly becomes aggressive and begins to verbally attack her mother, shaking all the while. The other customers look alarmed. Sally Fields realizes at once that Roberts is "low" and calmly takes over the situation. She grabs Roberts and calms people down. "It's all right, it's all right, she's just low. With all the excitement that's gone on, it's only natural. Get me some juice."

"I have a candy in my purse," pipes up a customer.

"No," insists Fields. "Juice is better; juice is better." Roberts becomes even more upset. Her reaction is sheer confusion and fright. Fields takes the juice and starts to feed her; Roberts, in confusion, spits it out and puts up a fight every step of the way. After Fields force-feeds her a little longer, Roberts starts to drink on her own, and utters an intelligible sentence. "Oh, she's making some sense now," coos Fields. "Yes, she is. She's starting to make sense."

In other words, the daughter's blood sugar is beginning to rise and the hypoglycemic symptoms that appeared out of nowhere are starting to dissipate.

Whether you notice your own mood changes or not, you, too, will feel "suddenly" unwell. By simply asking yourself, "Why is this happening?" you should be able to remember that it's a warning that your blood sugar is low, and reach for your snack pack (see page 105). Not everyone experiences the same warning symptoms, but here are some signs to watch for:

- pounding, racing heart;
- breathing fast;
- skin turning white;
- sweating (cold sweat in big drops);
- trembling, tremors or shaking;
- goose bumps or pale, cool skin;
- extreme hunger pangs;
- light-headedness (feeling dizzy or that the room is spinning);
- nervousness, extreme irritability or a sudden mood change;
- confusion;
- feeling weak or faint;
- headache;
- vision changes (seeing double or blurry vision);

Some people will experience no symptoms at all. If you've had a hypoglycemic episode without any warning symptoms, it's important for you to eat regularly, and to test your blood sugar. If you're experiencing frequent hypoglycemic episodes, diabetes educators recommend that by keeping your sugar above normal, you can prevent low blood sugar. In some cases of long-standing diabetes and repeated hypoglycemic episodes, experts note that the warning symptoms may not always occur. It's believed that in some people, the body eventually loses its ability to detect hypoglycemia and send adrenaline. Furthermore, if you've switched from an animal to human insulin, warning symptoms may not be as pronounced.

"Juice Is Better"

If you start to feel symptoms of hypoglycemia, stop what you're doing (especially if it's active) and have some sugar. Next, test your blood sugar to see what it reads. Regular food will usually do the trick. If your blood sugar is below 3.5 mmol/l, ingest some glucose. Sally Fields was right; real fruit juice is better when your blood sugar is low. The best way to get your levels back up to normal is to ingest simple sugar; that is, sugar that gets into your bloodstream fast. Half a cup of any fruit juice or one-third of a can of a sugary soft drink is a good source of simple sugar. Artificially sweetened soft drinks are useless. *It must have real sugar.* If you don't have fruit juice or soft drinks handy, here are some other sources high in simple sugar:

- 2 to 3 tablets of commercial dextrose, sold in pharmacies. If you're taking acarbose or combining it with an oral hypoglycemic agent or insulin, the only sugar you can have is dextrose (Dextrosol or Monoject), due to the rate of absorption.
- 3 to 5 hard candies (that's equal to about 6 Life Savers)
- 2 teaspoons of white or brown sugar (or 2 sugar cubes)
- 1 tablespoon of honey

Once you've ingested enough simple sugar, your hypoglycemic symptoms should disappear within 10 to 15 minutes. Test your blood sugar 10 minutes after having your sugar to see if your blood sugar levels are coming back up. If your symptoms don't go away, have more simple sugars until they do.

After a Low

If you've had a close call to the point where you experienced those adrenaline symptoms, be sure to have a snack or meal as soon as possible. If your next meal or snack is more than an hour away, eat half a sandwich or some cheese and crackers. That will ensure that your blood sugar levels don't fall again. Then, check your blood sugar levels after you eat to make sure your levels are where they should be. Try to investigate the cause of your episode by asking yourself the following:

1. Did you miss a meal or eat late? (Were you at one of those dinner parties where you came on time but everybody else arrived an hour later?)
2. Did you eat less than normal? (Are you sick or upset over something?)
3. Did you give yourself the right amount of pills or insulin?
4. Did you do anything physically active that you didn't plan in the last hour or so? (For instance, did someone ask you to help move some heavy object from one side of the room to the other?)
5. Did you remember to compensate for any exercising you did with the appropriate amount of carbohydrates? (See Chapter 6.)

Glucagon

Most people will be able to treat their low blood sugar without becoming unconscious. But on rare occasions, it can happen. And if that's the case, it's too late for juice, soft drinks and any other kind of sugar. That's where something known as a Glucagon Kit comes in. Glucagon is particularly useful for people who have little or no warning symptoms of low blood sugar and have previously lost consciousness from low blood sugar.

Glucagon is a hormone injected under the skin. Like insulin, glucagon is destroyed by the digestive system when it's taken orally. Glucagon causes an increase in blood glucose concentration; it basically stimulates the body to make glucose. It does this by forcing the liver to convert all its glycogen stores into glucose almost immediately after it's injected. You'll need about 1 mg of glucagon to do the trick. Glucagon works better in Type 2 diabetes than in Type 1; in Type 1, a glucagon injection has to be followed up by a carbohydrate snack after you've revived.

Glucagon will make you nauseous when you come to, so if glucagon is injected it's crucial to ingest simple sugars as soon as you wake. The simple sugar will replace the glycogen your liver releases, and will get rid of the nausea. Once you feel normal again, you should consume regular food. Get a prescription for a Glucagon Kit through your doctor; then purchase the kit at any pharmacy.

If you do not respond to glucagon, glucose will be administered intravenously in a hospital or ambulance.

People in states of starvation (anorexics) or who have chronic hypoglycemia will not benefit from glucagon because in those cases, there will be no glycogen stores in the liver ready for conversion into glucose.

Glucagon can also be administered intravenously by trained medical staff; in this case, it will take only about one minute to work. Injected under the skin, glucagon takes about 8 to 10 minutes to work its wonders.

The Third Person

The Glucagon Kit is for another person to use, who has been shown how to administer the drug to revive you. This may be someone close to you who is with you when you lose consciousness. The kit should have all the necessary instructions regarding giving injections. But here are the instructions just in case. Photocopy these instructions and post them in a safe place:

1. Inject 1 mg of glucagon anywhere under the skin. (The abdomen or thighs are good spots.)
2. Wait about 10 minutes for this person to regain consciousness. Call 9-1-1 if he or she does not regain consciousness in 15 minutes.
3. After this person wakes up, immediately give her or him about a half a cup of fruit juice or a third of a can of a sugary soft drink. The drink must contain sugar; artificially sweetened drinks will not work.
4. Continue feeding the drink to this person until he or she feels well enough to eat regular food.

For your wallet

Photocopy the following and carry it in your wallet as soon as you finish reading this chapter:

To whom it may concern:

These instructions will help you assist this person with diabetes, who has passed out because his or her blood sugar is too low.

1. If this person is conscious give him or her a form of simple sugar (juice, candies, table sugar, honey). If this person is unconscious, go to #2.

2. Do *not* give this person any food or drink or put anything in his or her mouth; he or she could choke.

3. Call 9-1-1 and say: "I'm with a person who has diabetes who has passed out from low blood sugar. I need someone to get here as soon as possible." Be sure to give a clear address with specific instructions about your location.

Recipe for Prevention

The recipe for preventing hypoglycemia or low blood sugar is the same one for preventing high blood sugar: frequent blood sugar monitoring if your doctor feels it's necessary (Chapters 2 and 3), following your meal plan (Chapter 5), following an exercise plan (Chapter 6) and taking your medication as prescribed (Chapters 2 and 3). Any changes in your routine, diet, exercise habits or medication dosages should be followed up by a period of very close blood sugar monitoring until your routine is more established.

Frequent episodes of hypoglycemia may also be a sign that your body is changing: you may be losing weight, thanks to those lifestyle changes you've made, and the dosage of pills that were prescribed to you when you weighed 190 may be too strong now that you're down to 145. Or, you may be taking too high an insulin dose.

A Snack Pack

Anybody with Type 1 or 2 diabetes should have a snack pack with them for emergencies or for unplanned physical activity. The pack should contain:

- juice (2 to 3 boxes or cans)
- sweet soft drinks—sweetened with real sugar, not sugar substitutes (2 cans)
- a bag of hard candies
- some protein and carbohydrates (packaged cheese/crackers)
- granola bars (great for after exercise)
- a card that says "I have diabetes." (See page 107.)

The Anti-hypoglycemic Snack Bar

With the emerging trend of "medical foods" or nutraceuticals, one company has invented a snack bar specifically designed to prevent hypoglycemia (particularly overnight) called Zbar™. It was well received by both the American and Canadian Diabetes Association. This snack bar contains 5 g of uncooked cornstarch, 22 g of carbohydrates, 7 g of protein and 2.5 g of unsaturated fat, for a total of 110 calories.

Uncooked cornstarch, you see, is more slowly digested, allowing your body to absorb glucose more gradually, preventing hypoglycemia. You could just eat plain, uncooked cornstarch, too, but that doesn't taste very good. One Zbar™ equals 1½ starch, defined by the Canadian Diabetes Association. You can get this bar in three flavours: chocolate, peanut butter and mandarin. I've tried them myself; I recommend the mandarin, which tastes a little bit like bubblegum. But as one diabetes educator said to me, "If you have diabetes, and you haven't been able to really have a treat, these bars taste pretty good." These bars are available through the Canadian Diabetes Association, as well as in drugstores, and retail at $1.50.

The makers of Zbar™ don't want you eating it unless you tell your doctor about it. The bar is intended primarily for people using insulin to control their diabetes (Types 1 or 2), to be eaten as your snack, or as part of your meal (dessert). Zbar™ is designed to *prevent* hypoglycemia, not as a form of treatment.

Wear Your Bracelets

All people with diabetes must wear a MedicAlert bracelet or necklace. The newer styles don't have that basic red lettering which announces to the world "I'm allergic or diabetic." The newer bracelet can be quite discreet, yet still have your medical information, personal ID number and a 24-hour emergency hotline number engraved on it. This crucial jewellery is yours for a one-time, upfront fee of $35.00. That will get you a lifetime membership into the Canadian MedicAlert Foundation, as well as a bracelet or necklace, and free updates on your information. You can reach Canadian MedicAlert Foundation at 1-800-668-6381.

Tell People You Have Diabetes

A crucial word about dealing with hypoglycemia: Tell people close to you, or who work closely with you, that you have diabetes. You never know when you might experience symptoms: at a family function (delayed meals are common during wedding receptions), at work, and so on. If you instruct people about symptoms of hypoglycemia and what to do, you'll have more bases covered should you experience an episode.

Your Diabetes ID Card

If you don't have the following information on you already, photocopy this section and put it in an obvious place in your wallet or on your person.

I have diabetes. If I am unconscious or if my behaviour appears unusual, it may be related to my diabetes or my treatment. I am not drunk. If I can swallow, give me sugar in the form of fruit juice, a sweet soft drink, candies or table sugar. Phone my doctor or the hospital listed below. Or phone 9-1-1 if I am unconscious.

Name_____

Address_____

_____

Phone Number _____

Chief Contact _____ Relation _____

My doctor's name is: _____

He or she can be reached at (phone number): _____

after hours: _____

My hospital: _____

My blood type is: ☐ A ☐ B ☐ AB ☐ O ☐ Rh+ ☐ Rh–

I wear: ☐ lens implants ☐ dentures ☐ contact lenses
☐ an artificial joint ☐ a pacemaker

I'm allergic to: _____

My Health Card/Insurance Number is: _____

My Group Insurance Number is: _____

Source: Adapted from *Health Record For People With Diabetes*, 1996, McNeil Consumer Products Company.

Chapter 5

HOW SWEET IT IS: COUNTING SUGAR, PLANNING MEALS

The diabetes meal plan is not just for people with diabetes; it's a healthy-eating plan that everyone in North America could be following. So when you begin to meal plan, not only will you be able to gain control of your condition, but the rest of your family may be able to prevent or delay it, too.

Only carbohydrates influence blood sugar levels, while cholesterol-containing foods increase blood *fat* levels—cholesterol and triglycerides. What lowers the sugar in your bloodstream are either exercise or medications you may be taking, such as oral hypoglycemic pills or insulin. Ideally, by balancing your food with activity, most of you will be able to control your diabetes.

How to know if you're balancing well and how to know what to eat so you can create this balance is all contained in this chapter.

A Few Good Foods

Before the discovery of insulin in 1921, there was the Allen Diet, a very low calorie diet that required low quantities of carbohydrates, followed by exercise.

Dr. Frederick Madison Allen, a leading diabetologist who spent 4 years working with diabetic patients at the Rockefeller Institute in New York City, published a 600-plus-page paper in 1919 called "Total Dietary Regulation in the Treatment of Diabetes." Allen's work showed that diabetes was largely a problem of carbohydrate metabolism. He introduced a radical approach to diabetes, the traces of which are apparent in current meal planning. It was known as the starvation treatment, which consisted of fasting followed by a gradual building up of diet. Allen's treatment also included exercise—now a vital aspect of diabetes treatment. The idea of emaciated patients fasting and exercising was controversial, but at the time it was the best treatment available without insulin. Although in some cases, Allen's patients did die of starvation, Allen ultimately prolonged the lives of many through his system of dietary regulation. Allen's diets were found to be more tolerable than any of the fad diabetes diets that were popular in Allen's day. Doctors were doing everything from feeding patients with diabetes as much sugar as possible to compensate for the sugar lost in the blood, to putting them on low-carbohydrate diets, which were so unappetizing that most patients wouldn't stick to it. Oatmeal diets, milk diets, rice diets and potato diets were also popular. The most logical diet, however, was the low-carbohydrate diet, which included recipes such as "thrice-boiled vegetables." Although this diet was effective in eliminating sugar from the urine (which produced the same effects of food rationing), it didn't seem to work with patients who had insulin-dependent or Type 1 diabetes.

Allen and his predecessors understood something central to diabetes meal planning; *carbohydrates were key*. And they are. Allen recognized the ability of carbohydrates to convert into glucose. The timing of this glucose conversion will affect how quickly and how high blood glucose level rise after eating. But what's changed drastically since the Allen Diet is that variety, quantity and timing of meals is crucial, too.

What to Eat

To live, you need three basic types of foods: carbohydrates, protein and fat. Carbohydrates are the main source of fuel for muscles. Protein is the "cell food" that helps cells grow and repair themselves. Fat is a crucial nutrient that can be burned as an alternative fuel in times of hunger or famine. Simple sugars that do not contain any fat, will convert quickly into energy or be stored as fat.

Your body will change carbohydrates into glucose for energy. If you eat more carbohydrates than you can burn, your body will turn the extra into fat. The protein your body makes comes from the protein you eat. As for fats, they are not broken down into glucose, and are usually stored as fat. The problem with fatty foods is that they have double the calories per gram compared with carbohydrates and protein, so you wind up gaining weight. Too much saturated fat, as discussed in Chapter 9, can increase your risk of developing cardiovascular problems. What we also know is that the rate at which glucose is absorbed by your body from starch and sugars is affected by other parts of your meal, such as the protein, fibre and fat. If you're eating only carbohydrates and no protein or fat, for example, your blood sugar will go up faster.

According to guidelines set out by the British Diabetic Association (BDA), at least 50 percent of your meals should be made up of complex carbohydrates (see Table 5.1). Canadian guidelines stipulate that your daily intake of protein (animal products) shouldn't exceed 20 percent (BDA guidelines stipulate 15 percent). And if you have a sweet tooth, the BDA recommends using artificial sweeteners instead of sugar.

TABLE 5.1

How Your Food Breaks Down

COMPLEX CARBOHYDRATES *(digest more slowly)*	DEFINED BY CDA
fruits*	Fruits & Vegetables
vegetables* (corn, potatoes, etc.)	Fruits & Vegetables or
Starch or Extra (see page 117)	Extras
grains (breads, pastas and cereals)	Starch
legumes (dried beans, peas, and lentils)	Starch

*Note: The following vegetables and/or herbs are Extra: artichokes, asparagus, mushrooms, bean sprouts, okra, onions, parsley, peppers, radish, celery, rapini, cucumber, shallots, eggplant, endive, tomato, kohlrabi, zucchini.

SIMPLE CARBOHYDRATES *(digest quickly)*	DEFINED BY CDA
fruits/fruit juices*	Fruits & Vegetables or Extra
sugars (sucrose, fructose, etc.)	Sugars or Starch
honey	Sugars or Starch
corn syrup	Sugars or Starch
sorghum	Sugars or Starch
date sugar	Sugars or Starch
molasses	Sugars or Starch
lactose	Milk

*Note: Lemon and lime juice are Extra. So are artificial sweeteners, clear coffee or tea.

PROTEINS *(digest slowly)*	DEFINED BY CDA
lean meats*	Protein
fatty meats*	Fats & Oils + Protein
poultry	Protein
fish	Protein
eggs	Protein
low-fat cheese	Protein
high-fat cheese	Fats & Oils + Protein
legumes	Starch
grains	Starch

*Note: Bouillon, broth or consommé are Extra. So are garlic, mustard, vinegar, herbs and spices, Worcester sauce, uncreamed horseradish and soy sauce.

TABLE 5.1 – *(continued)*

FATS *(digest slowly)*	DEFINED BY CDA
high-fat dairy products (butter or cream)	Fats & Oils
oils (canola/corn/olive/safflower/sunflower)	Fats & Oils
lard	Fats & Oils
avocados	Fats & Oils
olives	Fats & Oils
nuts	Fats & Oils
fatty meats	Fats & Oils

FIBRE *(doesn't digest; goes through you)*	DEFINED BY CDA
whole-grain breads	Starch
cereals (i.e., oatmeal)	Starch
all fruits	Fruits & Vegetables or Sugars
legumes (beans and lentils)	Starch & Protein
leafy greens	Extras
cruciferous vegetables	Extras

The American Diabetes Association guidelines state that a healthy diet should consist mainly of complex carbohydrates (roughly 50 percent) with about 30 percent of your energy from fat—and less than 10 percent from saturated fats. (See Chapter 9.)

Variety, variety, variety

Variety is the key to a good meal plan. If your meal contains mostly carbohydrates (50 to 55 percent), some protein (15 to 20 percent), not much fat (less than 30 percent) and limited sugar, you're eating well. See Table 5.1 for some examples of simple and complex carbohydrates, proteins and fat. (I think you know what sugar is, but there are examples provided there, too.) If you imagine the outside aisles of a supermarket, those contain the food items you need to eat. It's the middle aisles that have all the extras we don't need.

How Much to Eat

Meal plans recommended by registered dietitians are tailored to your individual goals and medication regimen. Men and women will usually require different quantities of food. The goal is to keep the supply of glucose consistent by spacing our your meals, snacks and activity levels accordingly. If you lose weight, this will allow your body to use insulin more effectively, but not all people with Type 2 diabetes need to lose weight. If you're on insulin, meals will have to be timed to match your insulin's peak (see Chapter 3). A dietitian can be helpful by prescribing an individualized meal plan that addresses your specific needs (weight control, shiftwork, travel, etc.).

Anatomy of a carbohydrate

Carbohydrates are like people; they can be simple or complex. Simple carbohydrates are found in any food that has natural sugar (honey, fruits, juices, vegetables, milk) and anything that contains table sugar or sucrose.

Complex carbohydrates are more sophisticated foods that are made up of larger molecules, such as grain foods, starches and foods high in fibre. The fibre foods, both soluble and insoluble (an important distinction), such as cereals, oatmeal or legumes, are discussed in Chapter 9.

All About Sugar

Sugars are found naturally in many foods you eat. Sucrose and glucose (table sugar), fructose (fruits and vegetables), lactose (milk products) and maltose (flours and cereals) are all naturally occurring sugars. What you have to watch out for is *added sugar*; these are sugars that manufacturers add to foods during processing or packaging. Foods containing fruit juice concentrates, invert sugar, regular corn syrup, honey or molasses, hydrolyzed lactose syrup or high-fructose corn syrup (made out of highly concentrated fructose through the hydrolysis of starch) all have added sugars. Many people don't realize, however, that pure, *unsweetened* fruit juice is still a potent source of sugar, even when it contains no added sugar. Extra lactose, dextrose and maltose are also contained in many of your foods. In other words, the products may have naturally occurring sugars anyway, and then *more* sugar is thrown in to enhance consistency, taste and so on. With the exception of lactose, which breaks down into glucose and galactose, all of these added sugars break down into fructose and glucose during digestion. To the body, no one sugar is more nutritional than the other; everything is broken down into either single sugars (called monosaccharides) or double sugars (called disaccharides), which are carried to cells through the bloodstream. See Table 5.2 for the complete sugar breakdown. The best way to know how much sugar is in a product is to look at the nutritional label for carbohydrates.

However, *how fast* that sugar is ultimately broken down and enters the bloodstream greatly depends on the amount of fibre in your food, how much protein you've eaten and how much fat accompanies the sugar in your meal. Theoretically, while the Canadian Diabetes Association guidelines allow you to substitute relative quantities of table sugar for starch, (fruit or milk in your meal plan) for example, 1 bread equals 3 teaspoons of sugar; 1 orange equals 2 teaspoons of sugar), this may be a tricky balancing act you'll need to discuss with your dietitian.

As far as your body is concerned, all sugars are nutritionally equal. Honey and table sugar, for instance, are nutritionally comparable. Ultimately, all the sugars from the foods you eat wind up as glucose; your body doesn't know whether the sugar started out as maltose from whole grain breads or lactose from milk products. Glucose then travels through your bloodstream to provide energy. If you have enough energy already, the glucose is stored as fat, for later. Sugars and starches (in equal "doses") affect blood sugar differently because of the time frame involved in glucose conversion. Sugars are converted faster than starches, so it's important to discuss sugar conversion with your dietitian.

TABLE 5.2
Sugar on the Table

What's in a sugar?

Fructose: a monosaccharide or single sugar. It combines with glucose to form sucrose and is $1\frac{1}{2}$ times sweeter than sucrose.

Glucose: a monosaccharide or single sugar. It combines with fructose to form sucrose. It can also combine with glucose to form maltose, and with galactose to form lactose. Slightly less sweet than sucrose.

High fructose corn syrup (HFCS): a liquid mixture of about equal parts glucose and fructose from cornstarch. Same sweetness as sucrose.

Sucrose: a disaccharide or double sugar made of equal parts glucose and fructose. Known as table or white sugar, sucrose is found naturally in sugar cane and sugar beets.

Why is sugar added?

Sugar is added to food because it can change consistencies of foods and, in some instances, act as a preservative, as in jams and jellies. Sugars can increase the boiling point or reduce the freezing point in foods; sugars can add bulk and density, make baked goods do wonderful things, including helping yeast to ferment. Sugar can also add moisture to dry foods, making them "crisp," or balance acidic tastes found in foods like tomato sauce or salad dressing. Invert sugar is used to prevent sucrose from crystallizing in candy, while corn syrup is used for the same purpose.

Since the 1950s, a popular natural sugar in North America has been fructose, which has replaced sucrose in many food products in the form of high fructose syrup (HFS), made from corn. HFS was developed in response to high sucrose prices, and is very cheap to make. In other parts of the world, the equivalent of high-fructose syrup is made from whatever starches are local, such as rice, tapioca, wheat or cassava. According to the International Food Information Council in Washington, D.C., the average North American consumes about 37 grams of fructose daily.

Going Shopping

Food shopping can be daunting because most foods are not purely carbohydrate, protein, fat or sugar, but often a mixture of two or three. That's where the Canadian Diabetes Association symbols come in. Instead of forcing you to eyeball the ingredients of your foods, the categories and CDA symbols (see page 117) are designed to do this for you. If you can count, you can plan a meal that has everything you need. A good meal plan will ensure that you are getting enough nutrients to meet your energy needs, and that your food is spread out over the course of the day. For example, if your meal plan allots for three meals with 1 to 2 snacks; meals should be spaced 4 to 6 hours apart so your body isn't overwhelmed. If you are obese, snacks will likely be discouraged because snacks can cause you to oversecrete insulin, and increase your appetite. A meal plan should also help you to eat consistently rather than bingeing one day and starving the next.

A good meal plan will also ensure that you're getting the vitamins and minerals you need without taking supplements such as iron, calcium, folic acid, vitamims A, B_1, B_2, B_3, C, D and E. By consuming a variety of foods from each of the four food groups (in Canada's Food Guide) at every meal, you'll be meeting your vitamin and mineral requirements.

Golden rules of diabetes meal plans:

- Eat three meals a day at fairly regular times (spaced 4 to 6 hours apart).
- Ask your dietitian to help you plan your snacks.
- Try to eat a variety of foods each day from all food groups.
- Learn how to gauge serving sizes; volume of bowls and glasses, and so on.
- Ask your dietitian or diabetes educator about how to adjust your diet if you're travelling (this depends on whether you're on medication, where you're going, what foods will be available, and so on.)

- Draw up a Sick Days Plan with your dietitian. This will depend on what your regular meal plan includes.
- Ask about any meal supplements, such as breakfast bars, sports bars or meal replacement drinks. How will these figure into your meal plan?
- Choose lower fat foods more often. (See Chapter 9.)

The Food Choice Values System

The first thing you need to learn before you shop for food is the Food Choice Values and Symbols, symbols developed by the Canadian Diabetes Association, which will tell you how various foods can be incorporated into your meal plan. This is different than the Food Exchange lists developed by the American Diabetes Association. (See Table 5.3 for the conversion, in case you're shopping in the United States.) The CDA has created seven symbols (colour and shape-coded) to represent various food groups. There are many crossovers, however (many of these food categories are a combination of carbohydrates, sugar or fat).

TABLE 5.3
Comparing the U.S. and Canadian Food Group Systems

AMERICAN DIABETES ASSOCIATION EXCHANGE SYSTEM	CANADIAN DIABETES ASSOCIATION CHOICE SYSTEM
1 Starch	1 Starch
1 Fruit	1½ Fruits & Vegetables
1 Vegetable	Fruits & Vegetables
1 Milk	2 Milk
(No equal food group)	Sugars
1 Lean Meat	1 Protein
1 Fat	1 Fats & Oils
Free Foods	Extra Vegetables

■ Starch Foods (breads, grains, cereals, pasta, corn, rice, potato)

◢ Fruits and Vegetables (all fruits and sweet vegetables, such as squash, carrots or peas)

◆ Milk (all milk and yogurt products; cheese not included)

[✱] Sugars (sweet)

[❷] Protein Foods (all lean meats, poultry, fish, eggs and cheeses)

[▲] Fats and Oils (anything high in fat, including butter, fatty meats, any oils, and so on.)

[++] Extras (all low-calorie foods such as leafy greens, herbs and spices, artificially sweetened and/or zero-calorie foods, all cruciferous veggies such as broccoli, and a few others.)

Your dietitian or diabetes educator will work with you to create an individual meal plan using food choices within the above food groups. One person, for example, may need 8 starch choices daily while another person may need 6. I cannot tell you in this book how many choices you can have; I can only explain how the foods are categorized.

A wide assortment of packaged goods have the CDA symbol on their labels as a courtesy to people with diabetes; this is not a legal requirement, however. Food manufacturers pay the Canadian Diabetes Association a fee to have their product evaluated and assigned the appropriate food choice symbols. Consumers often assume that CDA symbols mean that the product is better or more nutritious than products that do not carry those symbols. This assumption is false. CDA symbols on food packages are equivalent to the Braille symbols on elevator buttons; they're a courtesy to people with diabetes to assist in meal planning—that's all.

The Outside Aisles

What you need to live is usually found on the outside aisles of any supermarket or grocery store. Outside aisles simulate the foods you can buy at outdoor markets: fruits, vegetables, meat, eggs, fish, breads and dairy products. Natural fibre (both soluble and insoluble), discussed in Chapter 9, is also found in the outside aisles. (See Table 5.1 for a list of foods high in fibre.)

But remember: foods you buy in the outside aisles can also be high in fat unless you select wisely, all discussed in Chapter 9.

The Inside Aisles

These are not only the aisles of temptation, they may have complicated food labels. In Canada, ingredients on labels are listed according to weight, with the "most" listed first. If sugar is the first ingredient, you know the product contains mostly sugar. The lower sugar is on the list, the less sugar the product contains. The nutrition information on the label should also list the total amount of carbohydrates in a *serving* of the food. That amount includes both natural and added sugars.

Planning to pick up some cough syrup for that cold of yours when you hit the pharmacy section? How about vitamin pills? Check the sugar content first. Your pharmacist will recommend a sugar-free remedy.

Whenever a product says it is "calorie-reduced" or "carbohydrate-reduced" it means there are 50 percent less calories or carbohydrates compared to the original product. But something that was originally 7,000 calories isn't much better at 3,500!

"Cholesterol-free" or "low cholesterol" means that the product doesn't have any, or much, animal fat (hence, cholesterol). This doesn't mean "low fat." Pure vegetable oil doesn't come from animals but is pure fat!

TABLE 5.4
Commonly Used U.S. and Canadian Nutrient Claim Comparisons

CLAIM	U.S.	CANADA
"Low Calorie"	40 calories or less per serving.	50 percent less energy than a regular product and 15 calories or less per serving.
"Low Fat"	3 g of fat or less per serving.	3 g of fat or less per serving.
"Low Cholesterol"	20 mg of cholesterol or less per serving (in addition to saturated fat and total fat restrictions).	20 mg of cholesterol or less perserving (in addition to the saturated fat restrictions only).

A label that screams "low fat" means that the product has less than 3 g of fat per serving. In potato-chip country, that means about 6 potato chips. (*I don't know anybody who ever ate one serving of potato chips!*) So if you eat the whole bag of "low-fat" chips, you're still eating a lot of fat. Be sure to check serving sizes.

Products that are "light" (or lite) have 25 to 50 percent less of some ingredient in that product. It could be fat, cholesterol, salt, or sugar, or less food colouring, and therefore the designation is frequently misleading.

"Sugar-Free"

Careful! Sugar-free in the language of labels simply means "sucrose-free." That doesn't mean the product is *carbohydrate free*, as in: dextrose-free, lactose-free, glucose-free or fructose-free. Check the labels for all things ending in "ose" to find out the sugar content; you're not just looking for sucrose. Watch out for "no added sugar," "without added sugar" or "no sugar added." This simply means: "We didn't put the sugar in, God did." Again, reading the number of carbohydrates on the nutrition information label is the most accurate way to know the amount of sugar in the product. Nutrition claims in big, bold statements can be misleading.

Born in the U.S.A.

American labels that say "sugar-free" contain less than 0.5 g of sugars per serving, while a "reduced-sugar" food contains at least 25 percent less sugar per serving than the regular product. If the label also states that the product is not a reduced- or low-calorie food, or it is not for weight control, it's got enough sugar in there to make you think twice.

Serving sizes in the United States are also listed differently. Foods that are similar are given the same *type* of serving size defined by the U.S. Food and Drug Administration (FDA). That means that five cereals that all weigh X grams per cup, will share the same serving sizes.

Calories (how much energy) and calories from fat (how much fat) are also listed per serving of food in the United States. Total carbohydrate, dietary fibre, sugars, other carbohydrates (which means starches), total fat, saturated fat, cholesterol, sodium, potassium, and vitamin and minerals are given in Percent Daily values, based on the 2,000-calorie diet recommended by the U.S. government. (In Canada, Recommended Nutrient Intake (RNI) is used for vitamins and minerals).

Sweeteners

We gravitate toward sweet flavours because we start out with the slightly sweet taste of breast milk. A product can be sweet without containing a drop of sugar, thanks to the invention of artificial sugars and sweeteners. Artificial sweeteners will not affect your blood sugar levels because they do not contain sugar; they may contain a tiny amount of calories, however. It depends upon whether that sweetener is classified as nutritive or non-nutritive.

Nutritive sweeteners have calories or contain natural sugar. White or brown table sugar, molasses, honey and syrup are all considered nutritive sweeteners. *Sugar alcohols* (see page 124) are also nutritive sweeteners because they are made from fruits or produced commercially from dextrose. Sorbitol, mannitol, xylitol and maltitol are all sugar alcohols. Sugar alcohols contain only 4 calories per gram, like ordinary sugar, and will affect your blood sugar levels like ordinary sugar. It all depends on how much is consumed, and the degree of absorption from your digestive tract.

Non-nutritive sweeteners are sugar substitutes or artificial sweeteners; they do not have any calories and will not affect your blood sugar levels. Examples of non-nutritive sweeteners are saccharin, cyclamate, aspartame, sucralose and acesulfame potassium.

The Sweetener Wars

The oldest non-nutritive sweetener is saccharin, which is what you get when you purchase Sweet'n Low or Hermesetas. In Canada, saccharin can only be used as a tabletop sweetener in either tablet or powder form. Saccharin is 300 times sweeter than sucrose (table sugar) but has a metallic aftertaste. At one point in the 1970s, saccharin was also thought to cause cancer, but this was never proven.

In the 1980s, aspartame was invented, which is sold as NutraSweet. It was considered a nutritive sweetener because it was derived from natural sources (two amino acids, aspartic acid and phenylalanine), which means that aspartame is digested and metabolized the same way as any other protein foods. For every gram of aspartame, there are 4 calories. But since aspartame is 200 times sweeter than sugar, you don't need very much of it to achieve the desired sweetness. In at least 90 countries, aspartame is found in more than 150 product categories, including breakfast cereals, beverages, desserts, candy and gum, syrups, salad dressings and various snack foods. Here's where it gets confusing: aspartame is also available as a tabletop sweetener under the brand name Equal, and most recently, PROSWEET. An interesting point about aspartame is that it's not recommended for baking or any other recipe where heat is required. The two amino acids in it separate with heat and the product loses its sweetness. That's not to say it's harmful if heated, but your recipe won't turn out.

For the moment, aspartame is considered safe for everybody, including people with diabetes, pregnant women and children. The only people who are cautioned against consuming it are those with a rare hereditary disease known as phenylketonuria (PKU) because aspartame contains phenylalanine, which people with PKU cannot tolerate.

Another common tabletop sweetener is sucralose, sold as Splenda. Splenda is a white crystalline powder, actually made from sugar itself. It's 600 times sweeter than table sugar but is not broken down in your digestive system, so has no calories at all. Splenda can also be used in hot or cold foods, and is found in hot and cold beverages, frozen foods, baked goods and other packaged foods.

In the United States, you can still purchase Cyclamate, a non-nutritive sweetener sold under the brand name Sucaryl or Sugar Twin. Cyclamate is also the sweetener used in many weight control products and is 30 times sweeter than table sugar, with no after-taste. Cyclamate is fine for hot or cold foods. In Canada, however, you can only find cyclamate as Sugar Twin or as a sugar substitute in medication.

The newest sweeteners

The newest addition to the sweetener industry is acesulfame potassium (Ace-K), recently approved by Health Canada. About 200 times sweeter than table sugar, Ace-K is sold as Sunett and is found in beverages, fruit spreads, baked goods, dessert bases, tabletop sweeteners, hard candies, chewing gum and breath fresheners. While no specific studies on Ace-K and diabetes have been done, the only people who are cautioned against ingesting Ace-K are those on a potassium-restricted diet or people who are allergic to sulpha drugs.

Researchers at the University of Maryland have discovered another sweetener that can be specifically designed for people with diabetes. This sweetener would be based on D-tagatose, a hexose sugar found naturally in yogurt, cheese or sterilized milk. The beauty of this ingredient is that D-tagatose has no effect on insulin levels or blood sugar levels in both people with and without diabetes. Experts believe that D-tagatose is similar to acarbose (see Chapter 2) in that it delays the absorption of carbohydrates.

D-tagatose looks identical to fructose, and has about 92 percent of the sweetness of sucrose, except only 25 percent of it will be metabolized. Currently, D-tagatose is being developed as a bulk sweetener. It is a few years away from being marketed and sold as a brand-name sweetener, however.

Sugar alcohols

Not to be confused with alcoholic beverages, sugar alcohols are nutritive sweeteners, like regular sugar. These are found naturally in fruits or manufactured from carbohydrates. Sorbitol, mannitol, xylitol, maltitol, maltitol syrup, lactitol, isomalt and hydrogenated starch hydrolysates are all sugar alcohols. In your body, these types of sugars are absorbed lower down in the digestive tract, and will cause gastrointestinal symptoms if you use too much. Because sugar alcohols are absorbed more slowly, they were once touted as ideal for people with diabetes. But, since they are a carbohydrate, they still increase your blood sugar—just like regular sugar. Now that artificial sweeteners are on the market in abundance, the only real advantage of sugar alcohols is that they don't cause cavities. The bacteria in your mouth don't like sugar alcohols as much as real sugar.

According to the FDA, even foods that contain sugar alcohols can be labelled "sugar-free." Sugar alcohol products can also be labelled "Does not promote tooth decay," which is often confused with "low-calorie."

At the Liquor Store

The one thing missing from the CDA food choices is alcohol. As a food choice, alcohol is as fattening as a Fats & Oils choice (see Table 5.1), delivering about 7 calories per gram or 150 calories per drink. Many people with diabetes think they have to avoid alcohol completely because it converts into glucose. This is not so. Alcohol *alone* doesn't increase blood sugar since alcohol cannot be turned into glucose. It's the sugar *in* that alcoholic beverage that can affect blood sugar level. The problem with alcohol is that it's so darned fattening, something people with Type 2 diabetes may need to watch for. That said, alcohol has been proven to raise your "good" cholesterol (HDL). This fact was discovered in the late 1980s when researchers probed why France, with all its rich food, had such low rates of heart disease. It was the wine; red wine, in particular, was shown to decrease the risk of cardiovascular disease. But any alcohol will do this. So it's okay to have this stuff, so long as you *plan for it* with your dietitian, discuss it with your doctor, and *count it* as an actual food choice.

It's crucial to note that alcohol can cause hypoglycemia (low blood sugar), if you're on oral hypoglycemic agents or insulin. *Please* discuss the effects of alcohol and hypoglycemia with your health care team.

Fine Wine

Dry wines that are listed as (0), meaning no added sugar (in Ontario and British Columbia), or "dry" are fine to ingest if you are diabetic. Wine is the result of natural sugar in fruits or fruit juices fermenting. Fermentation means that natural sugar is converted into alcohol. A glass of dry red or white wine has calories (discussed below) but no sugar. And unless extra sugar is added to the wine, there's no way that alcohol will change back into sugar, even in your digestive tract. The same thing goes for cognac, brandy and dry sherry that contain no sugar.

On the other hand, a sweet wine listed as (3) in Ontario or British Columbia means that it contains 3 g of sugar per 100 ml or 3.5-oz portion. Dessert wines or ice wines are really sweet; they contain about 15 percent sugar or 10 g of sugar for a 2-oz serving. Sweet liqueurs are 35 percent sugar.

A glass of dry wine with your meal adds about 100 calories, or the equivalent calories of fat or oil. Half soda water and half wine (a spritzer) contains half the calories. When you cook with wine, the alcohol evaporates, leaving only the flavour. If your wine has no sugar, it counts as 2 Fats & Oils choices. If it has sugar, it counts as a Sugars choice plus 2 Fat & Oils choices (see Table 5.1).

At the Pub

If you're a beer drinker, you're basically having some corn, barley and a couple of teaspoons of malt sugar (maltose) when you have a bottle of beer. The corn and barley ferment into mostly alcohol and some maltose. Calorie-wise, that's about 150 calories per bottle plus 3 tsp of malt sugar. Beer can be defined as a 1 Sugar plus Fats & Oils choice.

A light beer has fewer calories but contains at least 100 calories per bottle. De-alcoholized beer still has sugar, and counts as 2 Fruits & Vegetables choice.

The Hard Stuff

The stiffer the drink, the fatter it gets. Hard liquors such as scotch, rye, gin and rum are made out of cereal grains; vodka, the Russian staple, is made out of potatoes. In this case, the grains ferment into alcohol. Hard liquor averages about 40 percent alcohol, but has no sugar. Nevertheless, you're looking at about 100 calories per small shot glass, so long as you don't add fruit juice, tomato or clamato juice, or sugary soft drinks. As bizarre as it sounds, a Bloody Mary or Bloody Caesar is actually a Fruit & Vegetables choice: potatoes and tomatoes!

The Glycogen Factor

If you recall from Chapter 4, glycogen is the stored sugar your liver keeps handy for emergencies. If your blood sugar needs a boost, the liver will tap into its glycogen stores and convert it into glucose. Alcohol in the liver *blocks* this conversion process. So, if you've been exercising and then go out with friends for a few drinks, unless you've eaten something after your exercise, you may need that glycogen. If you drink to the point of feeling tipsy, that glycogen can be cut off by the alcohol, causing hypoglycemia. What complicates matters even more is that your hypoglycemia symptoms can mimic drunkenness. This glycogen problem can affect both people with Type 1 or Type 2 diabetes because it can result when either insulin or oral hypoglycemic agents are used. (See Chapter 4 for details on hypoglycemia, and below for the alcohol/diabetes rules.)

Don't Drink and Starve

If you're going to drink, EAT! Always have food with your alcohol. Food delays absorption of alcohol into the bloodstream, providing you with carbohydrates and therefore preventing hypoglycemia.

Experts also recommend the following:

- Avoid alcohol when your blood sugar is high.
- Remember that two drinks a day is fine for someone with a healthy liver, but fewer is recommended for liver health.
- Choose dry wines or alcoholic beverages with no sugar. (Or rum and diet cola versus rum and cola.)
- Remember that juice has sugar; even tomato and clamato juice.
- Never substitute alcohol for food if you're taking insulin or pills.
- Don't be afraid to ask your dietitian about how to count your favourite wine or cocktail as a food choice. Again, as long as it's planned for, it's fine.
- Talk to your doctor about how to safely balance alcohol and insulin, and alcohol and oral hypoglycemic agents.

You need to exercise when you have diabetes. Meal planning is only one component of getting your blood sugar and weight under control. Exercise will allow your body to use the insulin you do make much more efficiently. In fact, many experts find that when their Type 2 diabetes patients stick to their meal plans and incorporate regular exercise into their routine, they may not need any medications or insulin to manage their diabetes. The next chapter will tell you how to make your body into a "lean mean insulin machine."

Chapter 6

THE LEAN, MEAN

INSULIN MACHINE

You are a lean mean insulin machine, although you may not realize it. The purpose of this chapter is to explain how exercise affects your body when you have diabetes—it is not, however, intended as a work-out program. Everyone needs to design a *do-able* exercise program that is appealing and convenient; for most people, that will mean combining some kind of simple stretching routine with some aerobic activity. As one expert aptly put it on her video, the program you *can* do is the one you *will* do.

Most people who have been sedentary most of their lives are intimidated by fitness clubs. Walking into a room filled with complex machines and fit, supple bodies is not an inviting atmosphere for somebody who doesn't understand how to program a StairMaster. And the "language" of exercise is intimidating, too. Not only do you need an anatomy lesson to understand which movements stretch which group of muscles, but you also need to take a crash course in cardiology to understand exactly how long you have to hyperventilate and have your pulse at X beats per minute—with the sweat pouring off you—before you burn any fat. The concept of "gaining muscle" over existing fat is also a hard one to grasp. (My question is always: "How come, if I've been doing my program for six months, I weigh *more* than when I started?")

Aerobics classes are another problem; many people (like me) are uncomfortable with their lack of finesse in public. And many aerobics classes assume that you've had formal training with the National Ballet of Canada; after all, you need the grace of a dancer to perform half the moves! So let me stress something before you begin reading: you're wearing all the equipment you will ever need to exercise. If you can breathe, stretch and walk, you can become a lean mean exercise machine without paying a membership fee.

What Does Exercise Really Mean?

The Oxford dictionary defines exercise as "the exertion of muscles, limbs, etc., especially for health's sake; bodily, mental or spiritual training." In the Western world, we have placed an emphasis on "bodily training" when we talk about exercise, completely ignoring mental and spiritual training. Only recently have Western studies begun to focus on the mental benefits of exercise. (It's been shown, for example, that exercise creates endorphins, hormones that make us feel good.) Meditation or other calming forms of mental and spiritual exercise have also been shown to improve well-being and health.

In the East, for thousands of years, exercise has focused on achieving mental and spiritual health *through* the body, using breathing and postures. Fitness practitioner Karen Faye maintains that posture is extremely important for organ alignment. Standing correctly, with ears over shoulders, and shoulders over hips, with knees slightly bent and head straight up naturally allows you to pull in your abdomen. According to Faye, many native cultures with people who balance baskets over their heads or do a lot of physical work with their bodies, are noted for correct postures and low rates of osteoporosis.

Nor should we ignore the aboriginal and Northern traditions known to improve mental health and well-being, such as traditional dances, active prayers that incorporate physical activity, circles that involve community and communication, and even sweat lodges, believed to help rid the body of toxins through sweating. These are forms of wellness activities that should be investigated.

The Meaning of Aerobic

If you look up the word "aerobic" in the dictionary, what you'll find is the chemistry definition: "living in free oxygen." This is certainly correct; we are all aerobes—beings that require oxygen to live. All that jumping around and fast movement is done to create faster breathing, so we can take in more oxygen into our bodies.

Why are we doing this? Because the blood contains *oxygen*! The faster your blood flows, the more oxygen can flow to your organs. But when your health care practitioner tells you to "exercise" or to take up "aerobic exercise" he or she is not referring solely to "increasing oxygen" but to exercising the heart muscle. The faster it beats, the better a workout it gets (although you don't want to overwork your heart, either).

Why we want more oxygen

When more oxygen is in our bodies, we burn fat, our breathing improves, our blood pressure improves and our hearts work better. Oxygen also lowers triglycerides and cholesterol, increasing our high-density lipoproteins (HDL) or the "good" cholesterol, while decreasing our low-density lipoproteins (LDL) or the "bad" cholesterol. This means that your arteries will unclog and you may significantly decrease your risk of heart disease and stroke. More oxygen makes our brains work better, so we feel better. Studies show that depression is decreased when we increase oxygen flow into our bodies. Ancient techniques such as yoga, which specifically improve mental and spiritual well-being, achieve this by combining deep breathing and stretching, which improves oxygen and blood flow to specific parts of the body.

With Type 2 diabetes, more oxygen in the body increases your cells' sensitivity to insulin, causing your blood-glucose levels to drop. More oxygen can also improve the action of insulin-producing cells in the pancreas. As you continue aerobic exercise, your blood sugar levels will become much easier to manage. You can also use exercise to decrease blood sugar levels in the short term, over a 24-hour period. People who are taking oral hypoglycemic pills may find that their dosages need to be lowered, or that they no longer need the medication.

Exercise has been shown to dramatically decrease the incidence of many other diseases, including cancer. Some research suggests that cancer cells tend to thrive in an oxygen-depleted environment. The more oxygen in the bloodstream, the less hospitable you make your body to cancer. In addition, since many cancers are related to fat-soluble toxins, the less fat on your body, the less fat-soluble toxins your body can accumulate.

Burning fat

The only kind of exercise that will burn fat is aerobic exercise because *oxygen burns fat*. If you were to go to your fridge and pull out some animal fat (chicken skin, red-meat fat or butter), throw it in the sink and light it with a match, it will burn. What makes the flame yellow is oxygen; what fuels the fire is the fat. That same process goes on in your body. The oxygen will burn your fat, however you increase the oxygen flow in your body (through jumping around or employing an established deep-breathing technique.)

Of course, when you burn fat, you lose weight, which can also cause your body to use insulin more efficiently, and lower your blood sugar levels. It may also cause your doctor to lower your dosage of oral hypoglycemics or stop your medication altogether.

The Western definition of aerobic

In the West, an exercise is considered aerobic if it makes your heart beat faster than it normally does. When your heart is beating fast, you'll be breathing hard and sweating and will officially be in your "target zone" or "ideal range" (the kind of phrases that turn many people off).

There are official calculations you can do to find this target range. For example, it's recommended that by subtracting your age from 220, then multiplying that number by 60 percent, you will find your "threshhold level"—which means "Your heart should be beating X beats per minute for 20 to 30 minutes." If you multiply the number by 75 percent, you will find your "ceiling level"—which means "Your heart should not be beating faster than X beats per minute for 20 to 30 minutes." But this is only an example. If you are on heart medications (drugs that slow your heart down, known as beta blockers), you'll want to make sure you discuss what "target" to aim for with your health care professional.

Finding your pulse

You have pulse points all over your body. The easiest ones to find are those on your neck, at the base of your thumb, just below your earlobe or on your wrist. To check your heart rate, look at a watch or clock and begin to count your beats for 15 seconds (if the second hand is on the 12, count until it reaches 15). Then multiply by 4 to get your pulse.

Borg's Rate of Perceived Exertion (RPE)

This doesn't refer to the Borg on Star Trek, but to the "Borg Scale of Perceived Exertion." This is a way of measuring exercise intensity without finding your pulse, and because of its simplicity, is now the recommended method for judging exertion. This Borg "scale" as it's dubbed goes from 6 to 20 (shown in Table 6.1). Extremely light activity may rate a "7" for example, while a very, very hard activity may rate a "19." What exercise practitioners recommend is that you do a "talk test" to rate your exertion, too. If you can't talk without gasping for air, you may be working too hard. You should be able to carry on a normal conversation throughout your activity. What's crucial to remember about RPE is that it is extremely individual; what one person judges a "7" another may judge a "10."

TABLE 6.1
Sample Borg Rate of Perceived Exertion Scales

SAMPLE A	SAMPLE B
6	0 Nothing at all
7 Very, very light	0.5 Very, very weak
8	1 Very weak
9 Very light	
10	2 Weak
11 Fairly light	3 Moderate
12	4 Somewhat strong
13 Somewhat hard	
14	5 Strong
15 Hard	6
16	7 Very strong
17 Very hard	
18	8
19 Very, very hard	9 Very, very strong
20	10 Maximum

Adapted from: Lea and Febiger, *Guidelines For Exercise Testing And Prescription* (American College of Sports Medicine, 1991: 70).

Other ways to increase oxygen flow

This will come as welcome news to people who have limited movement due to joint problems, arthritis, or other diabetes-related complications, ranging from stroke to kidney disease. You can increase the flow of oxygen into your bloodstream without exercising your heart muscle, by learning how to breath deeply through your diaphragm. There are many yoga-like programs and videos available that can teach you this technique, which does not require you to jump around. The benefit is that you would be increasing the oxygen flow into your bloodstream, which is better than doing nothing at all to improve your health, and has many health benefits, according to a myriad of wellness practitioners.

An "aerobic" activity versus active living

The phrase "aerobic activity" means that the *activity* causes your heart to pump harder and faster, and causes you to breathe faster, which increases oxygen flow. Activities such as cross-country skiing, walking, hiking and biking are all aerobic.

But you know what? Exercise practitioners hate the terms "aerobic activity" or "aerobics program" because it is not about what people do in their daily life. Health promoters are replacing these terms with the phrase "active living"—because that's what becoming un-sedentary is all about. There are many ways you can adopt an active lifestyle. Here are some suggestions:

- If you drive everywhere, pick the parking space further away from your destination so you can work some daily walking into your life.
- If you take public transit everywhere, get off one or two stops early so you can walk the rest of the way to your destination.
- Choose stairs more often over escalators or elevators.
- Park at the "Eaton's" side of the mall and then walk to "The Bay." Or vice versa.
- Take a stroll after dinner around your neighbourhood.
- Volunteer to walk the dog.
- On weekends, go to the zoo or get out to flea markets, garage sales, and so on.

What About Muscles?

Forty percent of your body weight is made from muscle, where sugar is stored. The muscles use this sugar when they are being worked. When the sugar is used up, the muscles, in a healthy body, will drink in sugar from your blood. After exercising, the muscles will continue to drink in glucose from your blood to replenish the glucose that was there before exercise.

But when you have insulin resistance, glucose from your blood has difficulty getting inside your muscles; the muscles act like a brick wall. As you begin to use and tone your muscles, they will become more receptive to the glucose in your blood, allowing the glucose in. Studies show that the muscles specifically worked out in a given exercise take up glucose far more easily than another muscle in the same body, which has not been worked out.

Doing weight-bearing activities is also encouraged because it builds bone mass and uses up calories. Building bone mass is particularly important; as Karen Faye tells me: "If you want a strong house, you need a strong frame!" Women who are vulnerable to osteoporosis (loss of bone mass) as a result of estrogen-loss after menopause (unless they are on hormone replacement therapy) will benefit from these activities. The denser your bones, the harder they are to break or sprain. As we age, we are all at risk for osteoporosis unless we've either been building up our bone mass for years, or are maintaining current bone mass. For information on osteoporosis, call your local office of The Osteoporosis Society of Canada.

By increasing muscular strength, we increase flexibility and endurance. For example, you'll find that the first time you ride your bike from home to downtown, your legs may feel sore. Do that same ride ten times, and your legs will no longer be sore. That's what's meant by building endurance. Of course, you won't be as out of breath, either, which is another way of building endurance.

Hand weights or resistance exercises (using rubber-band products or pushing certain body parts together) help increase what's called "lean body mass"—body tissue that is not fat. That is why many people find their weight does not drop when they begin to exercise. Yet, as your muscles become bigger, your body fat decreases.

Sugar and muscle
When you think "muscle," think "sugar." Every time you work any muscle in your body, either independent of an aerobic activity, or during an aerobic activity, your muscles use up glucose from your bloodstream as fuel. People with high blood sugar prior to muscle toning will find that their blood sugar levels are lower after the muscle has been worked.

On the downside, if you have normal blood sugar levels prior to working a muscle, you may find that your blood sugar goes too low after you exercise *unless* you eat something; this should be carbohydrates. In fact, your muscles prefer to use carbohydrates rather than fat as fuel. When your muscles use up all the sugar in your blood, your liver will convert glycogen (excess glucose it stores up for these kinds of emergencies) back into glucose and release it into your bloodstream for your muscles to use.

To avoid this scenario, eat before and after exercising if your blood sugar level is normal. How much you eat prior to exercising largely depends on what you're doing and how long you're going to be doing it. The general rule is to follow your meal plan, eating smaller, more frequent meals throughout the day to keep your blood sugar levels consistent.

Athletes without diabetes will generally consume large quantities of carbohydrates before an intense workout. In fact, it's a known strategy in the athletic world to eat 40 to 65 g of carbohydrate per hour to maintain blood glucose levels to the point where performance is improved. It's also been shown that glucose, sucrose, malto-dextrins or high fructose corn syrup during exercise can increase endurance. After a training session, athletes will typically consume more carbohydrates to replenish their energy and carry on throughout the day.

Athletes who have Type 1 diabetes do exactly the same thing, except they must be more careful about timing their food intake with insulin to avoid either too low or high blood sugar.

If your blood sugar is low, don't exercise at all as it may be life-threatening. Do not resume exercise until you get your blood sugar levels under control.

Exercises that can be hazardous

These activities, such as wrestling or weightlifting, are usually short but very intense. As a result, unless you fuel up ahead of time, they will force your body to use glycogen (see Chapter 4), which is the stored glucose your liver keeps handy. When you have diabetes, it's not a great idea to force your liver to give up that glycogen. This can actually increase your blood pressure and put you at risk for other health problems, including hypoglycemia. To avoid this, you'll need to eat some carbohydrates prior to these exercises, which will provide enough fuel to the muscles.

Getting Physical

More than 50 percent of all people with diabetes exercise less than once a week, and 56 percent of all diabetes-related deaths are due to heart attacks. This is terrible news, considering how beneficial and life-extending exercise can be. Reports from the United States show that one out of three American adults are overweight, a sign of growing inactivity. But, as mentioned earlier, the fitness industry has a done an excellent job of intimidating inactive people. Some people are so put off by the health-club scene, they become even more sedentary. This is similar to diet failure, where you become so demoralized because you "cheated" that you binge even more.

If you've been sedentary most of your life, there's nothing wrong with starting off with simple, even leisurely activities such as gardening, feeding the birds in a park or a few simple stretches. Any step you make towards being more active is a crucial and important step.

Experts also recommend that you find a friend, neighbour or relative to get physical with you. When your exercise plans include someone else, you'll be less apt to cancel plans or make excuses for not getting out there. Whomever you choose, teach this person how to recognize hypoglycemia just in case. (See Chapter 4.)

Things to Do Before "Moving Day"

1. *Choose an activity that's right for you.* Whether it's walking, chopping wood, jumping rope or folk dancing—pick something you enjoy. You don't have to do the same thing each time, either. Vary your routine to avoid monotony. Just make sure that whatever

activity you choose is continuous for the duration. Walking for
two minutes then stopping for three isn't continuous. It's also
important to choose an activity that doesn't aggravate a pre-
existing problem, such as eye problems. Lowering your head in a
certain way (as in touching your toes) or straining your upper
body can increase blood pressure and/or aggravate eye problems.
If foot problems are a concern, perhaps an activity that doesn't
involve walking, such as canoeing, is better. And so on.

2. *Choose the frequency.* Decide how often you're going to do this
   activity. (Twice, three or four times a week? or once a day?)
   Try not to let two days pass without doing something. And pick
   a duration. If you're elderly or ill, even a few minutes is a good
   start. If you're sedentary but otherwise healthy, aim for 20 to
   30 minutes.

3. *Choose the intensity level that's right for you.* This is easy to do if
   you're using an exercise machine of some kind by just setting the
   dial. If you're walking, the intensity would mean, how fast are you
   planning to walk, or how many hills will you be incorporating into
   your walk? In other words, how fast do you want your heart to beat?

4. *Work your activity into your meal plan.* Once you decide what
   kind of exercise you'll be doing, and for how long, see your dietitian about working your exercise into your current meal plan. You
   may need a small snack prior to and after exercise if you're planning to be active longer than 30 minutes. If you are overweight,
   you do not need to consume extra calories before exercising
   unless your blood sugar level is low.

5. *Tell your doctor what you're doing.* Your doctor may want to monitor
   your blood sugar more closely (or want you to do so), or adjust your
   medication. Don't do anything without consulting your doctor first.

Think Like a Cat

Ever watch a cat in action? Cats will never do anything before stretching. If stretching is your exercise, that's just fine; but if it's not the

focus of your activity, do some stretching before and after you get really active to reduce muscle tightness.

When Not to Exercise

Everyone can and should exercise, but your diabetes may get in the way at times, especially if you're taking insulin. So here are some alarm bells to listen for; if they go off, skip your exercise and do what you have to do to get back on track:

- Keep track of where you're injecting insulin. Insulin injected into an arm or leg that is being worked out will use up the insulin faster. Any signs of low blood sugar mean STOP!
- Check your blood sugar after 30 minutes to make sure it's still normal. If it's low, eat something before you resume exercising. (Blood sugar below 4 mmol/l is low; anything that's 3 mmol/l or less means you should stop exercising or not start exercising at all.)
- If your blood sugar level is high, exercise will bring it down, but if it's greater than 14 mmol/l, check your urine for ketones and don't exercise. When your body is stressed, the blood sugar level can go even higher.

Exercise Parental Duties

Obesity in childhood and adolescence is at an all-time high in North America. For example, the American National Health and Nutrition Examination Survey III (NHANES III) revealed that 21 percent of people 12 to 19 were obese, while as many as 40 percent of people in that age group were physically unfit. It wasn't until 1995 that the Dietary Guidelines for Americans even recommended physical activity. If you have Type 2 diabetes, unless you can encourage them to adjust their lifestyles early, your children will be at high risk for Type 2 diabetes as well. Old habits die hard—something you're learning the hard way. By making sure that your children appreciate the value and benefits of getting physical, you can help them avoid going through what you are. In fact, why don't you encourage your children to exercise right along with you?

TABLE 6.2
Suggested Activities

MORE INTENSE	LESS INTENSE
Skiing	Golf
Running	Bowling
Jogging	Badminton
Stair-stepping or stair-climbing	Croquet
Trampolining	Sailing
Jumping rope	Swimming
Fitness walking	Strolling
Race walking	Stretching
Aerobic classes	
Roller skating	
Ice skating	
Biking	
Weight-bearing exercises	
Tennis	
Swimming	

Source: Courtesy, Karen Faye, LPN, A.F.F.A., fitness practitioner

Chapter 7

DOWN THE

DIABETES ROAD

Why is it so important to manage your diabetes? Because many of the pre-existing conditions that led to your diabetes (see Chapter 1) can cause other complications down the road. On top of that, walking around with higher-than-normal blood sugar levels can lead to even more complications.

At least 40 percent of all people with Type 2 will develop another disease as a result of their diabetes. Many of you reading this may already be affected by some of the conditions discussed in this chapter. But if you've been newly diagnosed with Type 2 diabetes, you may not realize exactly how many other diseases can be triggered by it; after all, you may feel fine now. The purpose of this chapter is to simplify the complicated language of "complications" so you can see what's possible down the road, clearly read the road signs and perhaps take a different route. You'll find out why diabetes leads to other diseases, the diagnosis and treatment of each of those diseases, and what can be done to prevent complications.

Macro Versus Micro

The most important thing to grasp about diabetes complications is that there are two kinds of problems that can lead to similar diseases. The first kind of problem is known as a *macrovascular complication*. The prefix *macro* means LARGE, as in macroeconomics (studying an entire economic system as opposed to one company's economic structure). The word *vascular* means blood vessels—your veins and arteries, which carry the blood back and forth throughout your body. Put it together and you have "large blood vessel complications." But a plain-language interpretation of macrovascular complications would be: "BIG problems with your blood vessels."

If you think of your body as a planet, a macrovascular disease would be a disease that affects the whole planet; it is body-wide, or systemic. Cardiovascular disease is a macrovascular complication, which can cause heart attack, stroke, high blood pressure and body-wide circulation problems, clinically known as peripheral vascular disease (PVD). So your body, head to toe, is affected (see Head to Toe section, page 144).

A second type of problem is known as a *microvascular complication*. *Micro* means tiny, as in microscopic. Microvascular complications refer to problems with the smaller blood vessels (a.k.a. capillaries) that connect to various body parts. A plain-language interpretation of microvascular complications would be "Houston, we've got a problem." In other words, the problem *is* serious, but it's not going to affect the whole planet, just the spacecraft in orbit. Eye disease (clinically known as retinopathy) is a microvascular complication. Blindness is a serious problem, but you won't die from it. Nerve damage (neuropathy) is a microvascular complication that can affect your whole body: feet, eyes, sexual functioning, skin—but, again, you won't die from it.

The Combo Platter

Here's where complications get really complicated to understand: when macro *and* micro converge. This is what happens with kidney disease (clinically known as renal disease nephropathy). The high blood pressure that is caused by macrovascular complications, combined with the small blood vessel damage caused by microvascular complications, together, can cause kidney failure—something you *can* die from unless you have dialysis (filtering out the body's waste products through a machine) or a kidney transplant.

Who Gets Macrovascular Complications?

Macrovascular complications are caused, not only by too much blood sugar, but also by pre-existing health problems. People with Type 2 diabetes are far more vulnerable to macrovascular complications because they usually have contributing risk factors from way back when, such as high cholesterol and high blood pressure, both of which are discussed in Chapter 1. Obesity, smoking and inactivity can then aggravate those problems, resulting in major cardiovascular disease.

Warning signs of macrovascular complications

If you are obese, inactive, have Type 2 diabetes as well as high blood pressure and/or high cholesterol—these are the warning signs of macrovascular problems. The bomb is ticking. In this case, you should be working *right now* on making changes in your diet and lifestyle, and discuss whether you're a candidate for blood-pressure-lowering or cholesterol-lowering medication with your doctor. If you're a woman entering menopause, you should definitely consider hormone replacement therapy, which offers protection from heart disease, balancing the benefits of that against other risks. You may also want to look into more effective strategies to manage your obesity.

You also need to stay alert to signs of circulation problems, heart attack and stroke, which are discussed in detail below.

Who Gets Microvascular Complications?

People with Type 1 diabetes are very vulnerable to microvascular complications, but a good portion of people with Type 2 diabetes suffer from them, too. Microvascular complications are known as the sugar-related complications. The small blood vessel damage is caused by high blood sugar levels over long periods of time. The Diabetes Control and Complications Trial, referred to throughout this book and discussed in detail at the end of this chapter, showed that by keeping blood sugar levels as normal as possible, *as often as possible*, through frequent self-testing, microvascular complications can be prevented.

Warning signs of microvascular problems

Numbness in arms, face or legs, vision problems, bladder infections and other bladder problems are warning signs of microvascular problems. Specific alarm signals for each microvascular problem are discussed separately in the next section.

From Head to Toe

It's important to understand which parts of the body are vulnerable to macrovascular problems, microvascular problems, or both. Therefore, each subheading in this section will indicate "macro," "micro" or "both." People with Type 2 diabetes are far more likely to experience problems with the parts of their body exposed to "macro" and "both"; people with Type 1 diabetes are far more likely to suffer problems with the parts of their body exposed to "micro."

Your Brain (macro)

Cardiovascular disease puts you at risk for a stroke, which occurs when a blood clot (a clog in your blood vessels) travels to your brain and stops the flow of blood and oxygen carried to the nerve cells in that area. When that happens, cells may die or vital functions controlled by the brain can be temporarily or permanently damaged. Bleeding or a rupture from the affected blood vessel can lead to a very serious situation, including death. People with Type 2 diabetes are two to three times more likely to suffer from a stroke than people without diabetes.

Since the 1960s, the death rate from strokes has dropped by 50 percent. This drop is largely due to public-awareness campaigns regarding diet and lifestyle modification (quitting smoking, eating low-fat foods and exercising), as well as the introduction of blood-pressure-lowering drugs and cholesterol-lowering drugs, that have helped people maintain normal blood pressure and cholesterol levels.

Strokes can be mild, moderate, severe or fatal. Mild strokes may affect speech or movement for a short period of time only; many people recover from mild strokes without any permanent damage. Moderate or severe strokes may result in loss of speech, memory and paralysis; many people learn to speak again and learn to function with partial paralysis. How well you recover depends on how much damage was done. It's never too late to reduce the risk of stroke by quitting smoking and making even small changes in diet and lifestyle. Discuss with your doctor whether you're a candidate for medications that can control your blood pressure and cholesterol levels. Aiming for normal blood sugar levels as often as possible is also important. A considerable amount of research points to stress as a risk factor for stroke. The Heart section on page 151 suggests ways to cut down on stress.

Signs of a stroke

If you can recognize the key warning signs of a stroke, it can make a difference in preventing a major stroke or in the severity of a stroke.

Call 9-1-1 or get to Emergency if you suddenly notice one or more of the following symptoms:

- weakness, numbness and/or tingling in your face, arms or legs. (This may last only a few moments);
- loss of speech or difficulty understanding somebody else's speech. (This may last only a short time);
- severe headaches that feel different than any headache you've had before;
- feeling unsteady, falling a lot.

Alzheimer's disease

According to new research done at the Mayo Clinic and Mayo Foundation in Rochester, Minnesota, family members should become acquainted with early signs of Alzheimer's disease. This study showed that people with Type 2 diabetes were 66 percent more likely to develop Alzheimer's disease than those in the general population. The risk was more than double in men, and more than one-third in women. This study noted that it was unclear why there were differences in sex, but that the overall increase in Alzheimer's disease among people with Type 2 diabetes may be the result of common genetic predispositions. In other words, there may be some genes that go together in diabetes and Alzheimer's disease.

Your Nerves (micro)

When your blood sugar levels are too high for too long, you can develop a condition known as diabetic neuropathy or nerve disease. Somehow, the cells that make up your nerves are altered in response to high blood sugar. This condition can lead to foot amputations in people with diabetes. See the Feet section on page 159 for more details.

There are different groups of nerves that are affected by high blood sugar; keeping your blood sugar levels as normal as possible is the best way to prevent many of the following problems. Drugs that help to prevent chemical changes in your nerve cells can also be used to treat nerve damage.

Some nerve diseases

Polyneuropathy is a disease that affects the nerves in your feet and legs. The symptoms are burning, tingling and numbness in the legs and feet.

Autonomic neuropathy is a disease that affects the nerves you don't notice; the nerves that control your digestive tract (see Stomach section on page 153), blood pressure, sweat glands, overall balance and sexual functioning (see Sexual Organs section on page 156). Treatment varies depending on what's affected, but there are drugs that can control individual parts of the body, such as the digestive tract.

Proximal motor neuropathy is a disease that affects the nerves that control your muscles. This can lead to weakness, burning sensations in the joints (hands, thighs and ankles are the most common). These problems can be individually treated with physiotherapy and/or specific medication. When the nerves that control the muscles in the eyes (see Eyes section below) are affected, you may experience problems with your vision, such as double vision. Finally, nerve damage can affect the spine, causing pain and loss of sensation to the back, buttocks and legs.

Your Eyes (both)

Diabetes is the leading cause of new blindness in adults. Seventy-eight percent of people with Type 2 diabetes experience diabetes eye disease, clinically known as diabetic retinopathy. Microvascular complications damage the small blood vessels in the eyes. High blood pressure, associated with macrovascular complications, also damages the blood vessels in the eyes.

While 98 percent of people with Type 1 diabetes will experience eye disease within 15 years of being diagnosed, in Type 2 diabetes, eye disease is often diagnosed *before* the diabetes; in other words, many people don't realize they have diabetes until their eye doctors ask them: "Have you been screened for diabetes?" In fact, 20 percent of people with Type 2 diabetes already have diabetes eye disease before their diabetes is diagnosed.

What happens to the eyes?

Eighty percent of all eye disease is known as non-proliferative eye disease, meaning "no new blood vessel growth" eye disease. This is also called background diabetic eye disease. In this case, the blood vessels in the retina (the part of your eyeball that faces your brain, as opposed to your face) start to deteriorate, bleed or hemorrhage (known as microaneurysms) and leak water and protein into the centre of the retina, called the macula; this condition is known as macular edema, and causes vision loss, which sometimes is only temporary. However, without treatment, more permanent vision loss will occur.

Proliferative eye disease means "new blood vessel growth" eye disease. In this case, your retina says: "Since all my blood vessels are being damaged, I'm just going to grow *new* blood vessels!" This process is known as neovascularization. The problem is that these new blood vessels are deformed, or abnormal, which makes the problem worse, not better. These deformed blood vessels look a bit like Swiss cheese; they're full of holes and have a bad habit of suddenly bleeding out, causing severe damage without warning. They can also lead to scar tissue in the retina, retinal detachments and glaucoma, greatly increasing the risk of legal blindness.

Symptoms

In the early stages of diabetes eye disease, there are no symptoms. That's why you need to have a thorough eye exam every six months. As the eye damage progresses, you may notice blurred vision. The blurred vision is due to changes in the shape of the lens of the eye. During an eye exam, your ophthalmologist may notice yellow spots on your retina, signs that scar tissue has formed on the retina from bleeding. If the disease progresses to the point where new blood vessels have formed, vision problems may be quite severe, as a result of spontaneous bleeding or detachment of the retina. Other diabetes-related eye problems that may affect vision include cataracts and glaucoma.

How to protect yourself from diabetes eye disease

Early detection is your best protection! Using Type 1 rules is the best way to detect diabetes eye disease early and prevent vision loss. In other words, it's crucial to have frequent eye exams. Teens or young adults diagnosed with Type 1 diabetes should have semi-annual or annual eye exams. This way, eye disease can be detected before it affects vision permanently. The average person has an eye exam every five years. And if you're walking around with undiagnosed Type 2 diabetes, you can also be walking around with early signs of diabetes eye disease. So, as soon as you're diagnosed with Type 2 diabetes, get to an eye specialist for a complete exam and make it a yearly "gig" from now on.

During an eye exam, an ophthalmologist will dilate your pupil with eye drops, and then use a special instrument to check for:

- tiny red dots (signs of bleeding);
- a thick or "milky" retina, with or without yellow clumps or spots (signs of macular edema);
- a "bathtub ring" on the retina—a ring shape that surrounds a leakage site on the retina (also a sign of macular edema);
- "cottonwool spots" on the retina—small fluffy white patches in the retina (signs of new blood vessel growth, or more advanced eye disease).

Today, it's estimated that if everyone with impaired glucose tolerance (see Chapter 1) went for an eye exam once a year, blindness from diabetes eye disease would drop from 8 percent in this group to 1 percent.

Can you treat diabetes eye disease?

Not completely. A procedure known as laser photocoagulation can burn and seal off the damaged blood vessels, which stops them from bleeding or leaking. In the earlier stages of eye disease, this procedure can restore your vision within about six months. In most cases, however, laser surgery only slows down vision loss, rather than restoring vision. In other words, without the treatment, your vision will get worse; with the treatment, it will stay the same.

If new blood vessels have already formed, a series of laser treatments are done to purposely scar the retina. Since a scarred retina needs less oxygen, blood vessels stop re-forming, reducing the risk of further damage.

In more serious cases, surgery known as a vitrectomy is performed. In this procedure, blood and scar tissue on the retina are surgically removed.

If you're suffering from vision loss, a number of visual aids can help you perform daily tasks more easily. See the resources section at the back of this book for more details.

A word about smoking

Since smoking also damages blood vessels, and diabetes eye disease is a blood vessel disease, smoking will certainly aggravate the problem. Quitting smoking may help to reduce eye complications.

Eye infections

High blood sugar can predispose you to frequent bacterial infections, including conjunctivitis (pink-eye). Eye infections can also affect your vision. To prevent eye infections, make sure you wash your hands before you touch your eyes, especially before you handle contact lenses.

Your Teeth (micro)

High blood sugar levels get into your saliva, and then into your teeth. Cavities are caused by bacteria in plaque, which breaks down the starches and sugars to form acids that eventually break down your tooth enamel.

Moreover, damage to the blood vessels in your gums can lead to periodontal problems, while blood sugar levels naturally rise when you're fighting a gum infection (known as a periodontal infection),

such as an abscess. Preventing dental problems means the usual—
this order: regularly "rubber tipping" (massaging your gums with that
rubber tip at the end of your toothbrush, or buying a separate rubber-
tip instrument at the drugstore); flossing regularly; brushing regularly;
and rinsing regularly with a mouthwash that kills plaque and bacteria. You may also wish to use a fluoride rinse every night. Have your
teeth cleaned at least every six months, have an annual dental exam
and avoid sugary foods (which you should be doing anyway) that can
increase cavities.

Your Heart (macro)

Type 2 diabetes is often called "a heart attack about to happen."
When large blood vessels are damaged, it means cardiovascular
disease (a.k.a. heart disease).

The first sign of heart disease is angina, or chest pains. When
blood vessels get blocked due to hardening of the arteries (clinically
known as arteriosclerosis), not enough blood gets to the heart muscle,
causing it to die. That's what a heart attack is.

Peripheral vascular disease (meaning "fringe" blood-flow problems) is part of the heart disease story. PVD occurs when blood flow
to the limbs (arms, legs and feet) is blocked, which creates cramping, pains or numbness. *In fact, pain and numbing in your arms or
legs may be signs of heart disease or even an imminent heart attack.*

The way to prevent heart disease and peripheral vascular disease
is by modifying your lifestyle (stop smoking; eat less fat; get more
exercise). Blood-pressure-lowering medication and cholesterol-
lowering drugs are also an option if you have high blood pressure
and/or high cholesterol. And, finally, heart surgery is an option, which
includes angioplasty, laser treatment and bypass surgery. Smoking,
high blood pressure, high blood sugar and high cholesterol (called
the "catastrophic quartet" by one diabetes specialist) will greatly
increase your risk of heart disease. These problems are discussed in
detail in Chapter 1.

Type A and Type 2

Redford B. Williams, Jr., M.D., author of *The Trusting Heart*, documents that people with a Type A personality suffer from more heart disease than people who are calmer and more relaxed about life. The term "Type A personality" was coined in the early 1970s by researchers Meyer Friedman and Ray Rosenman. Type A people tend to be driven, overachieving, very competitive, easily upset and/or angered by everyday occurrences and, ultimately, have a hostile personality.

According to Williams's research, hostility is bad for your heart. This sentiment is echoed by renowned health expert Deepak Chopra, who, in numerous public appearances, has stated the shocking statistic that more heart attacks are recorded Monday mornings (the most stressful morning of the week) than on any other day of the week.

Physiologically, anger and hostility will raise your blood pressure (hence the term "red-faced with anger"). Many cardiologists are starting to list hostility as a risk factor for heart disease, along with smoking, obesity, high blood pressure and cholesterol, and a sedentary lifestyle.

Consider the following tips for becoming less hostile:

- Get into the habit of stopping yourself when you have a hostile thought. In other words, next time you're stuck in traffic, instead of cursing, honking and trying to furiously lane-change, just STOP getting upset and remind yourself that there's nothing you can do about the situation. Turn on the radio and "chill."
- Imagine the life of the person in front of you. If someone cuts in front of you in a line-up or in traffic, instead of erecting your middle finger and yelling, stop and ask yourself what's going on in that other person's life that caused him or her to cut you off. In other words, try to see that it's not personal.
- See the humour. Some situations are so ridiculous, laughing will get you further than ranting and raving. This includes things like terrible service, missing flight connections, and so on.
- Look upon your hostility as a character flaw you can work on. Some people are too shy; some people are too passive; you get angry too quickly. Seeing it and accepting it is a big step.

Your Stomach (micro)

When high blood sugar levels affect your nerve cells, this can include the nerves that control your entire gastrointestinal tract. In fact 30 to 50 percent of people with diabetes suffer from dysmotility, when the muscles in the digestive tract become uncoordinated, causing bloating, abdominal pain and reflux (heartburn). In this case, your doctor may prescribe a motility drug known as a prokinetic agent, a medication that can restore motility.

Your Kidneys (both)

Both micro- and macrovascular complications can lead to kidney problems. High blood pressure and high blood sugar can be a dangerous combination for your kidneys. About 15 percent of people with Type 2 diabetes will develop kidney disease, known as either renal disease or nephropathy. In fact, diabetes causes 40 percent of all end-stage renal disease (ESRD), the term used to describe kidney failure. Roughly 40 percent of all dialysis patients have diabetes.

What do your kidneys do all day?

Kidneys are the public servants of the body; they're busy little bees! If they go on strike, you lose your water service, garbage pickup and a few other services you don't even appreciate.

Kidneys regulate your body's water levels; when you have too much water, your kidneys remove it by dumping it into a large storage tank: your bladder. The excess water stays there until you're ready to "pee it out." If you don't have enough water in your body (or if you're dehydrated), your kidneys will retain the water for you to keep you balanced.

Kidneys also act as your body's sewage filtration plant. They filter out all the garbage and waste that your body doesn't need and dump it into the bladder; this waste is then excreted into your urine. The two waste products your kidneys regularly dump are *urea* (the waste product of protein) and *creatinine* (waste products produced by the muscles). In people with high blood sugar levels, excess sugar will get sent to the kidneys, and the kidneys will dump it into the bladder, too, causing sugar to appear in the urine.

Kidneys also balance calcium and phosphate in the body, needed to build bones. Kidneys operate two little side businesses on top of all of this. They make hormones. One hormone, called renin, helps to regulate blood pressure. Another hormone, called erythropoetin, helps bone marrow make red blood cells.

The macro thing

When you suffer from cardiovascular disease, you probably have high blood pressure. High blood pressure damages blood vessels in the kidneys, which interferes with their job performance. As a result, they won't be as efficient at removing waste or excess water from your body. And if you are experiencing poor circulation, which can also cause water retention, the problem is further aggravated.

Poor circulation may cause your kidneys to secrete too much renin, which is normally designed to regulate blood pressure, but in this case, increases it. All the extra fluid and the high blood pressure places a heavy burden on your heart—and your kidneys. If this situation isn't brought under control, you'd likely suffer from a heart attack before kidney failure, but kidney failure is inevitable.

The micro thing

When high blood sugar levels affect the small blood vessels, that includes the small blood vessels in the kidney's filters (called the nephrons). This condition known as *diabetic nephropathy*. In the early stages of nephropathy, good, usable protein is secreted in the urine. That's a sign that that the kidneys were unable to distribute usable protein to the body's tissues. (Normally, they would excrete only the waste product of protein—urea—into the urine.)

Another microvascular problem affects the kidneys: nerve damage. The nerves you use to control your bladder can be affected, causing a sort of sewage back-up in your body. The first place that sewage hits is your kidneys. Old urine floating around your kidneys isn't a healthy thing. The kidneys can become damaged as a result, aggravating all the conditions discussed so far in this section.

The infection thing

There's a third problem at work here. If you recall, frequent urination is a sign of high blood sugar. That's because your kidneys help to rid the body of too much sugar by dumping it into the bladder. Well, guess what? You're not the only one who likes sugar; bacteria, such as *e. coli* (the "hamburger bacteria"), like it, too. In fact, they thrive on it. So all that sugary urine sitting around in your bladder and passing through your ureter and urethra can cause this bacteria to overgrow, resulting in a urinary tract infection (UTI) such as cystitis (inflammation of the bladder lining). The longer your urethra is, the more protection you have from UTIs. Men have long urethras; women have very short urethras, however, and in the best of times, are prone to these infections—especially after a lot of sexual activity, which helped to coin the term "honeymoon cystitis." Sexual intercourse can introduce even more bacteria (from the vagina or rectum) into a woman's urethra due to the close space the vagina and urethra share. Women who wipe from back to front after a bowel movement can also introduce fecal matter into the urethra, causing a UTI.

Any bacterial infection in your bladder area can travel back up to your kidneys, causing infection, inflammation and a big general mess—again, aggravating all the other problems!

The smoking thing

In the same way that smoking contributes to eye problems (see Eyes section, page 147), it can also aggravate kidney problems. Smoking causes small vessel damage throughout your body.

Signs of diabetic kidney disease

Obviously, there are a lot of different problems going on when it comes to diabetes and kidney disease. If you have any of the following early warning signs of kidney disease, see your doctor as soon as possible:

- high blood pressure (see Chapter 1);
- protein in the urine (a sign of microvascular problems);
- burning or difficulty urinating (a sign of a urinary tract infection);
- foul-smelling or cloudy urine (a sign of a urinary tract infection);
- pain in the lower abdomen (a sign of a urinary tract infection);
- blood or pus in the urine (a sign of a kidney infection);
- fever, chills or vomiting (a sign of *any* infection);
- foamy urine (a sign of kidney infection);
- frequent urination (a sign of high blood sugar and/or urinary tract infection).

Treating kidney disease

If you have high blood pressure, getting it under control through diet, exercise or blood-pressure-lowering medication will help to save your kidneys. If you have high blood sugar, treating any UTI as quickly as possible with antibiotics is the best way to avert kidney infection, while drugs known as ACE inhibitors can help to control small blood vessel damage caused by microvascular complications.

If you wind up with kidney failure, or end-stage renal disease, dialysis or, in the worst case scenario, a kidney transplant are the only ways to treat kidney failure. Perhaps some day, cloning technology can be used to clone replacement organs, such as kidneys.

Your Sexual Organs (both)

The topic of sexual dysfunction is enormous. Therefore, the discussion here focuses on sexual dysfunction that is *directly* related to diabetes.

Men

Microvascular complications can lead to impotence, or erectile dysfunction (the new, politically correct term), because the small blood vessels responsible for causing an erection can be damaged, or the nerves controlling sexual response could be damaged. As well, macrovascular disease can affect the flow of blood to the penis.

In the first case, when nerves to the penis are damaged, blood flow is limited, preventing erection. Roughly 60 percent of all men with diabetes (Type 1 or 2) over age 50 suffer from impotence, which means that about 33 percent of all impotence is caused by diabetes.

To be considered impotent, you have to be unable to obtain or sustain an erection long enough to have intercourse—for a period of at least six months. In other words, we're not talking about one of those movie scenes where a frustrated couple lie in bed and the woman turns to the man, and says, "It happens," and the man replies, "Not to me." Premature ejaculation is also not considered to be impotence although it can happen when you are impotent. When a physical problem is at work, signs come on gradually. Over time, you'll notice that your penis becomes less rigid, until you are unable to obtain or sustain an erection completely.

Diagnosing diabetes-related impotence

Just because you have diabetes doesn't mean your impotence is caused by it. Therefore, to diagnose physical impotence, doctors will tell you to place a paper band around your penis before you go to sleep. Since all healthy men have erections during their sleep, if you wake up with a broken band, it means your impotence is not physical but psychological. If the band is intact upon waking, your problem is physical (although not necessarily related to diabetes—it could be hormonal).

Once it's established that you have a physical disorder at work, your doctor can rule out nerve damage versus blood vessel damage by checking out both. To check nerve damage, a test involving painless electrical current can measure your penis's response.

To check blood vessel damage, a device similar to testing blood pressure in your arm can be used on your penis. Or, a drug that bypasses your nerves can be injected into your penis to see if you can have an erection. If you can't, blood vessel damage is indeed the problem, and it's most likely a macrovascular problem. Ultrasound and a tracer dye can confirm impotence caused by macrovascular disease. This procedure allows the doctor to actually see whether the blood is flowing freely through the vessels into the penis.

Another physical cause of impotence is blood pressure-lowering medication, while smoking and alcohol are considered aggravating factors.

Treating physical impotence

If you know that your impotence is caused by microvascular complications, getting your blood sugar under control may improve the problem.

If that doesn't work, a variety of treatments are available that include:

- **Drug injections:** Various drugs can be injected into the penis prior to intercouse, which will increase blood flow and produce an erection for at least 30 minutes. Prolonged erection is a side effect, however. (In Europe, there is actually a problem of certain "patch" medications, intended for heart disease, being used by *healthy* men to prolong their normal erections!)

- **Vacuum devices:** A vacuum device is used to enlarge the penis, and then a tension band is placed around the penis to maintain the erection for intercourse. Bruising can occur if the rubber band is on longer than 20 minutes.

- **Penile implants:** Either an inflatable or semi-rigid rod is placed inside the penis to enable you to have an erection whenever you want.

- **Blood vessel surgery:** Blood vessels that are blocking blood flow to the penis can be corrected through surgery.

- **Yohimbine:** This is a sexual stimulant that increases nerve sensitivity in the penis; if nerve damage has occurred, you may want to ask your urologist about the benefits of this drug.

Sexual dysfunction in women

Diabetes can cause sexual dysfunction in the form of vaginal dryness due to high blood sugar levels. High blood sugar levels can also cause chronic yeast infections (the fungus candida albicans will overgrow when there is sugar), as well as urinary tract infections (see Kidneys section, page 153), which can make sexual intercourse uncomfortable. Diabetes will indirectly affect your sex life if your partner is suffering from diabetes-related impotence.

Your Feet (both)

Foot complications related to diabetes were dramatized in the mid-1980s film *Nothing In Common*, in which Jackie Gleason plays the ne'er-do-well diabetic father, and Tom Hanks plays the son who cannot accept him. In a heartbreaking scene, Tom Hanks is shocked to discover how ill his father really is when he finally sees his feet. They are swollen, purple and badly infected. Ultimately, the story ends with the father and son coming to terms as Gleason must undergo surgical amputation.

I share this example with you because many of us are used to ignoring and abusing our feet. We wear uncomfortable shoes, we pick at our calluses and blisters, we don't wear socks with our shoes, and so on. You can't do this anymore. Your feet are the targets of both macrovascular (large blood vessel) complications and microvascular (small blood vessel) complications. In the first case, peripheral vascular disease affects blood circulation to your feet. In the second place, the nerve cells to your feet, which control sensation, can be altered through microvascular complications. Nerve damage can also affect your feet's muscles and tendons, causing weakness and changes to your foot's shape.

The combination of poor circulation and no feeling in your feet means that you can sustain an injury to your feet and not know about it. For example, you might step on a piece of glass or badly stub your toe, and not realize it. If an open wound becomes infected, and you have poor circulation, the wound doesn't heal properly, infection could spread to the bone or gangrene could develop. In this situation, amputation may be the only treatment. Or, without sensation or proper circulation in them, your feet could be far more vulnerable to frostbite or exposure than they would be otherwise.

Diabetes accounts for approximately half of all non-emergency amputations, but all experts agree that doing a foot self-exam every day (see below) can prevent most foot complications from becoming severe. Those at most risk for foot problems are people who still smoke (smoking aggravates *all* diabetic complications), are over-weight (more weight on the feet), are over age 40 or have had dia-betes for more than ten years.

Signs of foot problems

The most common symptoms of foot complications are burning, tin-gling or pain in your feet or legs. These are all signs of nerve damage. Numbness is another symptom, which could mean nerve damage or circulation problems. If you do experience pain from nerve damage, it usually gets worse with time (as new nerves and blood vessels grow), and many people find that it's worse at night. Bed linens can actually increase discomfort. Some people only notice foot symptoms after exercising or a short walk. But many people don't notice imme-diate symptoms until they've lost feeling in their feet.

Other symptoms people notice are frequent infections (caused by blood vessel damage), hair loss on the toes or lower legs, or shiny skin on the lower legs and feet.

When you take off your socks at the end of the day, get in the habit of doing a foot self-exam. This is the only way you can have damage control on your feet. You're looking for signs of infection or potential infection triggers. If you can avoid infection at all costs, you will be able to keep your feet. Look for the following signs:

- reddened, discoloured or swollen areas (blue, bright red or white areas mean that circulation is cut off);

- pus;
- temperature changes in the feet or "hot spots";
- corns, calluses and warts (potential infections could be hiding under calluses; do not remove these yourself—see a podiatrist);
- toenails that are too long (your toenail could cut you if it's too long);
- redness where your shoes or socks are "rubbing" due to a poor fit. (When your sock is scrunched inside your shoe, the folds could actually rub against the skin and cause a blister.);
- toenail fungus (under the nail);
- fungus between the toes. (This is athlete's foot, common if you've been walking around barefoot in a public place.);
- breaks in the skin (especially between your toes), or cracks, such as in calluses on the heels; this opens the door for bacteria.

If you find an infection, wash your feet carefully with soap and water; *don't use alcohol*. Then see your doctor or a podiatrist (a foot specialist) as soon as possible. If your foot is irritated but not yet infected (redness for example from poor-fitting shoes but no blister yet), simply avoid the irritant—the shoes—and it should clear up. If not, see your doctor. If you're overweight and have trouble inspecting your feet, get somebody else to check them for the signs listed above. In addition to doing a self-exam, see your doctor to have the circulation and reflexes in your feet checked four times a year.

Foot rules to live by
- Walk a little bit every day; this is a good way to improve blood flow and get a little exercise!
- Don't walk around barefoot; wear proper fitting, clean cotton socks with your shoes daily, and get in the habit of wearing slippers around the house and shoes at the beach. If you're swimming, wear some sort of shoe (plastic "jellies" or canvas running shoes). This doesn't mean you have to look like the geek who

wears white sports socks with Greek sandals; there are lots of options. If it's cold out, wear woollen socks.

- Before you put on your shoes, shake them out in case your (grand)child's Lego piece, a piece of dry catfood or a pebble is in there.
- Wash your feet and lower legs every day in lukewarm water with mild soap. Dry them really well, especially between the toes.
- Trim your toenails straight across to avoid ingrown nails. Don't pick off your nails.
- No more "bathroom surgery" on your feet, which may include puncturing blisters with needles or tweezers, shaving your calluses and the hundreds of crazy things people do with their feet (but never disclose to their spouses).
- Baby your feet. When the skin seems too moist, use baby powder or a foot powder your doctor or pharmacist recommends (especially between the toes). When your feet are too dry, moisturize them with a lotion recommended by your doctor or pharmacist. The reason is simple: breaks in the skin happen if feet are too moist (such as between the toes) or too dry (such as cracking). Use a foot buffing pad on your calluses after bathing.
- When you're sitting down, feet should be flat on the floor. Sitting cross-legged, or in crossed-legged variations can cut off your circulation—and frequently does in people without diabetes.
- Wear comfortable, proper-fitting footwear. See Table 7.1 for tips about shoe shopping.

Treatment for open wounds on the feet or legs

To heal cuts, sores or any open wound, your body normally manufactures macrophages, special white blood cells that fight infection, as well as special repair cells, called fibroblasts. These "ambulance cells" need oxygen to live. If you have poor circulation, it's akin to an ambulance not making it to an accident scene in time because it gets caught in a long traffic jam.

TABLE 7.1
How to Shoe Shop For Health

To save your feet, you may not be able to save on your next pair of shoes. These are new shoe-shopping rules:

- Shoe-shop at the time of day when your feet are most swollen (such as afternoon). That way, you'll purchase a shoe that fits you in "bad times" as well as good times.
- Don't even think about high heels or any type of shoe that is not comfortable or that doesn't fit properly. Say goodbye to thongs. That strip between your toe can cause too much irritation.
- Buy leather; avoid shoes with the terms "man-made upper" or "man-made materials" on the label; this means the shoes are made of synthetic materials and your foot will not breathe. Cotton or canvas shoes are fine, as long as the in-sole is cotton, too. Man-made materials on the very bottom of the shoe are fine as long as the upper—the part of the shoe that touches your foot—is leather, cotton/canvas or something breathable.
- Remember that leather does, indeed, stretch. When that happens, the shoe could become loose and cause blisters. On the other hand, if the shoe is too tight and the salesperson tells you the shoe will stretch, forget it. The shoe will destroy you in the first few hours of wear, which sort of "defeets" the purpose.
- If you lose all sensation and cannot "feel" whether the shoe is fitting, make sure you have a shoe salesperson fit you.
- Avoid shoes that have been on display. A variety of people try these shoes on; you never know what bacteria and fungi these previously tried-on shoes harbour.

When wounds don't heal, gangrene infections can set in. Until recently, amputating the infected limb was the only way to deal with gangrene. But there is a new therapy available at several hospitals throughout Canada called Hyperbaric Oxygen Therapy (HBO), the procedure involves placing you in an oxygen chamber or tank, and feeding you triple the amount of oxygen you'd find in the normal atmosphere. To heal gangrene on the feet, you'd need about 30 treatments (several per day for a week or so). The result is that your tissues become saturated with oxygen, enabling the body to heal itself. In one research trial, 89 percent of diabetics with foot gangrene were healed, compared to 1 percent of the control group. This treatment sounds expensive, but it's much cheaper than surgery, which is why HBO is catching on.

Not everybody is an HBO candidate; and not everybody in Canada has access to this therapy. But if you're being considered for surgical amputation, you should definitely ask about HBO first.

Your Skin (micro)

High blood sugar levels, combined with poor circulation, puts the skin—on your whole body—at risk for infections ranging from yeast to open wound-related infections. You may form scar tissue, develop strange, yellow pimples (a sign of high fat levels in the blood), boils or a range of localized infections. Yeast can develop not just in the vagina, but in the mouth, under the arms, or anyplace where there are warm, fatty folds. And all skin, whether on the feet or elsewhere, can become dry and cracked, requiring a daily regimen of cleaning, moisturizing and protecting.

Preventing Complications

In earlier chapters, I make reference to a study known as the Diabetes Control and Complications Trial (DCCT). This study involved 1,441 people with Type 1 diabetes, who were randomly managed according to one of two treatment philosophies: "intensive" treatment and "conventional" treatment. Intensive treatments means frequently testing your blood sugar, and adding a short-acting insulin that requires three to four injections daily, or one dose of longer-acting insulin. The goal of this type of management is to achieve blood sugar levels that are as normal as possible as often as possible. Conventional treatment means controlling your diabetes to the point where you avoid feeling any symptoms of high blood sugar, such as frequent urination, thirst or fatigue, without doing very much, if any, self-testing.

The Results

The results of the DCCT were pretty astounding. So much so, that the trial, planned for a ten-year period, was cut short—a rare occurrence in research trials. The DCCT results were unveiled in 1993, at the American Diabetes Association's annual conference.

The people who were managed with intensive therapy were able to delay microvascular complications (all the conditions labelled "micro" or "both" above) between 39 percent to 76 percent. Specifically, eye disease was reduced by 76 percent; kidney disease by 56 percent; nerve damage by 61 percent and high cholesterol by 35 percent. Those are very significant results. Statistically, anything over 1 percent is considered "clinically significant." Wow! The overwhelming consensus among diabetes practitioners is that intensive therapy for people with Type 1 diabetes prolongs health and greatly reduces complications. Conventional therapy for Type 1 diabetes is now considered archaic, and even detrimental.

The National Institute of Diabetes and Digestive and Kidney Diseases (NIDDK) in the United States, reported similar findings. NIDDK research found that with intensive therapy, eye disease was still reduced by 76 percent; kidney disease by 50 percent; nerve disease by 60 percent; and cardiovascular disease (a macrovascular complication) by 35 percent.

What the DCCT Means for Type 2 Diabetes

The DCCT did not look at blood sugar control and macrovascular complications—the cardiovascular complications for which people with Type 2 diabetes are most at risk—even though it showed a significant reduction in cholesterol levels. In fact, the priorities of many specialists treating Type 2 diabetes are weight control, *not* sugar control. (A cholesterol-lowering drug can achieve far greater results on low cholesterol than the DCCT.)

As a result, the DCCT is now an area of controversy for Type 2 specialists. Should people with Type 2 diabetes be counselled to *intensively* control their blood sugar or not? Many specialists say: "No—losing weight and getting the diet under control is hard enough. Asking people to self-test their blood sugar three to four times per day is too much for most people with Type 2 diabetes." In other words, what's the point of avoiding microvascular complications when you're about to drop dead from a massive heart attack or stroke? Nevertheless, many specialists say that since the DCCT showed such overwhelming reductions in complications for Type 1, until more data is out, people with Type 2 diabetes should be intensively controlling their blood sugar.

If you are willing to test your blood sugar frequently, you have only something to gain; certainly nothing to lose, so long as it doesn't interfere with your weight control program.

In the United Kingdom, a DCCT-like study is under way to determine whether blood sugar control reduces macrovascular complications in Type 2 diabetes. The results were promised by 1996 and then 1997. As of this writing, the results are still not in. It is hoped that the British study will help to resolve the "sugar control" question for people with Type 2 diabetes in time for the next century.

In the meantime, preventing complications for Type 2 diabetes revolves around blood sugar control, low-fat eating and exercise (Chapters 5 and 6)—the same things that prevent Type 2 diabetes in the first place.

Chapter 8

TYPE 2 DIABETES

IN ABORIGINAL

CANADA

It's not possible to write a book about Type 2 diabetes without addressing the impact of this disease on Canada's aboriginal population.

The terms *aboriginal* or *native people* refer to people whose ancestors are indigenous to Canada. Those registered as "Indian" under the Indian Act were once referred to as "status" or "treaty Indians" but today are known as "people of the First Nations," with full political representation by the Assembly of First Nations. Over the last three decades as many as 40 percent of these people have moved off the reserves into large urban communities. The term "non-status Indians" refers to aboriginal people who are not registered as Indians under the Indian Act. This group is politically represented by the Council of Aboriginal Peoples. The Metis, aboriginal people of both French and aboriginal ancestry, are represented by the Metis National Council. Finally, the Inuit people in Canada, who live in the Northwest Territories and northern Quebec, are represented by the Inuit Tapirisat of Canada.

This chapter may read more like a history textbook than a health book, but it's not possible to understand the explosion of Type 2 diabetes in Canada's aboriginal population without some history.

Thirty-one percent of all aboriginal people over the age of 15 have a chronic health problem. According to extremely conservative estimates, Type 2 diabetes affects 6 percent of aboriginal adults overall, compared with 2 percent of all non-native adults. But on many reserves, such as Akwesasne, Quebec, near Cornwall, Ontario, *more than 75 percent of residents older than 35 have diabetes*, up from 50 percent in 1989. Because the symptoms of diabetes can be vague and develop slowly, many aboriginal people have the disease but do not realize it. For every known case of diabetes among aboriginal people, at least one goes undiagnosed. And when you consider that Type 2 diabetes was not a recognized health problem in this community until the 1940s, this is a staggering increase.

Aboriginal Canadians also suffer more end-stage renal disease (ESRD), a common complication of diabetes, discussed in Chapter 7, than non-native Canadians. Chronic renal failure among native people is 2.5 to 4.0 times higher than in the general Canadian population, mostly due to Type 2 diabetes. The United States reports similar statistics.

The native population is most at risk for this disease because of thrifty genes, which are discussed in Chapter 1 as well as further on in this chapter (see page 174). Centuries of living off the land, eating seasonally and indigenously bred metabolisms that weren't able to adapt to nutrient excess and a sedentary lifestyle. Yet prior to contact with Europeans, Canada's aboriginal people were leading the kind of healthy lifestyle that may ultimately prevent diabetes from developing in the first place.

Pre-European Canada

Aboriginal history in Canada is broken down into two periods: the pre-European or precontact period, and the postcontact period. We refer to the meeting of European and aboriginal societies as "first contact," just as they do in "Star Trek" episodes. But, unlike the fine officers who wear the Star Fleet uniform, Europeans failed miserably in their first contact mission because they could neither respect nor obey the famous Star Fleet Prime Directive: Never interfere with another culture. These first Europeans interfered, took over and ruined a culture, with both health and environmental consequences for *all* peoples.

At the time of their first contact with Europeans, aboriginal people enjoyed good health. Infections were rare, fevers were unheard of, while mental, emotional and physical vigour was status quo. For any ailment, a common remedy was to enter a smoke house and "sweat it out." (Today, natural-medicine gurus like Dr. Andrew Weil highly recommend weekly sweats in saunas or steam baths.)

Before being exposed to European food, aboriginal people lived on the ideal diet of seasonal foods native to Canada. Eating foods seasonably indigenous to the land is a concept widely written about in several disease-prevention health books, particularly by Eastern nutritionists, such as Mushio Kushi, the founder of macrobiotics. In pre-European Canada, there was no cholera, typhus, smallpox, measles, cancer or skin problems, while fractures were also rare. Mental illness among aboriginal people during this time was also unheard of. Interestingly, more than 500 drugs used in pharmaceuticals today were originally used by native people.

The Diseases

As European ships arrived in Canada, they brought with them a smorgasbord of strange and new bacteria and viruses, causing terrible epidemics among native people. (This is not unlike what happens to

Europeans when they go into Africa and Asia and are exposed to micro-organisms to which they have no immunity.) Many European explorers and settlers were weak and sick when they first met aboriginal people because they'd survived a long voyage in crowded, unsanitary ships with both contaminated drinking water and food that had gone bad. Nevertheless, thousands of aboriginal people got sick and died from infections they caught from Europeans. Influenza, measles, polio, diphtheria, smallpox and other diseases were brought to Canada from the public health disaster areas of Europe—*slums*! In a sense, the result was genocide as native people died by the thousands during the eighteenth and nineteenth centuries. And thus began an incredible transformation: healthy people became steadily unhealthy as more Europeans came to Canada. Sources of food and clothing from the land diminished, while centuries of a traditional economy dissolved. And worst of all, once-mobile, active people were confined to small plots of land with limited natural resources and poor sanitation. *Fit people became unfit*. Amidst this physical deterioration, centuries of spiritual practices and beliefs were actually outlawed as Christianity took over. With ceremonial and spiritual activity banned (elders and healers were prosecuted by Christians for engaging in unlawful spiritual ceremonies), self-respect and cultural pride began to disappear.

The 20th Century

The early twentieth century was one of the worst periods in Canadian aboriginal history. Epidemics and disease were rampant, and the Canadian government responded with feeble attempts to improve native health. From the end of the nineteenth century to the middle of the twentieth, semi-trained RCMP agents, missionaries and officers tried to administer health care. By 1930, the first nursing station was opened on a Manitoba reserve. Fearing the spread of tuberculosis from aboriginal communities into the general population, by 1950 the Canadian government was operating 33 nursing stations, 65 health centres and 18 small regional hospitals for registered Indians and

Inuit. Virtually all providers of health and social services for native people were non-native; people who had no knowledge of aboriginal healing skills, herbal medicines or other traditional treatments.

From disease to diseased environment

As waters became polluted and environmental raping of resources continued, the diseases changed from infectious to chronic. "Country food," traditional food indigenous to Canada, such as wild game, fish, root vegetables and fruit, whale meat and blubber (now known to contain omega–3 oils, which are linked to low levels of heart disease and cholesterol and, hence, are protective foods), became inherently more unavailable, forcing aboriginal people to eat the processed, refined foods of Europeans. Cut off from their habitat, fishing, hunting, ceremony and indigenous food supply, and exposed to infections, alcohol and overprocessed foods high in fat and sugar, aboriginal people developed poor eating habits, became obese and inactive: the main risk factors for Type 2 diabetes are obesity, poor eating habits and physical inactivity.

On the Akwesasne reserve, for example, diabetes exploded onto the population as Mohawks turned to fast food after their traditional diet of perch became contaminated with PCBs. Yellow perch were the bread and butter of the Mohawk diet for centuries until the 1950s, when the St. Lawrence Seaway was constructed and became polluted by industry. In 1980, scientists deemed the perch unsafe for human consumption. What's happened on Akwesasne has happened all over North America. Today, there's a project in place to raise healthy perch in tanks to replenish the once-healthy and traditional diet. These type of projects are springing up all over the country and are crucial in order to help contain the Type 2 diabetes epidemic among native peoples.

The issue of cash crops

Cash crops have further deteriorated indigenous food supplies. By the early twentieth century, chemical agriculture and factory farming revolutionized food production, which has had a detrimental effect on the traditional aboriginal diet. Canada's corn production over the last 40 years is a good example of the nutritional perils of over-farming.

Corn used to be the grain staple of Canada's aboriginal people in the Ganonoque region, and an industry controlled by them until the introduction of hybrid corn during the 1930s and early 1940s. Hybrid corn replaced the open-pollinated varieties that naturally flourished in Ontario. Before 1960, corn was a fairly minor crop in Canada, mostly limited to Ontario. But because of new technology and the development of better-yielding and earlier-maturing hybrids, corn boomed throughout the 1960s and 1970s, transforming from a regional crop into a cash crop as it became the most popular feed grain for livestock (beef, pork and poultry). By 1980, more than 30 percent of Ontario's 3.5 million hectares of cultivated farmland was seeded annually to corn. But corn is also used to make paper and cardboard, automobiles, clothing, absorbents (in diapers and sanitary napkins), non-petroleum-based plastics and even ethyl alcohol. The problem with this type of farming is that corn soon became the *only* crop on several farms, causing a number of environmental problems. The soils needed to plant corn each year became overworked and nutrient-poor, leading to crop failures and unstable farm income. Corn rootworm, a pest common to one type of corn, became rampant in the 1970s and early 1980s, necessitating the use of pesticides. But the more pesticides were used, the more resistant pests became, and the more exotic the pesticide concoctions became. Soon, these pesticides were detected in rivers and streams, getting into fish and groundwater, destroying important sources of food in that region and beyond.

The Impact of Poverty

Because poverty is also rampant among aboriginal people, the food supply is further diminished. In 1990, 54 percent of aboriginal people surveyed had a total annual income below $10,000. The proportion of single-parent families among aboriginal people was at least 19 percent in 1986, compared to 13 percent in the non-native population. Grocery bills are therefore a problem. Affordable items tend to be quick-energy, low-nutrient foods.

Food Availability and Familiarity

Another problem is the cost involved in transporting fresh vegetables and fruits to remote locations, where many aboriginal people reside. Shipping costs and poor supplier selection aggravate matters. There is a real problem in understanding how to shop for Western food, too. Reading labels and interpreting ingredients creates so much confusion that grocery shopping tours are now being conducted by volunteers. In the Sandy Lake Project, for example, people are shown how to walk down grocery aisles, select food and read labels. Projects regarding healthy food choices labelling are also being initiated.

Meanwhile, a lack of familiarity with European food preparation aggravates matters, too. In the same way that most Europeans would be unfamiliar with whale blubber recipes, many aboriginal people are not up on their lasagna or pot-roast recipes. Cooking methods for imported foods are also unfamiliar to many aboriginal people. Therefore, high-protein, low-fat foods and quality game meats (much lower in fat than livestock-raised meats, high in iron and vitamin C), have become replaced with starches, fats, sugar and alcohol. As mentioned above, the traditional diet of aboriginal people was far superior to today's. Today's diet, coupled with a sedentary lifestyle, is shown not only to increase the incidence of obesity and, hence, diabetes, but increases blood pressure and dental problems. Aboriginal people also boast an impressive list of heart diseases, cancer, infant morbidity and mortality in higher frequencies than non-aboriginal Canadians.

Genetics

To our genes, 200 years is an exceedingly short amount of time to ask our immune systems and metabolisms to adjust. Aboriginal people have not built up an immunity to "overnutrition" the way many non-native Canadians have. Europeans, for the most part, haven't lived nomadically for thousands of years, and have therefore developed metabolisms to adjust to more sedentary lifestyles, in response to urbanized living.

This is why it is said that aboriginal people have an inherited tendency toward diabetes, known as thrifty genes. Because aboriginal people lived seasonably, on indigenous diets, for so many centuries, their bodies are still behaving as though they were living in seventeenth-century Canada.

Healing Aboriginal Communities

As I have stressed throughout this book, diet is one of the most crucial aspects in managing Type 2 diabetes. Yet aboriginal people with Type 2 diabetes often do not understand the Canadian Diabetes Food Choice Values and symbols or the concept of meal planning. That's because the role of food is different in aboriginal culture. For one thing, there are strong cultural beliefs that equate health and prosperity with being overweight. The more central problem is that there is a lack of familiarity with many of the food items recommended on these meal plans in terms of cost and availability.

The traditional aboriginal diet consisted mostly of high-protein game meat with very few vegetables. In fact, fruits and vegetables are not usually available in the small stores on most reserves. And if they are, they are so expensive, nobody buys them.

As a result, projects such as the Northern Food, Traditional and Health Kit, which encourages traditional foods for health and well-being, was developed for the Northwest Territories. This kit is far more relevant for people with diabetes in this culture, and was developed by the Nutrition Section, Department of Health, Government of the Northwest Territories, after elders and Northern educators requested it. The kit incorporates traditional regional foods, cooking and preserving practices. Food items include small land mammals, sea mammals, three kinds of fish, sea urchins, fish eggs, birds, wild greens, berries and bannock. Pictures of the foods are in an accompanying booklet to increase comprehension, while a resource booklet provides a lot of background information, worksheets, posters and various other components to promote cultural pride in Northern foods and food preparation.

Traditional Healers

Treating diabetes in the aboriginal population is not possible within the current Western framework. Many aboriginal people with Type 2 diabetes usually do not follow a doctor's orders regarding medication, diet and exercise. But it's not because there's a problem with the patient; there is a problem with the way Western medicine is *communicating* with that patient.

Aboriginal people approach their health from a cultural perspective; the health of the culture and community is reflected in the individuals of that community. Therefore, telling an aboriginal person to "work out" every day is not as effective as planning, say, a community walk. Health and wellness programs must be connected to the health and wellness of the community and environment. Western-trained health care providers are beginning to recognize that they are woefully unequipped to deliver health care to the aboriginal community. In fact, aboriginal doctors and nurses have clearly identified that the diabetes educational and prevention materials available to their patients are not culturally relevant. Individual self-care can only take place if there is *community* self-care.

Nor does the West provide health care services in accordance with the Circle of Life or the Medicine Wheel, which has guided the health and wellness of aboriginal Canadians for generations. In fact, the Circle of Life is a far more progressive and sophisticated approach to health than Western medicine. It incorporates physical, emotional, social and spiritual aspects of health. The premise of the Circle of Life is that good health occurs when there is balance and harmony within the self, society and natural environment. When there is no harmony, there is ill health.

The West is only beginning to see that harmony and stress affect wellness; aboriginal Canadians already know this instinctively. Therefore, the role of spirituality is central to aboriginal health, while traditional healing methods and therapies can make an enormous contribution to managing diabetes in the aboriginal population.

The majority of traditional healers went underground when they were persecuted by Canadian governments and the Christian Church for using ceremonies, herbal treatments and other native therapies. By the 1960s, healers were almost wiped out. In the 1980s, some members of the Peguis First Nation community in Manitoba began exploring their cultural roots, and a new movement began to bring back the practices of traditional medicine. Today, in the decade of alternative medicine, traditional healing is encouraged by Western health care providers. Now, traditional healers come under the Non-Insured Health Benefits Program for aboriginal people. There is a movement for traditional healers to be recognized by the College of Physicians and Surgeons in each province. It is hoped that healing centres and lodges would be accessible in urban, rural and reserve settings to all aboriginal people, which would deliver integrated health and social services.

Aboriginal/Community Diabetes Programs

The most recent trend in treating aboriginal people with Type 2 diabetes is to combine Western medicine with Northern traditions. Right now, professional organizations such as the Native Physicians Association in Canada (NPAC), Native Psychologists in Canada (NPC) and the Aboriginal Nurses Association of Canada (ANAC) play a crucial role in marrying the West and North. The NPAC includes over 100 physicians of aboriginal ancestry; most members are women working in primary care, who are actively involved in aboriginal health.

In Ontario, underserviced aboriginal people with diabetes now have the Northern Diabetes Health Network, a special program that funds local initiatives in diabetes education. In the James Bay region (the Mushkegowuk Council), there is now a coordinator and dietitian, as well as four diabetes educators who are all aboriginal Canadians and who tailor education for the community. That means that culturally appropriate questions, such as, "Did you have any bannock (a traditional bread) today?" will be asked of patients.

There now exists the Diabetic Education Program for Native People, based on the Standards and Guidelines of the Canadian Diabetes Association, which includes a cultural component throughout.

The Sioux Lookout Diabetes Program (SLDP) serves Ojibway and Cree First Nations people from 30 remote communities in Northwestern Ontario—many of which can be reached only by plane. This program is establishing a registry of people with diabetes within the community and, by 1994, staffed a coordinator, two native diabetes educators, a nurse educator, five dietitians and support staff. These professionals travel to the communities to provide education; in the past, the communities were expected to come to one out-of-the-way hospital for education.

These kinds of community diabetes programs involve the community's input with respect to educational materials. Instead of pictures of people in aerobics classes, these materials show people doing familiar activities such as chopping wood. The materials are also translated into the community's first language—Cree versus English or French.

The SLDP program is a model for other aboriginal programs across North America. Health care providers, chiefs and councils, and people with diabetes welcome these community-relevant programs.

Healing Circles are also used to explain blood sugar monitoring in a blood-letting ceremony. Walking groups have also been started in a few communities; during these events the whole community becomes more active, not just one individual. Other culture-specific programs involve elders in diabetes education, who remind their community about traditions of food patterns and fitness. Traditional feasts are also used to teach diabetes education, using only traditional foods without any "Western" foods.

These programs have proven beyond a doubt that by closing gaps created through language barriers, diet, activity and environment (people learn better in their own communities), and by removing the intimidating Western health practitioner, aboriginal people can learn to manage their diabetes.

■ ■ ■

The issue of preventing diabetes, discussed in Chapter 9, is becoming more accepted as we look at diet and other lifestyle factors that trigger Type 2 diabetes in those who are genetically predisposed. Restoring Canada's lands and waters to their natural state, replenishing Canada's indigenous food supply, eating seasonal and more natural foods will help to heal all Canadians, while improving our spiritual and psychological health. Thousands of years of wisdom in food preservation, natural medicines, roots, herbs and spiritual healing already exist through aboriginal Canadians. This information is precious to anyone living in this climate and habitat. In short, if we can learn to reduce the incidence of Type 2 diabetes in our aboriginal population, perhaps we can help reduce the incidence of this disease in all Canadians.

Chapter 9

PREVENTION: LOW-FAT AND HEALTHFUL EATING

If you are at risk for Type 2 diabetes and want to prevent it, the best thing to do is to pretend you have the disease right now and design a meal plan in accordance with the Canadian Diabetes Association's guidelines. These guidelines will help you to eat a balanced diet and to reduce your fat intake, which will dramatically reduce the risk of Type 2 diabetes, or the risk of macrovascular complications (see Chapter 7) if you have already been diagnosed. Studies show that reducing dietary fat may also prevent colorectal cancer and estrogen-dependent cancers such as breast cancer.

When you begin to eat a balanced diet and reduce your fat intake, you'll notice that you're much more aware of the "organic matter" that goes into your mouth, be it animal, vegetable or mineral. Almost without exception, people who adopt a lower-fat diet will begin to incorporate less animal produce and more vegetable produce into their diets. This, by itself, makes a significant contribution to the environment (see Table 9.1). And once you begin to eat more fruits and vegetables, you may want to know whether they are organically grown or laden with pesticides. Therefore, this chapter includes information on organic produce. (And don't forget, many of those animals we eat are grazing on pesticides, which remain in their fat, which then winds up in ours!)

If, after reading the following information, you are unable to change your eating habits, it may be because you do not fully understand *why* you're eating. "Food Behaviour" discusses 12-step programs, the key to success for many people who are chronic overeaters.

The Skinny on Fat

Fat is technically known as *fatty acids*, which are crucial nutrients for our cells. We cannot live without fatty acids, or fat. Fat is therefore a good thing—in moderation. But, like all good things, most of us want too much of it. Excess dietary fat is by far the most damaging element in the Western diet. A gram of fat contains twice the calories as the same amount of protein or carbohydrate. Decreasing the fat in your diet and replacing it with more grain products, vegetables and fruit is the best way to lower your risk of Type 2 diabetes, cardiovascular problems and many other diseases. Fat in the diet comes from meats, dairy products and vegetable oils. Other sources of fat include coconuts (60 percent fat), peanuts (78 percent fat) and avocados (82 percent fat). There are different kinds of fatty acids in these sources of fats: saturated, unsaturated and transfatty acids (a.k.a. transfat), which is like a saturated fat in disguise. Some fats are harmful while others are considered beneficial to your health.

Understanding fat is a complicated business. This section explains everything you need to know about fat, and a few things you probably don't *want* to know.

TABLE 9.1
The Costs of High-Fat Eating

Our entire agricultural economy is designed to support livestock and animal products, which we consume in huge quantities. This is making us too fat, requires a large amount of resources to support its production and is ruining our environment. Land-animal food production uses:

- 85 percent of all cropland and 55 percent of all agricultural land in the United States;
- forestland and rangeland, through erosion and depletion;
- 80 percent of all piped water in the United States;
- pesticides, which pollute two-thirds of U.S. waters and more than half of U.S. lakes and streams;
- wildlife, through conversion and pre-emption of forest and rangeland habitats and through poisoning and trapping of predators;
- 14 percent of the U.S. energy budget, greater than twice the energy supplied by all our nuclear power stations;
- large amounts of scarce raw materials, such as aluminum, copper, iron, steel, tin, zinc, potassium, rubber, wood, petroleum products, used for processing, storing and packaging;
- 90 percent of our grains and legumes, and half of our fish catch feeds livestock;
- our incomes: meats cost 5 to 6 times as much as foods with equivalent amounts of vegetable protein; the average household spends roughly $7,500 annually on meat.
- 50 percent of the world's tropical forests to expand land for cattle production. The average hamburger is made from meat imported from Central or South America, or the loss of 55 square feet of rainforest;
- our ozone layer: the rainforest is the "lungs of planet," which absorbs excess carbon dioxide and clears methane, a greenhouse gas. Cattle, however, produce methane, while the clearing of rainforest interferes with our ecosystem;
- arable land: cloud seeding, which upsets natural atmospheric weather patterns and weather cycles, results in rapid loss of arable land and the spread of desert regions across Africa, Central Asia and parts of Latin America.

Source: Kushi, Mishio. *The Cancer Prevention Guide.* New York: St. Martin's Press, 1993.

TABLE 9.2
Fat Tips

- Whenever you refrigerate animal fat (as in soups, stews or curry dishes), skim the fat from the top before reheating and re-serving. A gravy skimmer will also help skim fats; the spout pours from the bottom, which helps the oils and fats to coagulate on top.
- Substitute something else for butter: yogurt (great on potatoes) or low-fat cottage cheese, or, at dinner, just dip your bread in olive oil with some garlic, Italian style. For sandwiches, any condiment without butter, margarine or mayonnaise is fine—mustards, yogurt, etc.
- Powdered non-fat milk is in vogue again; high in calcium, low in fat. Substitute it for any recipe calling for milk or cream.
- Dig out fruit recipes for dessert. Things like sorbet with low-fat yogurt topping can be elegant. Remember that fruit must be planned for in a diabetes meal plan.
- Season low-fat foods well. That way, you won't miss the flavour fat adds.
- Lower fat protein comes from vegetable sources (whole grains and bean products); higher fat proteins come from animal sources.

Saturated Fat

Saturated fat is solid at room temperature and stimulates cholesterol production in your body. In fact, the way the fat looks prior to ingesting it is the way it will look when it lines your arteries. Foods high in saturated fat include: processed meat, fatty meat, lard, butter, margarine, solid vegetable shortening, chocolate and tropical oils (coconut oil is more than 90 percent saturated). Saturated fat should be consumed only in very low amounts.

Unsaturated Fat

Unsaturated fat is partially solid or liquid at room temperature. This group of fats includes: monounsaturated fats, polyunsaturated fats and omega-3 oils (a.k.a. fish oil), which, in fact, even protect you against heart disease (see page 182). Sources of unsaturated fats include vegetable oils (canola, safflower, sunflower, corn) and seeds and nuts. To make it easy to remember, unsaturated fats come from plants, with the exception of tropical oils, such as coconut. The more liquid the fat, the more polyunsaturated it is, which, in fact, *lowers* your cholesterol levels. However, if you have familial hyperlipidemia (high cholesterol), which often occurs alongside diabetes, unsaturated fat may not make a difference in your cholesterol levels.

What Is a Triglyceride?

Each fat molecule is a link chain made up of glycerol, carbon atoms and hydrogen atoms. The more hydrogen atoms that are on that chain, the more saturated or solid the fat. If you looked at each fat molecule carefully, you'd find three different kinds of fatty acids on it: saturated (solid), monounsaturated (less solid, with the exception of olive and peanut oils) and polyunsaturated (liquid) fatty acids, or three fatty acids plus glycerol, chemically known as triglycerides (see Chapter 1).

The liver breaks down fat molecules by secreting bile (stored in the gallbladder)—its sole function. The liver also makes cholesterol (see Chapter 3). Too much saturated fat may cause your liver to over-produce cholesterol, while the triglycerides in your bloodstream will rise, perpetuating the problem. Too much cholesterol can clog your blood vessels, get into the bile and crystallize, causing gallstones and gallbladder disease.

Fish Fat (Omega-3 Oils)

The fat naturally present in fish that swim in cold waters, known as omega-3 fatty acids (crucial for brain tissue) or fish oils, are all polyunsaturated. They lower your cholesterol levels, and protect against heart disease. These fish have a layer of fat to keep them warm in cold water. Mackerel, albacore tuna, salmon, sardines and lake trout are all rich in omega-3 fatty acids. In fact, whale meat and seal meat are enormous sources of omega-3 fatty acids, which were once the staples of the Inuit diet (see Chapter 8). Overhunting and federal moratoriums on whale and seal hunting have dried up this once-vital source of food for the Inuit, which clearly offered real protection against heart disease.

Man-made Fats

An assortment of man-made fats have been introduced into our diet, courtesy of food producers who are trying to give us the taste of fat without all the calories or harmful effects of saturated fats. Unfortunately, man-made fats offer their own bag of horrors.

Trans-fatty acids (a.k.a. hydrogenated oils)

These are harmful fats that not only raise the level of "bad" cholesterol (LDL) in your bloodstream, but lower the amount of "good" cholesterol (HDL) that's already there. Trans-fatty acids are what you get when you make a liquid oil, such as corn oil, into a more solid or spreadable substance, such as margarine. Trans-fatty acids, you might say, are the "road to hell, paved with good intentions." Someone, way back when, thought that if you could take the "good fat"—unsaturated fat—and solidify it, so it could double as butter or lard, you could eat the same things without missing the spreadable fat. That sounds like a great idea. Unfortunately, to make an unsaturated liquid fat more solid, you have to add hydrogen to its molecules. This is known as *hydrogenation*, the process that converts liquid fat to semi-solid fat. That ever-popular chocolate bar ingredient, "hydrogenated palm oil" is a classic example of a trans-fatty acid. Hydrogenation also prolongs the shelf life of a fat, such as polyunsaturated fats, which can oxidize when exposed to air, causing rancid odours or flavours. Deep-frying oils used in the restaurant trade are generally hydrogenated.

Trans-fatty acid is sold as a polyunsaturated or monounsaturated fat with a line of copy like: "Made from polyunsaturated vegetable oil." Except in your body, it is treated as a saturated fat. This is why trans-fatty acids are a saturated fat in disguise. The advertiser may, in fact, say that the product contains "no saturated fat" or is "healthier" than the comparable animal or tropical oil product with saturated fat. So be careful out there: *read your labels*. The magic word you're looking for is hydrogenated. If the product lists a variety of unsaturated fats (monounsaturated X oil, polyunsaturated Y oil, and so on), keep reading. If the word hydrogenated appears, count that product as a saturated fat; your body will!

Margarine versus butter

There's an old tongue twister: "Betty Botter bought some butter that made the batter bitter; so Betty Botter bought more butter that made the batter better." Are we making our batters bitter or better with margarine? It depends.

Since the news of trans-fatty acids broke in the late 1980s, margarine manufacturers began to offer some less "bitter" margarines; some contain no hydrogenated oils, while others much smaller amounts. Margarines with less than 60 percent to 80 percent oil (9 to 11 g of fat) will contain 1.0 to 3.0 g of trans-fatty acids per serving, compared to butter, which is 53 percent saturated fat. You might say it's a choice between a bad fat and a *worse* fat.

It's also possible for a liquid vegetable oil to retain a high concentration of unsaturated fat when it's been partially hydrogenated. In this case, your body will metabolize this as some saturated fat and some unsaturated fat.

Fake fat

We have artificial sweeteners; why not artificial fat? This question has led to the creation of an emerging yet highly suspicious ingredient: *fat substitutes*, designed to replace real fat and hence reduce the calories from real fat without compromising the taste. This is done by creating a fake fat that the body cannot absorb.

One of the first fat substitutes was Simplesse, an All-Natural Fat Substitute, made from milk and egg-white protein, which was

developed by the NutraSweet Company. Simplesse apparently adds
1 to 2 calories per gram instead of the usual 9 calories per gram from
fat. Other fat substitutes simply take protein and carbohydrates and
modify them in some way to simulate the textures of fat (creamy,
smooth, etc.). All of these fat substitutes help to create low-fat products, discussed in Chapter 5.

The calorie-free fat substitute being promoted is called olestra,
developed by Procter and Gamble. It's currently being test marketed
in the United States in a variety of savoury snacks such as potato
chips and crackers. Olestra is a potentially dangerous ingredient that
most experts feel can do more harm than good. Canada has not yet
approved it.

Olestra is made from a combination of vegetable oils and sugar.
Therefore, it tastes just like the real thing, but the biochemical structure is a molecule too big for your liver to break down. So, olestra just
gets passed into the large intestine and is excreted. Olestra is more
than an "empty" molecule, however. It causes diarrhea and cramps
and may deplete your body of vital nutrients, including vitamins A,
D, E and K, necessary for blood to clot. If the FDA approves olestra for
use as a cooking-oil substitute, you'll see it in every imaginable high-
fat product. The danger is that instead of encouraging people to
choose nutritious foods, such as fruits, grains and vegetables over
high-fat foods, products like these encourage a high *fake*-fat diet
that's still too low in fibre and other essential nutrients. And the no-
fat icing on the cake is that these people could potentially wind up
with a vitamin deficiency, to boot. Products like olestra should make
you nervous.

The Incredible Bulk

For every action, there is an equal and opposite reaction. When you
decrease your fat intake, you should increase your bulk intake, or

fibre. As discussed in Chapter 5, complex carbohydrates are foods that are high in fibre. Fibre is the part of a plant your body can't digest, which comes in the form of both water soluble fibre (which dissolves in water) and water insoluble fibre (which does not dissolve in water but instead, absorbs water); this is what's meant by "soluble" and "insoluble" fibre.

Soluble versus Insoluble Fibre

Soluble and insoluble fibre do differ, but they are equally good things. Soluble fibre—somehow—lowers the "bad" cholesterol, or LDL, in your body. Experts aren't entirely sure how soluble fibre works its magic, but one popular theory is that it gets mixed into the bile the liver secretes and forms a type of gel that traps the building blocks of cholesterol, thus lowering your LDL levels. It's akin to a spider web trapping smaller insects. Sources of soluble fibre include oats or oat bran, legumes (dried beans and peas), some seeds, carrots, oranges, bananas and other fruits. Soybeans are also high sources of soluble fibre. Studies show that people with very high cholesterol have the most to gain by eating soybeans. Soybean is also a *phytoestrogen* (plant estrogen) that is believed to lower the risks of estrogen-related cancers (for example, breast cancer), as well as lower the incidence of estrogen-loss symptoms associated with menopause.

Insoluble fibre doesn't affect your cholesterol levels at all, but it regulates your bowel movements. How does it do this? As the insoluble fibre moves through your digestive tract, it absorbs water like a sponge and helps to form your waste into a solid form faster, making the stools larger, softer and easier to pass. Without insoluble fibre, your solid waste just gets pushed down to the colon or lower intestine as always, where it is stored and dried out until you're ready to have a bowel movement. High-starch foods are associated with drier stools. This is exacerbated when you "ignore the urge," as the colon will dehydrate the waste even more until it becomes harder and difficult to pass, a condition known as constipation. Insoluble fibre will help to regulate your bowel movements by speeding things along. It is also linked to lower rates of colorectal cancer. Good sources of insoluble fibre are wheat bran and whole grains, skins from various fruits and vegetables, seeds, leafy greens and cruciferous vegetables (cauliflower, broccoli or brussels sprouts).

Fibre and Diabetes

Soluble fibre helps delay glucose from being absorbed into your bloodstream, which not only improves blood sugar control but helps to control postmeal peaks in blood sugar, which stimulates the pancreas to produce more insulin. Fibre in the form of all colours of vegetables will also ensure that you're getting the right mix of nutrients. Experts suggest that you have different colours of vegetables daily—for example, carrots, beets and spinach. An easy way to remember what nutrients are in which vegetable is to remember that all green vegetables are for cellular repair; the darker the green, the more nutrients the vegetable contains. All red, orange and purplish vegetables contain antioxidants (vitamins A, C and E), which boost the immune system and fight off toxins. Studies suggest that vitamin C, for example, is crucial for people with Type 2 diabetes because it helps to prevent complications, as well as rid the body of sorbitol, which can increase blood sugar. Another study suggests that vitamin E helped to prevent heart disease in people with Type 2 diabetes by lowering levels of "bad" cholesterol, but this isn't yet conclusive. Other minerals, such as zinc and copper, are essential for wound healing. The recommendation is to eat all colours of vegetables in ample amounts to get your vitamins, minerals and dietary fibre. It makes sense when you understand diabetes as a disease of starvation. In starvation, there are naturally lower levels of nutrients in your body that can only be replenished through excellent sources of food.

Breaking Bread

For thousands of years, cooked whole grains was the dietary staple for all cultures. Rice and millet in the Orient; wheat, oats and rye in Europe; buckwheat in Russia; sorghum in Africa; barley in the Middle East; and corn in pre-European North America.

Whole-grain breads are good sources of insoluble fibre (flax bread is particularly good because flaxseeds are a source of soluble fibre, too). The problem is understanding what is truly "whole grain." For example, there is an assumption that because bread is dark or brown, it's more nutritious; this isn't so. In fact, many brown breads are simply enriched white breads dyed with molasses. ("Enriched" means that nutrients lost during processing have been replaced.) High-fibre pita breads and bagels are available, but you have to search for them. A good rule is to simply look for the phrase "whole wheat," which means that the wheat is, indeed, whole.

Food Behaviour

Just because you should decrease fat and increase fibre doesn't mean you can or will. In fact, for most people, eating is an emotionally fulfilling experience not a gastrointestinal one. Instead of eating when we're hungry, many of us eat when we experience a range of emotions from happiness and sadness to anger, boredom and frustration. The refrigerator solves everything from low self-esteem to sexual yearning. And for many, food is an addiction, just like alcohol. As one compulsive overeater writes:

> Food used to be my best friend; it was the most important thing in my life. Most people eat to live, I lived to eat. Food and I did everything together. The moment I woke up in the morning, I would run to greet my old friend. Often I would not even wait until morning, and I would wake up in the middle of the night for a quick visit. Everything else in life (parties, movies, dates, etc.) were just an excuse to be seen out in public with my friend. My pal also comforted me when I was alone, which seemed to be more and more.

Are You Addicted to Food?

If you answer yes to many of the following questions, which come directly from Overeaters Anonymous (OA), you may wish to consult them or an eating disorder clinic (see the resource section at the back of the book for numbers).

1. Do you eat when you're not hungry?
2. Do you go on eating binges for no apparent reason?
3. Do you have feelings of guilt and remorse after overeating?
4. Do you give too much time and thought to food?
5. Do you look forward with pleasure and anticipation to the time when you can eat alone?
6. Do you plan these secret binges ahead of time?
7. Do you eat sensibly before others and make up for it alone?
8. Is your weight affecting the way you live your life?
9. Have you tried to diet for a week (or longer), only to fall short of your goal?
10. Do you resent others telling you to "use a little willpower" to stop overeating?
11. Despite evidence to the contrary, have you continued to assert that you can diet "on your own" whenever you wish?
12. Do you crave to eat at a definite time, day or night, other than mealtime?
13. Do you eat to escape from worries or trouble?
14. Have you ever been treated for obesity or a food-related condition?
15. Does your eating behaviour make you or others unhappy?

The 12 Steps to Change

Food addiction, like other addictions, can be treated successfully with a 12-step program. For those of you who aren't familiar with this type of program, I've provided the text of "The 12 Steps" on page 191.

The 12-step program was started in the 1930s by an alcoholic, who was able to overcome his addiction by essentially saying, "God, help me!" He found other alcoholics who were in a similar position and through an organized, nonjudgemental support system, they overcame their addiction by realizing that "God" (a higher power, spirit, force, physical properties of the universe or intelligence) *helps those who help themselves*. In other words, you have to want the help. This is the premise of Alcoholics Anonymous—the most successful recovery program for addicts that exists.

People with other addictions have adopted the same program, using Alcoholics Anonymous and the "The 12 Steps and 12 Traditions," the founding literature for Alcoholics Anonymous. Overeaters Anonymous substitutes the phrase "compulsive overeater" for "alcoholic" and the word "food" for "alcohol." The theme of all 12-step programs is best expressed through the Serenity Prayer, the first line being "God grant me the serenity to accept the things I cannot change; change the things I can, and the wisdom to know the difference." In other words, you can't take back the food you ate yesterday or last year; but you can control the food you eat today instead of feeling guilty about yesterday. Here are the 12 Steps:

Step One: I admit I am powerless over food and that my life has become unmanageable.

Step Two: I've come to believe that a Power greater than myself can restore me to sanity.

Step Three: I've made a decision to turn my will and my life over to the care of a Higher Power, as I understand it.

Step Four: I've made a searching and fearless moral inventory of myself.

Step Five: I've admitted to a Higher Power, to myself and to another human being the exact nature of my wrongs.

Step Six: I'm entirely ready to have a Higher Power remove all these defects of character.

Step Seven: I've humbly asked a Higher Power to remove my shortcomings.

Step Eight: I've made a list of all persons I have harmed and have become willing to make amends to them all.

Step Nine: I've made direct amends to such people wherever possible, except when to do so would injure them or others.

Step Ten: I've continued to take personal inventory and, when I was wrong, promptly admitted it.

Step Eleven: I've sought through prayer and meditation to improve my conscious contact with a Higher Power, as I understand it, praying only for knowledge of Its will for me and the power to carry that out.

Step Twelve: Having had a spiritual awakening as the result of these steps, I've tried to carry this message to compulsive overeaters and to practice these principles in all my affairs.

■ ■ ■

Every 12-step program also has the 12 Traditions, which, essentially, is a code of conduct. To join an OA program, you need only to take the first step. Abstinence and the next two steps are what most people are able to do in a 6- to 12-month period before moving on. In an OA program, "abstinence" means three meals daily, weighed and measured, with nothing in between except sugar-free or no-calorie beverages, and sugar-free gum. Your food is written down and called in. The program also advises you to get your doctor's approval before starting. Abstinence is continued through a continuous process of one-day-at-a-time and "sponsors"—people who call you to check in, and whom you can call when the cravings hit. Sponsors are recovering overeaters who have been there and who can talk you through your cravings.

OA membership is predominantly female; if you are interested in joining OA and are male, you may feel more comfortable in an all-male group. Many women overeaters overeat because they have been harmed by men, and their anger is often directed at the one male in the room; this may not be a comfortable position if you're a male overeater. For this reason, OA is divided into all-female and all-male groups.

Food Pills

In countries where high-fibre and plant-rich diets are the norm, there are far lower rates of cancer, heart disease and diabetes. This fact has led to research into specific foods or food ingredients that you can now buy in pill or capsule form: garlic capsules, broccoli pills and hundreds of other food supplements have sprung onto the health food market. Should you be taking supplements or simply eating a healthy diet? The answer is boring, and not one you want to hear: eat a variety of good foods that are high in fibre and low in fat! The problem with taking a "plant pill" instead of eating the plant is that by taking the pill, you're missing out on other benefits, such as fibre, taste or the biochemical reaction that results from a known ingredient in the plant and the dozens of unknown ingredients.

Phytochemicals

Phytochemicals, or "plant chemicals" (*phyto* is Greek for "plant"), are the natural ingredients found in plant foods such as tomatoes, oats, soya, oranges and broccoli. As researchers strive for some magic wellness ingredient, they're finding all kinds of disease-fighting chemicals inside common fruits and vegetables. While phytochemicals, such as *isoflavones* (found in soybeans), *allylic sulphides* (found in garlic, onions and chives), *isothiocyanates* (found in cruciferous vegetables like brussels sprouts, cabbage and cauliflower), *saponins* (spinach, potatoes, tomatoes and oats), *lignin* and *alphalinolenic acid* (flaxseeds) sound exotic, you can easily get them by simply eating a variety of fruits, grains and vegetables.

Another hot phytochemical right now is *betaglucan* (found in legumes, oats and other grains). Betaglucan is believed to help prevent diabetes by delaying gastric emptying and by slowing down glucose absorption in the small intestine.

In fact, biologically engineered foods, which alter the natural genetic codes in vegetables (see below) may interfere with these natural phytochemicals.

Functional foods

Functional foods are foods that have significant levels of biologically active disease-preventing or health-promoting properties. Tomatoes, oatmeal, soy and garlic are all examples of functional foods because they contain phytochemicals. Functional foods are therefore different than nutraceuticals (from the words *nutrition* and *pharmaceutical*), which are manufactured health foods, such as dietary fibre drinks or Zbars™ discussed in Chapter 4.

In the next few years, you may even see tomato sauces or canned goods with a "functional food" label, touting, for example, that the food "may prevent prostate cancer" because it contains lycopene (a phytochemical in tomatoes, red peppers and red grapefruit).

TABLE 9.3
How To Get More Fruits and Vegetables*

- Go for one or two fruits at breakfast, one fruit and two vegetables at lunch and dinner, and a fruit or vegetable snack between meals.
- Consume many differently coloured fruits and vegetables. For colour variety, select at least three differently coloured fruit and vegetables daily.
- Put fruit and sliced veggies in an easy-to-use, easy-to-reach place (sliced vegetables in the fridge; fruit out on the table).
- Keep frozen and canned fruit and vegetables on hand to add to soups, salad or rice dishes.

*Fruits and vegetables must be planned for in a diabetes meal plan.

Source: Adapted from "Beyond Vitamins: Phytochemicals to help fight disease," *Health News*, June 1996, Volume 14, No. 3, by June V. Engel, Ph.D.

Changing Your Diet (and Helping the Environment Too!)

Note: This material is considered highly controversial by diabetes experts for good reason. It's difficult enough to stick to a meal plan (Chapter 5), without having to worry about pesticides, toxins and "saving the world" all at the same time. Yet, since many people reading this book are concerned about healthful eating, it's important to have some of this "nice to know" versus "need to know" information at hand—in case, some day, you want to know. I present this information based on numerous published works on healthful eating so you can make informed choices about your diet. But if you were to put down this book right now, rest assured that everything you need to know about managing Type 2 diabetes has now been provided. For those of you continuing on…

■ ■ ■

The American Association of Advancement of Science stated that a diet centred on whole-grain cereals and vegetables rather than meat, poultry and dairy, would benefit our entire way of life, making more land, water, fuel and mineral use available, which would in turn have positive effects on inflation, employment and international trade. For example, in 1991, researchers at the California Institute of Technology reported that a meat-based diet was actually ruining the environment. According to research, cooking meat contributes to air pollution by releasing hydrocarbons, furans, steroids and pesticide residues. Interestingly, a major source of smog in Los Angeles is smoke from *barbecued beef*! On Earth Day 1992, an international coalition of environmental groups pledged to help lower beef consumption by 50 percent by the year 2002. The plan is to move toward a diet centred on whole grains and vegetables.

Animal Farm

Here are some other things to consider about animal farms.

Sulphonamides and penicillin, first used to a limited extent in the 1930s and 1940s, were routinely added to feed by the late 1950s, when farmers began raising animals in concentrated areas to meet increased demands. (Tight quarters triggered the spread of disease, necessitating antibiotics.) Today, antibacterial, antiparasitic drugs and hormones are in widespread use in meat-producing farms. Anabolic hormones or steroids are used to increase growth and muscle in cattle (so we can have our thick, juicy steaks). A few years ago, the European Community banned the raising or importing of any animal that was given hormones. The United States and Canada continue to use growth hormones.

When you see statements such as "low incidence" or "acceptable levels" of drug residue in animals, it means that the said meat or milk has drugs in it. It's like saying "acceptable levels of toxins," when, in fact, NO LEVEL of toxin should be acceptable! The U.S. Food and Drug Administration has defined "no residue" as a level of drug that presents no more than one in a million risk of cancer over a lifetime; that's not the same thing as "no level of drug."

TABLE 9.4
Meat Tips

- Broil, grill or boil meat instead of frying, baking or roasting it. (If you drain fat and cook in water, baking/roasting should be fine.)
- Trim off all visible fat from meat before and after cooking.
- Adding flour, breadcrumbs or other coatings to lean meat adds FAT.
- Try substituting low-fat turkey meat for red meat.

Bovine somatotropin (BST)

It gets worse. Bovine somatotropin, or BST, is a hormone that causes cows to overproduce milk. And when that happens the cows can become engorged and develop a bacterial infection called mastitis, necessitating the use of even more antibiotics. Although the FDA has concluded that milk and meat from BST-treated cows are safe for human consumption, Canada has not yet approved it. We don't know whether BST can cross over into humans and affect our own lactation hormones, nor do we know what effect "mastitis milk" or the antibiotics used to treat mastitis may have on us. Clear labelling guidelines of BST milk products must also be introduced before they are sprung onto unsuspecting milk consumers.

Mad cows

An almost biblical lesson in eating foods that are not indigenous can be seen with the revolting tale of mad cow disease, or *bovine spongiform encephalopathy* (BSE). BSE is an infectious disease that causes degenerative changes in the brains of cattle, and degenerative brain disease in humans who ingest "mad cow" brains. This is not old news, but ongoing news. BSE is passed on to the cow through other animal brains, commonly sheep with a sheep disease known as *scrapies* (although humans cannot get this disease by eating sheep with scrapies).

In nature, the only way a cow can contract this disease is to eat the brain of an infected animal, which wouldn't happen because cows are vegetarian. In the interest of cost-effective farming, agriculture began using animal parts (slaughterhouse waste, dead pets and road kill) in cattle feed. This brain disease was passed on to "Cow Zero" when Cow Zero unwittingly ate a piece of another animal brain, probably a sheep who was a carrier of the infection. Cow Zero gets slaughtered and becomes a hamburger. Its leftover brain parts get mixed into another sack of cattle feed and Cow Number 1 eats infected Cow Zero's brain parts and *also* becomes infected. The cycle continues as the cows eat one another's brains—something that Mother Nature never meant to happen. Ultimately, when a human being eats the hamburger made with ground beef, which may have some remnants of mad cow brains and spinal cords (through the slaughtering and meat-recovery process), he or she may contract mad cow disease as well.

What's truly frightening is that BSE has a five-year incubation period. So even if you became a vegetarian today, the hamburger you ate three years ago could still have infected you. And, in that time period, BSE can spread to other animals in many other countries that use slaughtered-cattle products in their feed. Mad cows have been identified in Canada, Denmark, France, Germany, Ireland, the Netherlands, Oman, Portugal and Switzerland.

One way to prevent BSE from spreading, or to prevent similar types of agricultural atrocities, is to stop eating cows. If you don't want to give up red meat, support organic growing, which is committed to ethical farming practices and raising cattle the old-fashioned way: feeding them good, organic feed.

Vegging Out

By simply becoming more vegetarian, you can actually change the world, lessening the demand for meat. Cleaning up the environment starts at your own kitchen table, in your own house, not in the House of Parliament.

It's estimated that at least 7 to 10 percent of North Americans practise some strain of vegetarianism. Semi-vegetarians, like myself, eat poultry, fish, eggs and dairy foods. Pesco-vegetarians eat fish, eggs and dairy foods; lacto-ovo-vegetarians eat eggs and dairy foods. Stricter forms of vegetarianism include ovo-vegetarians, who do not eat dairy but will consume eggs; lacto-vegetarians will not eat eggs but will have dairy; and vegans, who will not eat any sort of animal-derived foods.

When you compare the health of vegetarians to that of the general population, vegetarians have lower rates of heart disease, colon cancer, colitis (inflammation of the colon), hypertension, Type 2 diabetes and obesity. Keep in mind that becoming more vegetarian isn't a licence to overdo it on high-fat, meatless food, either. You should still choose lower fat dairy products if you are still eating dairy. See Table 9.5 for details.

TABLE 9.5
Milk Tips

In North America, we consume a lot of milk. Know what you're getting:

- Whole milk is made up of 48% calories from fat.
- 2% milk gets 37% of its calories from fat.
- 1% milk gets 26% of its calories from fat.
- Skim milk is completely fat-free.
- Cheese gets 50% of its calories from fat, unless it's skim milk cheese.
- Butter gets 95%of its calories from fat.
- Yogurt gets 15% of its calories from fat, unless it's low-fat yogurt.

Indigenous Eating

Earlier, I discussed how the loss of ecology and environment has led to an epidemic of diabetes in aboriginal Canadians. However, there are many reasons to support an indigenous diet. Eastern health practitioners (from Asia and India—*not* Nova Scotia), maintain that the right diet is based on where you live. Canadians need no further proof than to look at the traditional aboriginal diet, discussed in Chapter 8. In hotter climates, such as India and other tropical regions, lighter diets based on grains and vegetables, and even certain spices, are more conducive to good health.

Eating seasonally

Eating foods that are seasonal to our own habitat ensures that we are getting the most bang from our produce. Food begins to lose its natural phytochemicals (or healthful properties) when it travels long distances in refrigeration units. Since most of us don't have the luxury of living on a farm, we may feel that we haven't much choice in controlling the produce that is in our local grocery stores. But, does it seem "natural" for Winnipeg to eat tropical fruits in January, or for Tokyo to turn into a steak-and-potatoes society? What are the consequences of this?

For one thing, there may be some health-related reasons that we plant in the spring, harvest and preserve in the fall and make soups in the winter. Eastern nutritionist Mushio Kushi advises against foods that are not in harmony with the seasons. In cold weather, for example, food that is cooked longer—soups and stews—is considered better than salads and tropical fruits; in summer, lighter fare is healthier than heavy meats and starches.

Epidemiologists observe that as we send our meat and dairy to vegetarian-based societies, we notice that the incidence of Western diseases, such as Type 2 diabetes, rises. Yet, as we meat-eaters adopt a more vegetarian diet, which need not mean tropical but rather *indigenous* fruits and vegetables and a wide variety of nuts we can grow right here in Canada, we see a decrease in disease.

Discovering Canadian roots

According to many horticulturists and organic growers, the future of farming is learning how to grow *native plants* from seed, which is called *sustainable farming*. This isn't anything new but, rather, centuries old! Sustainable farming creates a sustainable vegetation system or "web" that keeps rebuilding upon itself for decades to come. Planting in this way helps to renew and protect soil, allowing the diverse range of organisms—some even pests—to coexist within the food chain. You see, when the food chain is left intact, parasites are taken care of by their natural predators, or natural repellents. Organic farmers therefore practise what's known as *companion planting*, which is simply ethical "biological pest management." In other words, if Vegetable A is always pestered by Beetle X, you simply plant Vegetable B next to it, which together with Vegetable A produces an odour that turns off Beetle X so that it doesn't go near either plant. Or you can plant Herb A next to Vegetable A, which is a more tempting treat for Beetle X. Vegetable A grows beautifully, Weed A gets devoured and then you simply hand-pick Weed A and throw it out at the end of the season. Companion planting is used to confuse insects, repel them or trap them. Companion planting is also used to make crops healthier. Vegetable A, for example, will grow better when it's beside Herb A for reasons not completely understood.

Why not just use pesticides?

Pesticides cause mutations in wildlife and humans, and have definitively and scientifically been shown to cause cancer. By mutating and destroying wildlife, the food chain is dying off, which has led to disastrous consequences for planetary health. The entire pesticide story is, however, another big book. But, for the purposes of this chapter, all you need to understand is that by eating more indigenous and seasonable foods, you are supporting an enormous network of organic growers and farmers, who, in the next century, will be leading the way for sustaining and maintaining life on earth. We simply cannot continue to eat as we once did. It makes us fat; it makes us sick; and it can trigger Type 2 diabetes if you are genetically predisposed. Not only that, it wastes billions of acres of arable farmland that could be used to feed people nutritious foods; and it wastes billions of dollars of natural resources we can't afford to lose.

But I don't want to be a farmer!

You don't have to be a farmer to eat organic produce. Hundreds of organic farmers, united under the Canadian Organic Growers Association, will be happy to sell you their organic produce, from vegetables and beef to clothing (made with cotton that was grown without pesticides). By buying organic spinach instead of spinach that was sprayed with endosulphan (a pesticide), you are supporting organic farming, eating well and saving the world, all at the same time. To find out where your organic farmers are, contact your local chapter of the Canadian Organic Growers Association, listed in the resource section at the back of the book.

As for your supermarket's produce, many supermarkets are getting into the organic act. In fact, a chain of U.S. supermarkets, called Bread and Circus, sells only organic produce. To get your local supermarkets to disclose where your produce was grown, how it was raised or where it swam, demand labelling that provides this information. You can exert your consumer power (and you do have power!) by contacting the head office of your supermarket and asking to speak to the head of Consumer Relations, Public Relations or Marketing. You can also exert pressure by calling manufacturers' 1-800/1-888 numbers that appear on your food labels, starting a news-group or banning products to help change standards. You have a right to a label that reads: This produce sprayed with Pesticide A. In fact, by calling Agriculture and Agrafood Canada at 613-952-8000, you can find out:

- what your produce has eaten, and whether it was injected with anything;
- what waters your fish has swum in; and
- what your grown produce was sprayed with.

In your own backyard

While yes, you do have a beautiful flower garden, which may be the envy of all your neighbours, if you're using pesticides you're part of the problem, not the solution, as they said in the 1960s. Contact the Canadian Organic Growers Association for literature on organic insecticides and fungicides for lawns and gardens, as well as for companion planting tips for the backyard (such as planting garlic beside roses).

■ ■ ■

You now know how to manage Type 2 diabetes, prevent further complications and lower your risk of Type 2 diabetes. I've also assembled several useful tables and charts that can help you trim fat, lower cholesterol and choose the least toxic vegetables. Don't forget to browse through the glossary and resource section! And don't forget exercise. I wish you all good luck, good health and a long and happy life.

GLOSSARY

Note: This list is not exhaustive. These are not literal dictionary definitions, but rather definitions created solely for the context of this book. Any resemblance to definitions found in other glossaries or dictionaries is purely coincidental.

Adrenaline: a hormone your body secretes that creates "fright-or-flight" symptoms of increased heart rate, sweating, nervousness, dizziness, and so on.

Aerobic activity: any activity that causes the heart to pump harder and faster, causing you to breathe faster, which increases the level of oxygen in the bloodstream.

Alpha-glucosidase inhibitors (a.k.a. acarbose or Prandase): a drug that delays the breakdown of sugar in your meal.

Andrologist: a doctor who specializes in male reproductive problems.

Anorexia nervosa: "a loss of appetite due to mental disorder." People with anorexia refuse to eat any food at all, starving themselves.

Antioxidants: vitamins A, C, E and beta-carotene, found in coloured (i.e., non-green) fruits and vegetables. Antioxidants prevent the oxidation of cell membranes, which can lead to cancer; they are the "cancer-fighting GIs."

Autoimmune disease: a disease in which the body produces antibodies to its own tissues, seen in Type 1 diabetes.

Betaglucan: a phytochemical found in legumes, oats and other grains that is believed to help prevent diabetes by delaying gastric emptying and by slowing down glucose absorption in the small intestine.

Biguanides (Metformin): an oral hypoglycemic agent that helps the body's insulin work better.

Binge-eating disorder (BED): refers to compulsive overeating, or bingeing without purging.

Bulimia nervosa: bingeing followed by purging in the form of self-induced vomiting, laxative/diuretic abuse or abusing other medications to induce weight loss.

Carbohydrates: the building blocks of most foods, which provide energy to the body to fuel the central nervous system; they help the body use vitamins, minerals, amino acids and other nutrients.

Certified Diabetes Educator (CDE): a dietitian, nurse, pharmacist, social worker or any other health care professional who has taken a diabetes educator certification course; teaches diabetes patients about diet and management.

Cholesterol: a whitish, waxy fat made in vast quantities by the liver. (See also HDL; LDL.)

Community Health Representative (CHR): Someone from the community who works with you and your family, as well as with other health care professionals, to educate you about various health issues, including diabetes.

Complex carbohydrates: more sophisticated foods that have larger molecules in them, such as grain foods and foods high in fibre.

Creatinine: waste products produced by the muscles and released by the kidneys.

Cystitis: urinary tract infection (UTI) resulting in an inflammation of the bladder lining.

Dextrose tablets: tablets that contain pure dextrose to boost the blood sugar level quickly, in case of hypoglycemia.

Diabetes: also known as hyperglycemia, which means high blood sugar, a condition where blood sugar levels are too high, usually defined by a fasting blood sugar level of over 7.8 mmol/l.

Diabetes specialist: an endocrinologist (hormone specialist) who subspecializes in diabetes.

Diabetic ketoacidosis (DKA): an emergency situation that can lead to death; signs of DKA include frequent urination, excessive thirst, excessive hunger and a fruity smell to your breath.

Diabetic neuropathy: diabetic nerve disease; occurs when the cells that comprise nerves are altered in response to high blood sugar.

Diabetic retinopathy: diabetes eye disease, characterized by damage to the back of the eye, or retina.

Diastolic pressure: one of the readings in a blood pressure measurement; the pressure occurring when the heart rests between contractions.

Dysmotility: occurs when the muscles in the digestive tract become uncoordinated, causing bloating, abdominal pain and reflux (heartburn).

Edema: water retention.

End-stage renal disease: a term used to describe kidney failure.

Erythroepoetin: a hormone produced by the kidneys that helps bone marrow to make red blood cells.

Fasting blood glucose readings: what your blood sugar levels are before you've eaten (normally between 3 to 5 mmol).

Fatty acids: crucial nutrients for cells, which also regulate hormone production.

Fibre: part of a plant that cannot be digested, which can lower cholesterol levels or improve regularity; also causes a slower rise in glucose levels, which lowers the body's insulin requirements.

Fructose: a monosaccharide or single sugar that combines with glucose to form sucrose and is $1\frac{1}{2}$ times sweeter than sucrose.

Functional foods: foods that have significant levels of biologically active disease-preventing or health-promoting properties.

Gastroenterologist: a doctor who is a G.I. (gastrointestinal) specialist.

Gerontologist: a doctor who specializes in diseases of the elderly.

Gestational diabetes mellitis (GDM): a type of diabetes that occurs usually between the 24th and 28th week of pregnancy; it simply means "diabetes during pregnancy" and generally takes the form of Type 2.

Gestational hypertension: high blood pressure during pregnancy.

Glucagon: a hormone that, when injected under the skin, causes an increase in blood glucose concentration.

Glucose: a monosaccharide or single sugar that combines with fructose to form sucrose; can also combine with glucose to form maltose, and with galactose to form lactose; slightly less sweet than sucrose.

Glycosuria: sugary urine, a symptom of very high blood sugar.

Glycosylated hemoglobin levels: detailed blood sugar test that checks for glycosylated hemoglobin (glucose attached to the protein in red blood cells), known as glycohemoglobin or HbA_{1c} levels; this test can determine how well blood sugar has been controlled over a period of two to three months by showing what percentage of it is too high.

Guar gum: a high source of fibre made from the seeds of the Indian cluster bean. When you mix guar with water, it turns into a gummy gel, which slows down the digestive system, similar to acarbose.

HDL: high-density lipoproteins, known as the "good" cholesterol.

High fructose corn syrup (HFCS): a liquid mixture of about equal parts glucose and fructose from cornstarch, which has the same sweetness as sucrose.

Human insulin: a kind of insulin that is identical to the insulin that is normally produced by the human body.

Hydrogenation: process that converts liquid fat to semi-solid fat, adding hydrogen.

Hyperglycemia: high blood sugar; also known as "diabetes, "a condition where blood sugar levels are too high; defined by a fasting blood sugar level of over 7.8 mmol/l.

Hyperinsulinemia: when the pancreas produces too much insulin; a condition caused by insulin resistance.

Hypertension (a.k.a. high blood pressure): the tension or force exerted on the artery walls; a condition that damages the small blood vessels as well as the larger arteries.

Hypertensive drug: a drug designed to lower blood pressure, sometimes called a "blood thinner."

Hypoglycemia: means low blood sugar; defined by a blood sugar level less than 4 mmol/l, any time.

Impaired glucose tolerance (IGT): what many doctors refer to as the "gray zone" between normal blood sugar levels and "full-blown diabetes."

Impotence: the inability to obtain or sustain an erection long enough to have intercourse, for a period of at least six months.

Insulin: a hormone made by the islets of Langerhans, a small island of cells afloat in the pancreas, that regulates blood sugar levels.

Insulin lispro: an insulin analogue ("synthetic copycat") that is very short-acting.

Insulin resistance: occurs when the pancreas is making insulin but the cells are not responding to it.

Insulin shock: occurs when low blood sugar is caused by insulin therapy.

Intensive insulin therapy: a treatment program involving close monitoring of blood sugar levels combined with taking short-acting insulin prior to meals.

Islets of Langerhans: one of two cell systems located inside the pancreas, which secretes insulin.

Isokinetic exercise: an activity such as wrestling or weightlifting that is short but intense.

Ketones (a.k.a. ketone bodies): a poisonous by-product produced when there is not enough glucose in the cells and the body burns fat as an alternate fuel; this situation can occur when blood sugar levels are 14 mmol/l at any one time.

Lancet: tiny needle used to prick the finger for a blood sample.

Laser photocoagulation: a procedure that can burn and seal off damaged blood vessels, stopping them from bleeding or leaking; this can restore vision in the earlier stages of diabetes eye disease.

LDL: low-density lipoproteins, known as the "bad" cholesterol.

Lean body mass: body tissue that is not fat.

Leptin: a hormone currently being used to treat obesity (a leptin deficiency is thought to cause weight gain); also being tested as a preventative drug for Type 2 diabetes.

Macrosomia: a condition that occurs in gestational diabetes, when high blood sugar levels cross the placenta and feed the fetus too much glucose, causing it to grow too fat and large for its gestational age; technically defined by a birth weight greater than 4,000 g; babies with macrosomia are usually not able to fit through the birth canal because their shoulders get stuck (known as shoulder dystocia).

Macrovascular complication: a "large blood vessel complication," one that is body-wide, or systemic, such as cardiovascular problems.

Maturity-onset diabetes of the young (MODY): rare form of non-insulin-dependent Type 2 diabetes developed in a person under age 30.

Mellitus: Latin for "honey"; added to the term "diabetes" because in the past, diabetes was diagnosed through sweet-tasting urine.

Microvascular complication: a problem with the smaller blood vessels (a.k.a. capillaries) that connect to various body parts, such as eyes.

mmol: "millimole," a unit of measurement that counts molecular volume per litre.

Modifiable risk factor: a risk factor that can be changed by alterations in lifestyle or diet.

Monosodium glutamate (MSG): the sodium salt of glutamic acid; an amino acid that occurs naturally in protein-containing foods such as meat, fish, milk and many vegetables.

Nephrologist: a kidney specialist.

Neurologist: a nerve and brain specialist.

Non-nutritive sweeteners: sugar substitutes or artificial sweeteners, such as saccharin and sucralose, that do not have any calories and will not affect blood sugar levels.

Nutritive sweeteners: sweeteners such as table sugar, molasses and honey, which have calories or contain natural sugar.

Obesity: when you weigh more than 20 percent of your ideal weight for your age and height.

Omega-3 fatty acids: naturally present in fish that swim in cold waters; crucial for brain tissue, all polyunsaturated; not only lower cholesterol levels, but are also said to protect against heart disease.

Ophthalmologist: an eye specialist.

Oral glucose tolerance test: Standard method of diagnosing impaired glucose tolerance (IGT) or diabetes; blood sugar is tested every 30 minutes for two hours following a period of fasting.

Oral hypoglycemic agents (OHAs): drugs that help the pancreas release more insulin or help the insulin work more effectively.

Orlistat: an anti-obesity drug that blocks the absorption of almost one-third of the fat one consumes.

Pancreas: a bird-beak-shaped gland situated behind the stomach; secretes insulin and glucagon produced by the islets of Langerhans.

Pancreatitis: inflammation of the pancreas; occurs when the pancreas's digestive enzymes attack your own pancreas.

Peripheral vascular disease (PVD): occurs when the blood flow to the limbs (arms, legs and feet) is blocked, causing cramping, pains or numbness.

Phytochemicals: "plant chemicals" (phyto is Greek for "plant"); disease-fighting or protective chemicals found in plant foods such as tomatoes, oats, soya, oranges and broccoli.

Polydipsia: excessive thirst.

Polyphagia: excessive hunger.

Polyuria: excessive urination.

Postprandial: "postmeal" or after a meal, as in postprandial blood sugar levels.

Premixed insulin: when both short-acting insulin and intermediate-acting insulin are mixed together.

Primary care doctor: the doctor you see for a cold, flu or an annual physical; the doctor who refers you to specialists; general and family practitioners (GPs and FPs) or internists are common primary care doctors.

Renin: a hormone produced by the kidneys that helps to regulate blood pressure.

Risk marker: a risk factor that cannot be changed, such as age or genes.

Saturated fat: a solid fat at room temperature (from animal sources) that stimulates the body to produce LDL, or "bad" cholesterol.

Secondary diabetes: occurs when diabetes surfaces as a side effect of a particular drug or surgical procedure; also called "iatrogenic" or "clinically caused" diabetes.

Soluble fibre: fibre that is water-soluble, or dissolves in water.

Stroke: occurs when a blood clot travels to the brain and stops the flow of blood and oxygen carried to the nerve cells in that area, at which point, cells may die or vital body functions controlled by the brain may be temporarily or permanently damaged.

Sucrose: A disaccharide or double sugar made of equal parts glucose and fructose; known as table or white sugar; found naturally in sugar cane and sugar beets.

Sugar alcohols: nutritive sweeteners that are half as sweet as sugar; found naturally in fruits or manufactured from carbohydrates (i.e., Sorbitol).

Sulphonylureas: an oral hypoglycemic agent that helps the pancreas release more insulin.

Systolic pressure: one of the readings in a blood pressure measurement; the pressure occurring during the heart's contraction.

Thiazoladinediones (troglitazone or Rezulin): an agent that make the cells more sensitive to insulin.

Traditional healer: a vital health care professional within the aboriginal population.

Trans-fatty acids (a.k.a. hydrogenated oils): harmful, man-made fats that not only raise the level of "bad" cholesterol (LDL) in the bloodstream, but also lower the amount of "good"cholesterol (HDL) that's already there; produced through the process of hydrogenation.

Triglycerides: a combination of saturated, monounsaturated and polyunsaturated fatty acids and glycerol.

Type 1 diabetes: insulin-dependent diabetes mellitus (IDDM), a disease usually diagnosed before age 30, in which the pancreas stops producing insulin; Type 1 diabetes, also known as juvenile diabetes, requires daily insulin injections for life.

Type 2 diabetes: "non-insulin-dependent diabetes mellitus" (NIDDM), also called "late-onset" or "mature-onset" diabetes because it's usually diagnosed after age 45; either the body is not producing enough insulin or the insulin it does produce cannot be used efficiently.

Unsaturated fat: known as "good fat" because it doesn't cause the body to produce "bad" cholesterol and increases the levels of "good" cholesterol; partially solid or liquid at room temperature.

Urea: the waste product of protein released by the kidneys.

BIBLIOGRAPHY

General

American Diabetes Association. Online information. Document ID: ADA035, 1995.

Guthrie, Diana, RN, PhD, and Richard A. Guthrie, MD, *The Diabetes Sourcebook* (1996, Lowell House, Los Angeles).

The Better Health & Medical Network Collective Work & Database. Transmitted to the Internet: 8/18/97.

"What Is Diabetes?" Canadian Diabetes Association, February 2, 1996. CDA Document ID: ADA037.

Historical Background

"Glory Enough For All: The Discovery of Insulin." Film. 1988, Gemstone Productions Ltd. and Primedia Productions, Ltd.

Best, Henry, B.M., "Charles Herbert Best: 1899–1978." *Diabetes Dialogue*, (Vol. 43, No. 4) Winter 1996.

Bliss, Michael, "Rewriting Medical History." *Journal of History of Medicine and Allied Sciences, Inc.*, 1993, Volume 48: 253–274.

Bliss, Michael, *Banting: A Biography* (1984, McClelland & Stewart, Toronto).

Bliss, Michael, *The Discovery of Insulin* (1982, McClelland & Stewart, Toronto).

Maltman, Grant, "Banting: Co-discoverer of Insulin and . . . Artist." *Diabetes Dialogue*, (Vol. 41, No. 4) Winter 1994.

Maltman, Grant, "The Birth of an Idea." *Diabetes Dialogue*, (Vol. 42, No. 4) Winter 1995.

Williams, Michael, J., "Macleod: The Co-discoverer of Insulin." *Proceedings of the Royal College of Physicians of Edinburgh*, July 1993, (vol. 23, No. 3).

Chapter 1

"A Jelly Bean Glucose Test." *American Baby*, April 1996: 6.

"Blood Pressure: Check it out." *Countdown USA: Countdown to a Healthy Heart*, Allegheny General Hospital and Voluntary Hospitals of America, Inc., 1990.

"Diabetes Implants Tested." *Los Angeles Daily News*, January 23, 1997.

"Diabetes Raises Dementia Risk." Reuters, Thursday February 13, 1997.

"Diabetes: Facts and Figures." *News from the VIP*, No. 2, Fall 1995. Vitamin Information Program, Fine Chemicals Division of Hoffman-La Roche Ltd.

"Diets Slow Reaction Times." Reuters, Tuesday April 8, 1997.

"Double Trouble." *Countdown USA: Countdown to a Healthy Heart*, Allegheny General Hospital and Voluntary Hospitals of America, Inc., 1990.

"Feeding Your Child for a Lifetime." Reuters, Thursday April 10, 1997.

"Flick Your Risk: By Tossing Out Those Cigarettes, You Can Slash Your Chances of Heart Disease." *Countdown USA: Countdown to a Healthy Heart*, Allegheny General Hospital and Voluntary Hospitals of America, Inc., 1990.

"Folic Acid Surveys Say Consumer Awareness Is Low." *News from the VIP*, No. 2, Fall 1995. Vitamin Information Program, Fine Chemicals Division of Hoffman-La Roche Ltd.

"Get Off The Diet Rollercoaster." *Countdown USA: Countdown to a Healthy Heart*, Allegheny General Hospital and Voluntary Hospitals of America, Inc., 1990.

"Guidelines for the Nutritional Management of Diabetes in Pregnancy." A position statement by the Canadaian Diabetes Association, (Vol. 15, No. 3) September 1991.

"Obese Children May Lack Antioxidants." Reuters Health Summary, Tuesday April 22, 1997.

"Obesity Hormone May Prevent Diabetes." Reuters Health Summary, Tuesday April 29, 1997.

"Study Finds That Teens Who Had Less Salt As Infants Have Lower Blood Pressure." Associated Press, April 8, 1997.

"Study Ranks Cities by Pudginess of Residents." The Associated Press, March 4, 1997.

"Study: You Can Lose Weight and Cigarettes." Reuters, Thursday June 19, 1997.

"The Fat Trap." *Countdown USA: Countdown to a Healthy Heart*, Allegheny General Hospital and Voluntary Hospitals of America, Inc., 1990.

"VIP Conference on Elderly Attracts Canadian Media." *News from the VIP*, No. 2, Fall 1995. Vitamin Information Program, Fine Chemicals Division of Hoffman-La Roche Ltd.

"We're Winning: By Changing Lifestyles, We're Proving Every Day That Coronary Disease Can Be Beaten." *Countdown USA: Countdown to a Healthy Heart*, Allegheny General Hospital and Voluntary Hospitals of America, Inc., 1990.

"What's Your Type?" *News from the VIP*, No. 2, Fall 1995. Vitamin Information Program, Fine Chemicals Division of Hoffman-La Roche Ltd.

"What You Should Know About MSG." International Food Information Council, 1100 Connecticut Avenue N.W., Suite 430, Washington D.C. 20036, September 1991.

"Bayer Launches Major International Research Project into Prevention of Diabetes." Media Release, March 5, 1997.

"Living Well." Patient information. Canadian Diabetes Association, distributed 1997.

"Mature Lifestyles: High Blood Pressure." Patient information. Health Watch/Shoppers Drug Mart, distrubuted 1997.

"Nutrition News." *Diabetes Dialogue*, (Vol. 44, No. 1) Spring 1997.

Anderson, Pauline. "Researchers predict 'beginning of the end' of diabetes." *The Medical Post*, August 22, 1995.

Canadian Diabetes Association. "Health...The Smoke-Free Way." *Equilibrium*, (Issue 1) 1996.

Costin, Carolyn, MA, MEd, MFCC, *The Eating Disorder Sourcebook* (1996, Lowell House, Los Angeles).

Gauthier, Serge G., MD, FRCPC, and Patricia H. Coleman, MS, RPDt, Reviewers. "Nutrition and Aging." *The Lederle Letter*, (Vol. 2, No. 2) April 1993, Lederle Consumer Health Products Department.

Marliss, Errol B., MD, FRCPC, and Rejeanne Gougeon, PhD, Msc, DtP, Reviewers. "Focus on Women: Dieting as a Possible Risk Factor for Obesity." *The Lederle Letter*, (Vol. 2. No. 4) August 1993, Lederle Consumer Health Products Department.

Marliss, Errol B., MD, FRCPC, Rejeanne Gougeon, PhD, Msc, DtP, and Sandra Schwenger, HBSc, RPDt, Reviewers. "Weight-Reducing Diets May Compromise Nutrition." *The Lederle Letter*, (Vol. 1, No. 3) August 1992, Lederle Consumer Health Products Department.

Mihill, Chris. "New Fears over Link Between Cow's Milk and Diabetes." *The Guardian*, October 4, 1996.

Neergaard, Lauran, "Study Finds Low Hormone Levels May Encourage Weight Gain." Associated Press, May 14, 1997.

Reddy, Sethu, MD, "Smoking and Diabetes." *Diabetes Dialogue*, (Vol. 42, No. 4) Winter 1995.

Wanless, Melanie, BASc, "The Weight Debate." *Diabetes Dialogue*, (Vol. 44, No. 1) Spring 1997.

Yankova, Diliana, MD, "Diabetes in Bulgaria." Diabetes Dialogue, (Vol. 44, No.1) Spring 1997.

Chapter 2

"Diabetes: What is it?" *Equilibrium,* Canadian Diabetes Association, (Issue 1) 1996.

"Improving Treatment Outcomes in NIDDM: The Questions and Controversies." *The Diabetes Report*, Issue 1, Vol. 2, 1996.

"Insulin and Type 2 Diabetes." *Equilibrium,* Canadian Diabetes Association, (Issue 1) 1996.

"Monitoring Your Blood Sugar." *Equilibrium,* Canadian Diabetes Association, (Issue 1) 1996.

"New Developments in the Management of Type II Diabetes." *The Diabetes Report*, Issue 2, Vol. 1, 1995.

"New Perspectives in the Management of NIDDM." *The Diabetes Report,* Issue 3, Vol. 1, 1996.

"Pills for Diabetes?" *Equilibrium,* Canadian Diabetes Association, (Issue 1) 1996.

"Pills for Treating Diabetes." Pamphlet. Canadian Diabetes Association, 1996.

"Understanding Type 2 Diabetes: Guidelines for a Healthier You." Patient information. Bayer Inc. Healthcare Division, distributed 1997.

"Your Blood Sugar Level...What Does It Tell You?" Patient information. Lilly Diabetes Care, 1997.

"7 Key Factors for Real World Accuracy in the Real World." Patient information from MediSense Canada Inc., distributed 1997.

"7 Key Steps to Control Your Diabetes." Patient information from MediSense Canada Inc., distributed 1997.

"Advocacy in Action." *Diabetes Dialogue*, (Vol. 43, No. 3) Fall 1996.

"All About Insulin: Novolin Care." Patient information manual from Novo Nordisk Canada Inc.

"Balancing Your Blood Sugar: A Guide for People with Diabetes." Patient information. Canadian Diabetes Association, distributed 1997.

"Blood Glucose Monitoring: Guidelines to a Healthier You." Patient information from Bayer Inc. Healthcare Division, distributed 1997.

"Blood Sugar Testing Diary." Patient information. Becton Dickinson Consumer Products, 1996.

"Dextrolog: For Recording Blood and Urine Glucose Test Results." Booklet. Bayer Inc. Healthcare Division, distributed 1997.

"Diabetes Education." Patient information. Canadian Diabetes Association, distributed 1997.

"First New Insulin in 14 Years Approved for Use in Canada." Media release. Eli Lilly of Canada Inc./Boehringer Mannheim Canada, October 9, 1996.

"Following the Patient with Chronic Disease." *Patient Care Canada*, (Vol. 7, No. 5) May 1996: 22–38.

"Glucometer Elite." Patient information. Bayer Healthcare Division, 1995.

"How Adults are Learning to Manage Diabetes with Their Lifestyle." *The Globe and Mail*, Friday November 1, 1996.

"Health Record for People with Diabetes." Patient information booklet. The Canadian Diabetes Association/Lifescan Canada, Ltd., McNeil Consumer Products Company, 1996.

"How to Choose Your New Blood Glucose Meter." Patient information. LifeScan Canada Inc., distributed 1997.

"Insulin Management Information." Patient information from Eli Lilly and Co., distributed 1997.

"Insulin: Guidelines to a Healthier You." Patient information. Bayer Inc. Healthcare Division, distributed 1997.

"Is Your Insulin as Easy to Use as Humulin?" Patient information. Eli Lilly of Canada Inc., distributed 1997.

"Keeping Well with Diabetes: Novolin Care." Patient information. Novo Nordisk Canada Inc., 1996.

"Ketone Testing: Guidelines to a Healthier You." Patient information. Bayer Inc. Healthcare Division, distributed 1997.

"MediSense Blood Glucose Sensor." Product monograph, 1995.

"Monoject: Diabetes Care Products." Patient information. Sherwood Medical Industries Canada Inc., distributed 1997.

"Non-Insulin Dependent Diabetes Mellitus." Patient information. National Pharmacy Continuing Education Program and Bayer Inc., February 1997.

"One-touch Profile: For Complete Diabetes Management." Patient information. LifeScan Canada Inc., distributed 1997.

"Real-World Factors That Interfere with Blood-Glucose Meter Accuracy." Patient information from MediSense Canada Inc., 1996.

"Reducing Your Risk of Diabetes Complications." Patient information. MediSense Canada Inc., distributed 1997.

"Research, Improvement in Products Never Stop in Health Industry." *The Globe and Mail*, November 1, 1996.

"Surestep." Patient information. LifeScan Canada Inc, distributed 1997.

"The Accu-Chek Advantage System." Patient information. Eli Lilly of Canada Inc., distributed 1997.

"Travelling with Diabetes." Patient information. Canadian Diabetes Association, March 1996.

"Type II Diabetes." Shoppers Drug Mart Education Series NIDDM, Vol. 95, 11.

"What Is Intensive Diabetes Management?" Patient information. Diabetes Clinical Research Unit of Mount Sinai Hospital Toronto for Sherwood Medical Industries Canada Inc., distributed 1997.

"Your Blood Sugar Level...What Does It Tell You?" Patient information. Eli Lilly of Canada Inc., distributed 1997.

Antonucci, T., et al., Impaired Glucose Tolerance Is Normalized by Treatment with the Thiazolidinedione. *Diabetes Care*, (Vol. 20, No. 2) February 1997: 188–193.

Brubaker, Patricia L, PhD, "Glucagon-like Peptide-1." *Diabetes Dialogue*, (Vol. 41, No. 4) Winter 1994.

Cattral, Mark, MD, MSc, FRCSC, "Pancreas Transplantation." *Diabetes Dialogue*, (Vol. 43, No. 4) Winter 1996.

Chaddock, Brenda, CDE, "Blood-Glucose Testing: Keep Up with the Trend." *Canadian Pharmacy Journal*, September 1996: 17.

Helwick, Caroline, "Apnea, Diabetes Linked." *The Medical Post*, May 28. 1996.

Joyce, Carol, MD, "What's New in Type 2." *Diabetes Dialogue*, (Vol. 43, No. 3) Fall 1996.

Kumar, S., et al., Troglitazone, An Insulin Action Enhancer, Improves Metabolic Control in NIDDM Patients. *Diabetologia*, (Vol. 30, No. 6) June 1996: 701–709.

Leiter, Lawrence A., MD, FRCP(C), FACP, "Acarbose: New Treatment in NIDDM Patients, *New Drugs/Drug News*, Ontario College of Pharmacists, Vol. 14, No. 2.

Novolin Product Monograph, 1997.

Prochaska, James O., PhD, "A Revolution in Diabetes Evaluation." Excerpted from the Canadian Diabetes Association Conference, 1995.

Ryan, David, PhD, "At the Controls." *Diabetes Dialogue*, (Vol. 43, No. 3) Fall 1996.

Sinclair, A.J., Bsc, MD, MRCP(UK), "Rational Approaches to the Treatment of Patients with Non-Insulin-Dependent Diabetes Mellitus. *Practical Diabetes Supplement*, (Vol. 10, No. 6), November/December 1993.

Whitcomb, Randall, MD, "The Key to Type 2." *Diabetes Dialogue*, (Vol. 43, No. 4) Winter 1996.

Yale, Jean-François, MD, "Glucose Results: Plasma or Whole Blood?" *Monitor*, Vol. 1, No. 2, Medisense Canada Inc.

Zinman, Bernard, MD, FRCP, FACP, "Insulin Analogues." *Diabetes Dialogue*, (Vol. 43, No. 4) Winter 1996.

Chapter 3

"All About Insulin." Booklet. Novo Nordisk Canada Inc., 1996.

"Balancing Your Blood Sugars: A Guide for People with Diabetes." Booklet. Canadian Diabetes Association, 1996.

"FDA Approves Drug to Reduce Insulin Needs for Some Diabetics." The Associated Press, January 30, 1997.

"Following the Patient with Stable Chronic Disease: Type II Diabetes Mellitus." *Patient Care Canada*, (Vol 7. No. 5) May 1996.

"Get the Best Out of Life." Patient information. Canadian Diabetes Association, distributed 1997.

"Grieving Necessary to Accept Diabetes." *Diabetes Dialogue*, (Vol. 41 No. 3) Fall 1994.

"How to Take Insulin." Patient information. Monoject Diabetes Care Products, distributed 1997.

"Is Your Insulin As Easy to Use as Humulin?" Patient information manual from Eli Lilly of Canada Inc., distributed 1997.

"Managing Your Diabetes with Humalog." Booklet. Eli Lilly and Company, 1997.

"Non-Insulin-Dependent Diabetes Mellitus." Booklet. National Pharmacy Continuing Education Program, February 1997.

"Practical Advice for the Prandase Patient." Booklet. Bayer Inc. Healthcare Division, distributed 1996.

"Seven Tips for Your Sick Day Blues." *Equilibrium*, Canadian Diabetes Association, (Issue 1) 1996.

"Your Diabetes Healthcare Team." *Equilibrium*, Canadian Diabetes Association, (Issue 1) 1996.

"Report on the Second International Conference on Diabetes and Native Peoples." Prepared by the First Nations Health Commission, Assembly of First Nations, November 1993.

"Safety First." Patient information. Becton Dickinson and Co. Canada Inc., distributed 1997.

"What You Should Know About Humulin." Booklet. Eli Lilly of Canada Inc., distributed 1997.

Abbott Hommel, Cynthia, PHEC, "The SUGAR Group," *Diabetes Dialogue*, (Vol. 41, No. 3) Fall 1994.

Appavoo, Donna, RD, Rayanne Waboose, RN, and Stuart Harris, MD, CCFP, ACPM, "Sioux Lookout Diabetes Program," *Diabetes Dialogue*, (Vol. 41, No. 3) Fall 1994.

Augustine, Freda, "Helping My People." *Diabetes Dialogue,* (Vol. 41, No. 3) Fall 1994.

Badley, Wendy, RN, "Across the Country." *Diabetes Dialogue,* (Vol. 41, No. 3) Fall 1994.

Barnie, Annette, RN , "'At Risk' in Northern Ontario: Looking for Answers in the Sioux Lookout Zone". *Diabetes Dialogue,* (Vol. 41, No. 3) Fall 1994.

Barwise, Kim, RN, BScN, CDE, and Sota, Danielle, "Two Views." *Diabetes Dalogue,* (Vol. 43, No. 3) Fall 1996.

Chaddock, Brenda, CDE, "Doing the Things That Make a Difference." *Canadian Pharmacy Journal,* July/August 1996.

Clarke, Peter V., MD, FRCP(C), FACP, "Hemoglobin A_{1c} Test Helps Long-Term Diabetes Management." *Monitor,* Vol. 1, No. 1, Medisense Canada Inc.

Doyle, Patricia, RN, RN, CDE, "Insulin—The Facts." Canadian Diabetes Association, 1995.

Dutcher, Lisa, RN, RN, "A Wholistic Approach to Diabetes Management." *Diabetes Dialogue,* (Vol. 41, No. 3) Fall 1994.

Foxman, Stuart (adapted), "Human vs. Beef/Pork Insulin," *The Report of the Ad Hoc Committee on Beef–Pork Insulins* by Nahla Aris-Jilwan, MD, Pierre Malheux, MD, Tina Kader, MD, Alain Boisvert, B Pharm, DPH, MSc, and Sara Meltzer, MD. Adapted by Stuart Foxman, Canadian Diabetes Association, June 6th, 1996.

Houlden, Robyn, MD, FRCPC, "Health Beliefs in Two Ontario First Nations Populations." *Diabetes Dialogue,* (Vol. 41, No. 4) Winter 1994.

Kewayosh, Alethea, "The Way We Are: The Eye of the Storm—A First Nations Perspective on Diabetes." *Diabetes Dialogue,* Fall 1994.

Rowlands, Liz and Denis Peter, "Diabetes—Yukon Style." *Diabetes Dialogue,* (Vol. 41, No. 3) Fall 1994.

Tetley, Deborah, "Fish Farmer Hopes to Tame Diabetes on Akwesasne." *The Toronto Star,* April 12, 1997.

Chapter 4

"Low Blood Sugars: Your Questions Answered." *Equilibrium,* Canadian Diabetes Association, (Issue 1) 1996.

"Prandase: A New Approach to NIDDM Therapy." Patient information booklet. Bayer Inc. Healthcare Division, distributed 1997.

"Acarbose (Prandase)." *New Drugs/Drug News,* Ontario College of Pharmacists Drug Information Service Newsletter, (Vol. 14, No. 2) March/April 1996.

"Novolin ge: Insulin, Human Biosynthetic Antidiabetic Agent." Product Monograph for Novo Nordisk Canada Inc., 1997.

"Pills for Treating Diabetes." Patient information. Canadian Diabetes Association, March 1996.

"Prandase (Acarbose) Tablets." Product monograph. Bayer Inc. Healthcare Division, April 14, 1997.

Halvorson, Mary, Kaufman, Francine and Kaufman, Neal. "A Snack Bar Containing Uncooked Cornstarch to Diminish Hypoglycaemia." American Diabetes Association 56th Scientific Sessions, 1996.

Jeffrey, Susan. "Uncooked Cornstarch Snacks Aid Diabetics." *The Medical Post*, November 12, 1996.

Korytkowski, Mary, MD, "Something Old, Something New." *Diabetes Spectrum*, (Vol. 9) November 4, 1996.

Martin, Cheryl, BSc Pharm, "Acarbose (Prandase)." *Communication*, March/April 1996:38.

Schoepp, Glen, BSP, "What Is the Role of Acarbose (Prandase) in Diabetes Management?" *Pharmacy Practice*, (Vol. 12, No. 4) April 1996: 37–38.

White Jr., John R., Pharm, "The Pharmacologic Management of Patients with Type II Diabetes Mellitus in the Era of New Oral Agents and Insulin Analogs." *Diabetes Spectrum*, (Vol. 9, No. 4) 1996.

Zbar Clinical Product Information. Baker Cummins Inc., 1997.

Chapter 5

"IFIC Review: Intense Sweeteners: Effects on Appetite and Weight Management." International Food Information Council, 1100 Connecticut Avenue N.W., Suite 430, Washington D.C. 20036, November 1995.

"Position of the American Dietetic Association: Use of Nutritive and Non-nutritive Sweeteners." *Journal of the American Dietetic Association* 93: 816–822, 1993.

"Q&A on Low-Calorie Sweeteners." *The Diabetes News*, (Vol. 1, Issue 2) Spring 1997.

"What You Should Know About Aspartame." International Food Information Council, 1100 Connecticut Avenue N.W., Suite 430, Washington D.C. 20036, November 4, 1996.

"What You Should Know About Sugars." International Food Information Council, 1100 Connecticut Avenue N.W., Suite 430, Washington D.C. 20036, May 1994.

"You Are What You Eat." *Equilibrium*, Canadian Diabetes Association, (Issue 1) 1996.

"Alcohol and Diabetes—Do They Mix?" Booklet. Canadian Diabetes Association, 1996.

"Choosing Your Sweetener." Product information. PROSWEET Canada, 1997.

"Cooked Food Byproducts May be Hazardous to Diabetics." *The Medical Post*, July 2, 1996.

"Nutrition for Diabetes." Patient information manual from Novo Nordisk Canada Inc., 1996.

"Nutrition News." *Diabetes Dialogue*, (Vol. 44, No. 1) Spring 1997: 56.

"Pocket Partner: A Guide to Healthy Food Choices." Booklet. Canadian Diabetes Association, distributed 1997.

"Pocket Serving Sizer." Patient Information. Canadian Diabetes Association, distributed 1997.

"PROSWEET: The Low Calorie Pure Sugar Taste Sweetener." Product information. PROSWEET Canada, 1997.

"Sucralose Overview." Product information from Splenda (brand sweetener) Information Centre, 1997.

"Sweet Promise from Sugar Substitute?" *The Medical Post*, July 2, 1996.

"You Have Diabetes...Can You Have That?" Booklet. Canadian Diabetes Association, 1995.

Allsop, Karen F., and Janette Brand Miller. "Honey Revisited: A Reappraisal of Honey in Preindustrial Diets. *British Journal of Nutrition*, 1996; 75: 513–520.

Beyers, Joanne, RD, "How Sweet It Is!" *Diabetes Dialogue*, (Vol. 42, No. 1) Spring 1995.

Chabun, Roxanne, RD, and Debbie Stiles, RD, "Bar None." *Diabetes Dialogue*, (Vol. 43, No. 3) Fall 1996.

Chaddock, Brenda, CDE, "The Right Way to Read a Label." *Canadian Pharmacy Journal*, May 1996.

Cronier, Claire, MSc RD, "Sweetest Choices." *Diabetes Dialogue*, (Vol. 44, No. 1) Spring 1997.

Gabrys, Jennifer, Bsc Pharm CDE, "Ask the Professionals." *Diabetes Dialogue*, (Vol. 43, No. 4) Winter 1996.

Gordon, Dennis, "Acarbose: When It Works/When It Doesn't." *Diabetes Forecast*, February 1997.

Kermode-Scott, Barbara. "NIDDM Affecting Huge Numbers, Says Expert." *Family Practice*, March 11, 1996.

Kuczmarski, R.J., K.M. Flegal, S.M. Campbell, and C.L. Johnson, "Increasing Prevalence of Overweight Among U.S. Adults: The National Health and Nutrition Examination Surveys, 1960 to 1991." *Journal of the American Medical Association*, (Vol. 272) 1994: 205–211.

Musgrove, Lorraine, RN, CDE, "Ask the Professionals." *Diabetes Dialogue*, (Vol. 44, No. 1) Spring 1997.

Seto, Carol, RD, CDE, "Nutrition Labelling—U.S. Style." *Diabetes Dialogue*, The Canadian Diabetes Association, (Vol. 42, No. 1) Spring 1995.

Chapter 6

"Physical Activity." *Equilibrium,* Canadian Diabetes Association, (Issue 1) 1996.

"Exercise: Guidelines to a Healthier You." Patient information. Bayer Inc. Healthcare Division, distributed 1997.

"Food and Exercise: Guidelines to a Healthier You." Patient information. Bayer Inc. Healthcare Division, distributed 1997.

"Spring at Last!" *The Diabetes News,* prepared by the LifeScan Education Institute, Spring 1996.

Bonen, Arent, PhD, "Fueling Your Tank." *Diabetes Dialogue,* (Vol. 42, No. 4) Winter 1995.

Chaddock, Brenda, CDE, "Activity is Key to Diabetes Health." *Canadian Pharmacy Journal,* March 1997.

Chaddock, Brenda, CDE, "Foul Weather Fitness: The Hardest Part is Getting Started." *Canadian Pharmacy Journal,* March 1996.

Chaddock, Brenda, CDE, "The Magic of Exercise." *Canadian Pharmacy Journal,* September 1995.

Clarke, Bill. "Action Figures." *Diabetes Dialogue,* (Vol. 43, No. 3) Fall 1996.

Farquhar, Andrew, MD, "Exercising Essentials." *Diabetes Dialogue,* (Vol. 43, No. 3) Fall 1996: 6–8.

Hunt, John A., MB, FRCPC, "Fueling up." *Diabetes Dialogue,* (Vol. 41, No. 4) Winter 1994.

Kaptchuk, Ted and Micheal Croucher, *"The Healing Arts: A Journal Through the Faces of Medicine."* The British Broadcasting Corporation, London, 1986.

Musgrove, Lorraine, RN, CDE, "Ask the Professionals." *Diabetes Dialogue,* (Vol. 44, No. 1) Spring 1997: 60,61.

The Challenge: Newsletter of the International Diabetic Athletes Association, (Vol. 11, No. 1) Spring 1997.

Todd, Robert, "The Sporting Life." *Diabetes Dialogue,* (Vol. 43, No. 4) Fall 1996.

Chapter 7

"Anger with an A Spells Trouble." *Countdown USA: Countdown to a Healthy Heart,* Allegheny General Hospital and Voluntary Hospitals of America, Inc., 1990.

"Complications: The Long-Term Picture." *Equilibrium,* Canadian Diabetes Association, (Issue 1) 1996.

"Hostility and Heart Risk." Reuters Health Summary, Tuesday April 22, 1997.

"The Agony of De-Feet." *Equilibrium,* Canadian Diabetes Association, (Issue 1) 1996.

"Watch Your Step." Booklet. Norvo Nordisk Canada, Inc., 1996.

"Diabetes and Kidney Disease." Patient information. The Kidney Foundation of Canada, 1995.

"Diabetes and Non-Prescription Drugs: Guidelines to a Healthier You." Patient information. Bayer Inc. Healthcare Division, distributed 1997.

"Diabetes." Patient information. Pharma Plus, distributed 1997.

"Diabetes: An Undetected Time-Bomb." *CARP News*, April 1996.

"High Blood Pressure and Your Kidneys." Patient information. The Kidney Foundation of Canada, 1995.

"How to Cope with a Brief Illness: A Guide for the Person Taking Insulin." Patient information from the Canadian Diabetes Association, March 1996.

"It Takes Two: A Couple's Guide to Erectile Dysfunction." Patient information. Pharmacia and Upjohn, distributed 1997.

"Kidney Stones." Patient information. The Kidney Foundation of Canada, 1995.

"Micral-S Kidney Chek." Patient information. Eli Lilly of Canada/ Boehringer Mannheim Canada Inc., distributed 1997.

"Nutrition News." *Diabetes Dialogue*, (Vol. 44, No. 1) Spring 1997.

"Organ Donation: Have You Thought About It?" Patient information. The Kidney Foundation of Canada, 1995.

"Preventing the Complications of Diabetes: Guidelines to a Healthier You." Patient information. Bayer Inc. Healthcare Division, distributed 1997.

"Taking Care of Your Feet: Guidelines to a Healthier You." Patient information. Bayer Inc., Healthcare Division, distributed 1997.

"Travelling with Diabetes." Booklet. Canadian Diabetes Association, 1996.

"Treating Kidney Failure." Patient information. The Kidney Foundation of Canada, 1995.

"Urinary Tract Infections." Patient information. The Kidney Foundation of Canada, 1995.

"Your Kidneys." Patient information. The Kidney Foundation of Canada, 1993.

Armstrong, David G., DPM, Lawrence A. Lavery, DPM, MPH, and Lawrence B. Harkless, DPM, of the Department of Orthopaedics and the Diabetic Foot Research Group at the University of Texas Health Science Center, San Antonio Treatment-based Classification System for Assessment and Care of Diabetic Feet. *Journal of the American Podiatric Medical Association*, (Vol. 87, No. 7) July 1996.

Bril, Vera, MD, FRCP(C), "Diabetic Neuropathy—Can It Be Treated?" *Diabetes Dialogue*, (Vol. 41, No. 4) Winter 1994.

Graham, Joan, RN, BPA, "Impotence—The Complication No One Wants to Talk About." Canadian Diabetes Association, 1995.

Lebovitz, Harold E., MD, "Acarbose, an Alpha-Glucosidase Inhibitor, in the Treatment of NIDDM. *Diabetes Care,* 19 (Suppl. 1) 1996: 554–561.

Linden, Ron, BSc, MD, CCFP, "Hyperbaric Medicine." *Diabetes Dialogue,* (Vol 43, No. 4) Fall 1996.

Little, Margaret, RN, CDE, "Step Right Up." *Diabetes Dialogue,* Vol. 43, No. 3) Fall 1996.

Musgrove, Lorraine, RN, CDE, "Ask the Professionals." *Diabetes Dialogue,* (Vol. 44, No.1) Spring 1997.

Schwartz, Carol, MD, FRCS(C), "An Eye-Opener." *Diabetes Dialogue,* (Vol. 43, No. 4) Winter 1996.

Chapter 8

"Combining the Old and the New." *Caring for the Earth: A Strategy for Sustainable, Living IUCN—The World Conservation Union.* United Nations Environment Programme, World Wide Fund For Nature, Gland, Switzerland, 1991.

"Discovery of Insulin Marked Turning Point in Human History." *The Globe and Mail,* Friday, November 1, 1996.

"Health and Healing, Inroads of Chronic Disease," Vol. 3, Ch. 3, *Final Report on Royal Commission on Aboriginal Peoples.* Posted to the Internet at: www.libraxus.com.

"The Ad Hoc Technical Committee Working Group on Development of Management Principles and Guidelines for Subsistence Catches of Whales by Indigenous (Aboriginal) Peoples." *International Whaling Commission and Aboriginal/Subsistence Whaling: April 1979 to July 1981.* Special Issue 4, International Whaling Commission, Cambridge, England.

"Trapped by Furs" Presentation at the Symposium, *Conflicting Interests Of Animal Welfare and Indigenous Peoples.* January 17, 1997, Erasmus University, Rotterdam, Finn Lynge.

"CMA's Submission to the Royal Commission on Aboriginal Peoples," in *Canadian Medical Association Bridging the Gap: Promoting Health and Healing for Aboriginal Peoples in Canada.* Ottawa: The Association, 1994: 9–17.

Canadian Institute of Child Health, "Aboriginal children." In *The health of Canada's Children: A CICH profile,* 2nd ed. Ottawa: The Institute, 1994: 131–48.

Canadian Task Force on the Periodic Health Examination, "The Canadian Guide to Clinical Preventive Health Care." Ottawa: Health Canada, 1994.

Corn and the Environment—Historical Perspectives. Ontario Corn Produers Association (OCPA) Corn and Environment Index Homepage, 1997.

Cox, Bruce Alan, Ed., *Native People, Native Lands: Canadian Indians, Inuit and Metis*. (Carleton University Press, Ottawa, 1988.)

Creighton, Donald, *The Forked Road: Canada 1939–1957* (1976, Mc-Clelland & Stewart, Ltd, Toronto)

Fox, Mary Lou. "Zeesbakadapenewin: Words of an Elder Grandmother About the Sugar Disease." *Diabetes Dialogue*, (Vol. 41, No. 3) Fall 1994.

MacMillan, Harriet L., MD, FRCP(C), Angus B. MacMillan, MD, FRCP(C), David R. Offord, MD, FRCP(C), Jennifer L. Dingle, MBA, "Aboriginal Health." *Canadian Medical Association Journal* 1996; 155: 1569–1578.

McCarten, James, "Toxic or Not, Inuit Stand by Whale Meat." *The Edmonton Journal*, Thursday December 28, 1995.

Morrison, Bruce. R., and C. Roderick Williams, *Native Peoples Canadian Experience* (1986, McClelland & Stewart, Ltd., Toronto).

Mulvad, Gerth, MD, and Henning Sloth Pedersen Mulvad, MD, "Orsoq—Eat Meat and Blubber from Sea Mammals and Avoid Cardiovascular disease." *Inuit Whaling*, published by Inuit Circumpolar Conference, June 1992, Special Issue.

Orton, David, "Rethinking Environmental—First Nations Relationships." *Canadian Dimension*, (Vol. 29, No. 1) February–March 1995.

Orton, David, "Some Limitations of a Left Critique and Deep Dilemmas in Environmental—First Nations Relationships." Learned Societies Conference, June 5, 1995, in Montreal, on the Environment and the Relations with First Nations, co-sponsored by the Society for Socialist Studies and the Environmental Studies Association of Canada.

Postl, B., J. Irvine, S. MacDonald, and M. Moffatt, "Background Paper on the Health of Aboriginal Peoples in Canada." *Canadian Medical Association*. Bridging the gap: promoting health and healing for aboriginal peoples in Canada. Ottawa, 1994: 19–56.

Spicer, Kay, "Traditional Foods of Aboriginal Canadians." *Diabetes Dialogue*, (Vol. 41, No. 3) Fall 1994.

Tookenay, Vincent F., MD, "Improving the Health Status of Aboriginal People in Canada: New Directions, New Responsibilities." *Canadian Medical Association Journal*, (Vol. 155) 1996: 1581–1583.

Thompson, John Herd with Allen Singer, *Canada 1922–1939: Decades of Discord* (1985, McClelland & Stewart, Ltd., Toronto).

Chapter 9

"10 Tips to Healthy Eating." American Dietetic Association and National Center for Nutrition and Dietetics (NCND), April 1994.

"Antibiotics in Animals: An Interview with Stephen Sundlof, DVM, PhD."

International Food Information Council, 1100 Connecticut Avenue N.W., Suite 430, Washington D.C. 20036, 1997.

"Getting to the Roots of a Vegetarian Diet," Vegetarian Resource Group, Baltimore, MD, 1997.

"Health Record for People with Diabetes." Patient Information. Canadian Diabetes Association, distributed 1997.

"Heart Disease and Stroke." Patient information. The Heart and Stroke Foundation of Ontario, distributed 1997.

"High-Carbohydrate Diet Not for Everyone." Reuters, Wednesday April 16, 1997.

"How Do I Choose a Healthy Diet?" Patient information. The Heart and Stroke Foundation of Ontario, distributed 1997.

"Oats Are In." *Countdown USA: Countdown to a Healthy Heart*, Allegheny General Hospital and Voluntary Hospitals of America, Inc., 1990.

"Putting Fun Back into Food," International Food Information Council, 1100 Connecticut Avenue N.W., Suite 430, Washington D.C. 20036, 1997.

"Q&A About Fatty Acids and Dietary Fats." International Food Information Council, 1100 Connecticut Avenue N.W., Suite 430, Washington D.C. 20036, 1997.

"Sorting Out the Facts About Fat," International Food Information Council, 1100 Connecticut Avenue N.W., Suite 430, Washington D.C. 20036, 1997.

"The Heart Healthy Kitchen." *Countdown USA: Countdown to a Healthy Heart*, Allegheny General Hospital and Voluntary Hospitals of America, Inc., 1990.

"How Adults Are Learning to Manage Diabetes with Their Lifestyle." *The Globe and Mail*, November 1, 1996.

"Nutrition News." *Diabetes Dialogue*, (Vol. 43, No. 4) Winter 1996.

"Nutrition News." *Diabetes Dialogue*, (Vol. 44, No. 1) Spring 1997.

"Olestra: Yes or No?" Excerpted from the University of California at Berkeley Wellness Letter, c. Health Associates, 1996, in *Diabetes Dialogue*, (Vol. 43, No. 3) Fall 1996.

"Proper Knowledge of a Healthy Diet Makes Huge Difference." *The Globe and Mail*, November 1, 1996.

"The Antioxidant Connection: Visiting Speakers Discuss Immunity, Diabetes." Published by the Vitamin Information Program of Hoffman-La Roche Ltd., September 1995.

Allard, Johane P., MD, FRCP(C), Excerpts from "International Conference on Antioxidant Vitamins and Beta-Carotene in Disease Prevention: a Canadian Perspective." 1996.

Berndl, Leslie, RD, MSc, "Understanding Fat." *Diabetes Dialogue*, (Vol. 42, No. 1) Spring 1995.

Britt, Beverley, "Pesticides and Alternatives." Excerpted from the Canadian Organic Growers Toronto Chapter's Spring Conference: 1–4.

Christrup, Janet, "Nuts About Nuts: The Joys of Growing Nut Trees." *Cognition*, July 1991: 20–22.

Cunningham, John J., PhD, FACN, "Vitamins, Minerals and Diabetes." Excerpted from Canadian Diabetes Association Conference, 1995.

Deutsch, Nancy, "Vitamin C Stores Critical for Diabetics." *Family Practice*, November 11, 1996.

Engel, June V., PhD, "Beyond Vitamins: Phytochemicals to Help Fight Disease." *Health News*, June 1996, Volume 14, University of Toronto.

Engel, June, PhD, "Eating Fibre." *Diabetes Dialogue*, (Vol. 44, No. 1) Spring 1997.

Fraser, Eliabeth, RD, CDE, and Clarke, Bill. "Loafing Around." *Diabetes Dialogue*, (Vol. 44, No. 1) Spring 1997.

Gabrys, Jennifer, Bsc Pharm, CDE, "Ask the Professionals." *Diabetes Dialogue*, (Vol. 43, No. 4) Winter 1996.

Harrison, Pam. "Rethinking Obesity." *Family Practice*, March 11, 1996.

Ho, Marian, MSc, RD, "Learning Your ABCs, Part Two." *Diabetes Dialogue*, (Vol. 43, No. 3) Fall 1996.

Hunter, J.E., and Applewhite, T.H., "Reassessment of Trans Fatty Acid Availability in the U.S. Diet." *American Journal of Clinical Nutrition*, 54: 363–9, 1991.

Hurley, Jane, and Schmidt, Stephen, "Going with the Grain." *Nutrition Action*, October 1994:10–11.

IFIC Review: Uses and Nutritional Impact of Fat Reduction Ingredients, International Food Information Council, 1100 Connecticut Avenue N.W., Suite 430, Washington D.C. 20036, October 1995.

Kea, David. "Herd Health: The Biggest Reward of Ecological Dairy Farming." *Cognition*, Winter 1992/93: 26–27.

Kock, Henry, "Restoring Natural Vegetation as Part of the Farm." *Gardening without Chemicals '91*, Canadian Organic Growers Toronto Chapter, April 6, 1991.

Kushi, Mishio, *The Cancer Prevention Guide*. New York: St. Martin's Press, 1993.

Lichtenstein, A.H., et al., "Hydrogenation Impairs the Hypolipidemic Effect of Corn Oil in Humans." *Arteriosclerosis and Thrombosis* 13: 154–161, 1993.

Lichti, Janice, C., D.C. "Mind Boosters." *Healing Arts Magazine*, March 1996: 14–15.

Little, Linda. "Vitamin E May Help Cut Diabetics' Risk of Heart Disease." *The Medical Post*, May 14, 1996, 5.

Rifkin, Jeremy, "Playing God with the Genetic Code." *Health Naturally*, April/May 1995: 40–44.

Ruggiero, Laura, PhD, "Helping People with Diabetes Change: Practical Applications of the Stages of Change Model." Professional Information. LifeScan Education Institute, distributed 1997.

The Receptor, Canadian Association for Familial Hypercholesterolemia, (Vol. 7, No. 3) Fall/Winter 1996.

Toronto and Region Organic Directory. Canadian Organic Growers, Toronto Chapter.

Willett, W.C., et al., "Intake of Trans Fatty Acids and Risk of Coronary Heart Disease Among Women." *Lancet* 341: 581–5, 1993.

Wormworth, Janice, "Toxins and Tradition: The Impact of Food-Chain Contamination on the Inuit of Northern Quebec." *Canadian Medical Association Journal*, (Vol. 152, No. 8) April 15, 1995.

WHERE TO GO
FOR MORE INFORMATION

Note: This list was compiled from dozens of sources. Because of the volatile nature of many health and non-profit organizations, some of the addresses and phone numbers below may have changed since this list was compiled. Many of these organizations have e-mail addresses, some of which are not made public. Please review "Diabetes Online" at the end of this list.

Canadian Diabetes Association

National Office
15 Toronto St., Suite 800
Toronto, Ont.
M5C 2E3
ph. (416) 363-3373
fax (416) 363-3393

British Columbia/Yukon Division
1091 West 8th Ave.
Vancouver, B.C.
V6H 2V3
ph. (604) 732-1331/
1-800-665-6526
fax (604) 732-8444

Manitoba Division
102-310 Broadway
Winnipeg, Man.
R3C 0S6
ph. (204) 925-3800/
1-800-782-0175
fax (204) 949-0266

New Brunswick Division
165 Regent St., Suite 3
Fredericton, N.B.
E3B 7B4
ph. (506) 452-9009/
1-800-884-4232
fax (506) 455-4728

Newfoundland/Labrador Division
354 Water St., Suite 217
St. John's, Nfld.
A1C 1C4
ph. (709) 754-0953
fax (709) 754-0734

Nova Scotia Division
6080 Young St., Suite 101
Halifax, N.S.
ph. (902) 453-4232
fax (902) 453-4440

Prince Edward Island Division
P.O. Box 133
Charlottetown, P.E.I.
C1A 7K2
ph. (902) 894-3005
fax (902) 368-1928

Saskatchewan Division
104-2301 Avenue C.N.
Saskatoon, Sask.
S7L 5Z5
ph. (306) 933-4446/
1-800-996-4446
fax (306) 244-2012

*Association Diabete Québec
(Quebec CDA Affiliate)*
5635 Sherbrooke Ave. East
Montreal, Que.
H1N 1A2
ph. (514) 259-3422
fax (514) 259-9286

Alberta/NWT Division
Suite 1010, Royal Bank Building
10117 Jasper Ave. N.W.
Edmonton, Alta.
T5J 1W8
ph. (403) 423-1232/
1-800-563-0032
fax (403) 423-3322

**The Canadian Dietetic
Association**
480 University Ave., Suite 601
Toronto, Ont.
M5G 1V2
ph. (416) 596-0857
fax (416) 596-0603

**Canadian National Institute
for the Blind**
National Office
320 McLeod St.
Ottawa, Ont.
K2P 1A3
ph. (613) 563-4021
fax (613) 563-1898

**Canadian Podiatric
Medical Association**
2 Sheppard Ave. East, Suite 900
Willowdale, Ont.
M2N 5Y7
ph. (416) 927-9111/
1-888-220-3338
fax (416) 733-2491

Health Information Centre
Ontario Ministry of Health
6th Floor, 2195 Yonge St.
Toronto, Ont.
M4S 2B2
ph. (416) 327-4327/
1-800-268-1153

**Heart and Stroke
Foundation of Ontario**
(Heart & Stroke Healthline)
ph. 1-800-360-1557
Local Toronto: (416) 631-1557

**Juvenile Diabetes
Foundation Canada**
89 Granton Dr.
Richmond Hill, Ont.
L4B 2N5
ph. (905) 889-4171/
1-800-668-0274
fax (905) 889-4209

The Kidney Foundation of Canada
National Branch
5165 Sherbrooke Ave. West, Suite 300
Montreal, Que.
H4A 1T6
ph. 1-800-361-7494

MedicAlert
250 Ferrand Dr., Suite 301
Postal Station Don Mills,
Box 9800,
Toronto, Ont.
M3C 2T9
ph. 1-800-668-1507
Local Toronto: (416) 696-0267

Food/Nutrition:
Canadian Organic Growers Inc.
National Branch
Box 6408, Station J
Ottawa, Ont.
K2A 3Y6

National Institute of Nutrition
302–265 Carling Ave.
Ottawa, Ont.
K1S 2E1
ph. (613) 235-3355
fax (613) 235-7032

Diabetes Education Hospitals

Note: This list is not exhaustive; it is intended as a "starting point" for English-speaking Canadians looking for specific hospitals across the country that provide diabetes education.

Ontario
Diabetes Education Centre
Doctors Hospital
340 College St., Suite 560
Toronto, Ont.
M5T 3A9
ph. (416) 963-5288
fax (416) 923-1370

Mount Sinai Hospital
600 University Ave.
Toronto, Ont.
M5G 1X5
ph. (416) 586-4800
fax (416) 586-8785

Tri-Hospital Diabetes Education Centre (TRIDEC)
(All Toronto Hospital patients referred here)
Women's College Hospital
60 Grosvenor St.
Toronto, Ont.
M5S 1B6
ph. (416) 323-6170
fax (416) 323-6085

Diabetes Care and Research Centre
Chedoke McMaster Hospitals
McMaster Division
1200 Main St. West
Hamilton, Ont.
L8S 4J9
ph. (905) 521-2100 Ext. 6818
fax (905) 521-2653

Education Department
Hamilton Civic Hospitals
General Division
Robert Panchyson, BScN
237 Barton St. East
Hamilton, Ont.
L8L 2X2
ph. (905) 527-4322 Ext. 6245

Hamilton Civic Hospitals
(Patient Teaching)
711 Concession St.
Hamilton, Ont.
L8V 1C3
ph. (905) 527-4322 Ext. 2024,
paging 2110
fax (905) 575-2641

Diabetes Education Centre
Kitchener-Waterloo Health Centre
Grand River Hospital
835 King St. West
Kitchener, Ont.
N2G 1G3
ph. (519) 749-4300
fax (519) 749-4317

Sioux Lookout Diabetes Program
Box 163, 73 King St.
Sioux Lookout, Ont.
P8T 1A3
ph. (807) 737-4422
fax (807) 737-2603
E-mail: slktdiab@sioux-
lookout.lakeheadu.ca

Lawrence Commanda Diabetes
Education & Resource Centre
Ken Goulais, Resource Clerk
24 Semo Rd.
Garden Village, RR #1,
Sturgeon Falls, Ont.
P0H 2G0
ph. (705) 753-3355
fax (705) 753-4116

Porcupine Health Unit
Teresa Taillefer
Bag 2012
Timmins, Ont.
P4N 8B2
ph. (705) 267-1181
fax (705) 264-3989

Quebec
SMBD Jewish General Hospital
Diabetes Clinic
Pav. E104
3755 Cote St. Catherine
Montreal, Que.
H3T 1E2
ph. (514) 340-8222, Loc. 5787
fax (514) 340-7529

B.C.
University of Northern
British Columbia
Department of Community Health
3333 University Way
Prince George, B.C.
V29 4Z9
ph. (250) 960-5671
fax (250) 960-5743

S. Okanagan Diabetes
Education Program
S. Okanagan Health Unit
740 Carmi Ave.
Penticton, B.C.
V2A 8P9
ph. (250) 770-3492
fax (250) 770-3470

Diabetes Education Program
1305 Summit Ave.
Prince Rupert, B.C.
V8J 2A6
ph. (250) 624-0294
fax (250) 627-1244

Western Canada
Manitoba Health
(Teaching text for Type 2 diabetes
and Aboriginal Population)
303–800 Portage Ave.
Winnipeg, Man.
R3G 0N4
ph. (204) 945-6735
fax (204) 948-2040

Royal University Hospital
103 Hospital Dr.
Saskatoon, Sask.
S7N 0W0
ph. (306) 655-2615
fax (306) 655-1044

Mista Hia Regional
Health Authority
Grande Prairie Health Unit
10320–99 St.
Grande Prairie, Alta.
T8V 6J4
ph. (403) 532-4441
fax (403) 532-1550

University of Alberta Hospitals
2F2 Metabolic Centre
Brenda Cook, R.D.
8440–112 St.
Edmonton, Alta.
T6G 2B7
ph. (403) 492-6696
fax (403) 492-8291

Clinical Nutrition Services
Foothills Hospital
1403–29th St. N.W.
Calgary, Alta.
T2N 2T9
ph. (403) 670-1522
fax (403) 670-1848

Maritimes
Nova Scotia Diabetes Centre
Queen Elizabeth II Health
Science Centre
Gerrard Hall, 5303 Morris St.,
2nd Floor
Halifax, N.S.
B3J 1B6
ph. (902) 496-3722
fax (902) 496-3726

Outside Canada:
American Association of
Diabetes Educators
444 N Michigan Ave., Suite 1240
Chicago, Ill. 60611
ph. (312) 644-2233 or
1-800-TEAMUP4 (832-6874)
(Diabetes Educator Access Line)

The American Diabetes Association
ADA National Service Center
1660 Duke St.
Alexandria, Va. 22314
ph. (703) 549-1500

American Dietetic Association and
National Center for Nutrition and
Dietetics (NCND) Consumer
Nutrition Hot Line
ph. (312) 899-0040
fax (312) 899-1979

International Diabetic
Athletes Association
1647-B West Bethany Home Road
Phoenix, Ariz. 85015
ph. (602) 433-2113

International Diabetes
Federation (IDF)
1 Rue Defacqz
B–1000
Brussels, Belgium
ph. 32-2-538-5511
fax 32-2-538-5114

Toll-Free Hotlines:
The Becel Heart Health
Information Bureau
ph. 1-800-563-5574
fax 1-800-442-3235

LifeScan TELELIBRARY
1-800-847-SCAN (7226)

LifeScan Customer Care Line
1-800-663-5521

Lilly/BMC Diabetes Care
ph. 1-800-361-2070
fax (514) 668-7009

McNeil Consumers
ph. 1-800-561-0070

Novo Nordisk Canada Inc.
ph. 1-800-465-4334/
(905) 629-4222
fax (905) 629-2596

Monoject Diabetes Care Products
Sherwood Medical Industries
Canada Inc.
ph. 1-800-661-1903

Pharma Plus Pharma Answers
Phone Line
(24 hour access to a pharmacist)
ph. 1-800-511-INFO

Diabetes Online

Through the internet, you can participate in newsgroups and bulletin boards (public forums) on diabetes information. These can be accessed through either independent internet providers, or through an interactive computer service, such as CompuServe, Prodigy or America Online (AOL).

Literature searches are great ways of getting specific information. Medline—free from The National Library of Medicine in the U.S. at http://www.n/m.nih.gov/databases/freemedl.html— is the best for search service for medical journal articles (many of which are extremely technical). Compuserve, Prodigy or America Online all give you access to Medline. Medline is also available through many public and university libraries all over Canada.

Another way of accessing good information is through a web browser, such as Netscape. By web browsing, you can go to various sites in cyberspace to find your information. When you don't know the e-mail address, you can use a search engine, such as Yahoo! or Webcrawler, to search for what you want by simply typing in your topic. The more specific you can be in your search, the better. For example, if you want information on nerve damage, don't type "nerves" but "diabetes nerve damage" or "diabetic neuropathy." A search engine is essentially an "index" to the Internet. When you go to a site, you can save or print the information, and the site may even lead you to other valuable internet sources. A good guide to get is *Internet For Dummies*, which will walk you through internet access step by step.

A Few Sites To Get You Started:
Note: some of these addresses may have changed since this list was compiled.

http://www.diabetes.ca/cda
The Canadian Diabetes
Association
(See above for address)

http://www.diabetes.org
The American Diabetes
Association
ADA National Service Center
(See above for address)

http://www.idf.org
International Diabetes
Federation (IDF)
(See above for address)

http://www.joslin.harvard.edu
Joslin Diabetes Center

http://www.niddk.nih.gov/
DiabetesDocs.html
The National Institute of Health
(general information on diabetes
in the United States)

http://www.getnet.com/~idaa/
International Diabetic
Athletes Association
(See above for address)

http://www.aadenet.org/
American Association of Diabetes
Educators (AADE)
(See above for address)

http://www.konnections.com/
eyedoc/index.html
Diabetic Retinopathy (information
provided by eyecare specialists)

http://www.footandankle.com
Foot and Ankle Web Index
(provides links to a wealth of
podiatry-related information
on the web)

http://www.achoo.com
(on-line internet directory of
health care information)

http://hpb1.hwc.ca
Canadian Medical Association
On-line
(provides information on a wide
range of health-related topics)

INDEX